Routledge Revivals

The Ethnography of Malinowski

Bronislaw Malinowski is one of the founding fathers of modern social anthropology and the innovator of the technique of prolonged and intensive fieldwork. His writings about the Trobriand Islands of Papua were in their time the most formative influence on the work of British social anthropologists and are of perennial interest and importance. They produced a revolution in the aims and field techniques of social anthropologists, and the method he created is that now normally used by anthropologists in the field.

Malinowski's field material remains compulsory reading for students. First published in 1979, this book draws from the major monographs of Malinowski to compile a selection of his writings on the Trobriand Islanders. In presenting a concise Trobriand ethnography in one volume, Dr Young gives balanced coverage of economic life, kinship, marriage and land tenure, and to the system of ceremonial exchange known as the Kula. He also provides, in an introductory essay, a critical assessment of Malinowski the ethnographer, and gives a brief account of the Trobriands in a modern perspective.

The Ethnography of Malinowski

Malinowski

The Trobriand Islands 1915-18

Edited by
Michael W. Young

Routledge
Taylor & Francis Group

First published in 1979
by Routledge & Kegan Paul Ltd

This edition first published in 2017 by Routledge
2 Park Square, Milton Park, Abingdon, Oxon, OX14 4RN
and by Routledge
711 Third Avenue, New York, NY 10017

Routledge is an imprint of the Taylor & Francis Group, an informa business

Introduction, and selection of material
© 1979 Michael W. Young

Publisher's Note
The publisher has gone to great lengths to ensure the quality of this reprint but
points out that some imperfections in the original copies may be apparent.

Disclaimer
The publisher has made every effort to trace copyright holders and welcomes
correspondence from those they have been unable to contact.

A Library of Congress record exists under LC control number: 78040938

ISBN 13: 978-1-138-06397-6 (hbk)
ISBN 13: 978-1-315-16067-2 (ebk)
ISBN 13: 978-1-138-06400-3 (pbk)

The ethnography of Malinowski
The Trobriand Islands 1915–18

edited by

Michael W. Young

First published in 1979
by Routledge & Kegan Paul Ltd
11 New Fetter Lane, London EC4P 4EE

Published in the USA by
Routledge and Kegan Paul Inc.
in association with Methuen Inc.
29 West 35th Street, New York NY 10001

Set in Compugraphic English Times
and printed in Great Britain by
Hartnoll Print
Bodmin, Cornwall

British Library Cataloguing in Publication Data

Malinowski, Bronislaw

The ethnography of Malinowski.
1. Ethnology – Trobriand Islands
I. Title II. Young, Michael W
301.29'95'3   GN671.N5   78–40938

ISBN 0 7100 0013 8
ISBN 0 7100 0100 2 Pbk

Contents

Illustrations

* The original captions to these plates have been modified or slightly shortened.

Illustrations

Acknowledgments

Grateful acknowledgment is made to the following for permission to reproduce the material indicated:

The Royal Anthropological Institute of Great Britain and Ireland for extracts from 'Kula: the circulating exchange of valuables in the archipelagoes of Eastern New Guinea', *Man*, 20, 1920, 97–105, article 51 (chapter 7, section 4).

Routledge & Kegan Paul Ltd and E. P. Dutton for extracts from *Argonauts of the Western Pacific*, 1922 (chapter 7, sections 1–3, chapters 8 and 9).

Routledge & Kegan Paul Ltd and Paul R. Reynolds, Inc. for extracts from *The Sexual Life of Savages*, 1929 (chapters 3 and 4, chapter 5, sections 1–5, 7–9).

Paul R. Reynolds, Inc. for extracts from *Coral Gardens and their Magic* (vol. 1), 1935 (chapters 1 and 2, chapter 5, section 6, chapter 6).

Introduction

I

The Trobriand Islands are a cluster of coral atolls which lie some 100 miles due north of the eastern tail of Papua New Guinea. They are inhabited by a people of Melanesian stock who speak an Austronesian language unique to themselves, though it is related to others in the region. The Trobriand Islands were named by the French explorer D'Entrecasteaux in 1793, but it was Bronislaw Malinowski who placed them firmly on the anthropological map. He lived there for two years during 1915–18 and subsequently wrote prolifically about the islanders' language, culture and society. His major monographs, all classics, are: *Argonauts of the Western Pacific* (1922), an account of the system of ceremonial exchange known as the Kula; *The Sexual Life of Savages* (1929), a study of Trobriand courtship, marriage and domestic life; *Coral Gardens and their Magic* (1935), which deals with horticulture and land tenure (vol. I), and with the language of magic and gardening (vol. II). In two short monographs, *Baloma: the Spirits of the Dead in the Trobriand Islands* (1916) and *Crime and Custom in Savage Society* (1926), Malinowski examined, respectively, Trobriand magico-religious beliefs and the principles underlying social control in Trobriand society. In addition to these works Malinowski wrote a great deal more which was directly inspired by his Trobriand researches. For example, *Sex and Repression in Savage Society* (1927) invokes Trobriand familial relations in an attempt to modify Freudian theory. The substance of most of his articles and longer essays on the Trobriands, however, was usually tidily incorporated into one or another of the major monographs.

More than forty years after its completion, Malinowski's Trobriand corpus remains the most famous, if not the most copious and exhaustive, ethnography in the anthropological literature. The

1

Trobrianders have occupied a place in the limelight of academic debate and generally enjoyed a fame out of all proportion to their numbers or the size of their miniscule islands. This has been due to two things: first, the uniqueness and exotic appeal of the Trobrianders themselves, whose culture has indeed proved to be richer than so many of their Melanesian neighbours, and second, the tireless and insistent publicity given to them by Malinowski. Like an impresario he conducted them to the centre of almost every anthropological (and popular) controversy: the nature of the family, the ignorance of physiological paternity, free love and adolescent sterility, the roots of the Oedipus Complex, the 'meaning' of kinship terminology, the rationality of magic, the sources of law and order, the interpretation of mythology, the mainspring of economic incentives, the function of ritual . . . There was practically nothing in Human Nature and Society about which the Trobrianders, through Malinowski's erudite advocacy, did not have something interesting to say.

Fame is not synonymous with familiarity, however, and it is unusual today for non-specialist readers to tackle more than one or two of the monographs. Reasons for this are not hard to find, for set against their individual scientific value and literary virtues, they are, as a body of writings, disjointed, riddled with internal redundancies and saturated with tiresome, outdated polemics. Malinowski has frequently been criticised for failing to present a coherent, synoptic account of Trobriand culture, from which the latter might be seen (in Clyde Kluckholn's words) 'not from the vantage point of the Kula or of sex or of garden magic, but from a more embracive perspective which helps us to understand the interrelationships of these various "institutional systems"' (1943:213). Malinowski regretted this lack himself, and in 1929 blamed illhealth and the urgent need to establish his doctrine of functionalism, both of which had required him to work up his material in piecemeal fashion (Firth 1957:10). But there were also theoretical inhibitions. It is clear from the *apologia* with which he concluded his last book on the Trobriands that he regarded 'an ultimate theoretical assessment' of the various institutions his monographs had dealt with as transcending 'the proper task of the fieldworker' (1935(I):455). Such coy restraint is uncharacteristic, and it is more plausible to suppose that it was his oft-noted inability to think in terms of social systems, rather than a self-confessed 'methodological puritanism', which prevented him from writing a generalised account of Trobriand culture.

The present volume makes no claim to substitute for the omission. Obviously, the required synopsis would need to have been born of the mind and pen of Malinowski himself; it cannot be effected by any scissors-and-paste synthesis. It seemed worth while, however, to attempt to reduce by judicious paring the 2,500-odd pages of the Trobriand corpus to a wieldy number, which would then constitute an 'essential' Trobriand ethnography between two covers. There could be no question, of course, of assembling anything like a 'total' ethnography within the limits of a single volume, and much of interest and value has had to be sacrificed. Thus, I have ruthlessly omitted detailed descriptions of technology, gardening activities, sexual behaviour, much mythology and magic, and all linguistic material. Another victim, alas, has been the 'imponderabilia of everyday life' (including case material) which gave such colour to Malinowski's narratives but added so inordinately to their length. It may be protested, not unjustly, that with the excision of purple passages, polemical tilts and rhetorical asides, little will remain of the idiosyncratic flavour of Malinowski's style. If this is so (and the reader must judge), it is regrettable but necessary, for the purpose of this book is to offer a concise ethnography of the Trobriands in Malinowski's own words, rather than an anthology of Malinowski's Trobriand writings. This is a fine but crucial distinction.

Other notable deletions I have been forced to make are the many disquisitions on fieldwork practice and method which introduced, concluded or otherwise punctuated Malinowski's monographs. Here again, I must plead that they are not as directly relevant to the 'function' of this book as they were to his own when he wrote them. In their original contexts they were impassioned and didactic declarations of a revolutionary fieldworker's manifesto – as influential within the profession as anything he ever wrote. Partly to redress this omission, I give below some attention to his prescriptions for fieldwork in offering an assessment of his accomplishments as an ethnographer.

Since his death in 1942, much has been written about Malinowski's life and works. A major evaluation was the collection of essays by twelve of his most distinguished pupils, published under the title *Man and Culture* (Firth 1957a). (This work should be referred to for a comprehensive bibliography of Malinowski's writings, plus a list of other items which had been published about him before 1957.) A great number of additional critiques, assessments and intellectual portraits have appeared during the last twenty years by American, British and French authors, notably: Harris (1968), Hatch (1973), Métraux (1968), Stocking (1974), Symmons-Symonolewicz (1958, 1959, 1960), Voget (1975) and Wax (1972); Barnes (1963), Forge (1972), Jarvie (1964), Kuper (1973), Leach (1966a, 1966b) and Richards (1969); Lombard (1972) and Panoff (1972). Much of this literature is highly critical of Malinowski's theorising; his British intellectual descendants, particularly, have been less than kind to him. But then, he himself gave no quarter to his own antecedents. This literature is also testimony to the fact that, for all his failings, his memory is still remarkably green. In great measure this is due to his Trobriand works. He gave them vitality and they in turn assure him of his immortality.

II

Bronislaw Malinowski was born of aristocratic parentage in Poland in 1884. He studied mathematics and physics at the University of Cracow and in 1908 was awarded a PhD. Shortly afterwards he turned his interests to anthropology – converted, he was later to claim, by reading Frazer's *Golden Bough*. In 1910 he went to England and studied under Edward Westermarck and C. G. Seligman at the London School of Economics, where he wrote his first book, *The Family Among the Australian Aborigines* (1913). With Seligman's help he obtained finance to undertake field research in New Guinea. He visited Australia on the way, and was there when the Great War began. As an Austrian subject he was technically an enemy alien, but the Australian authorities permitted him to proceed to the Territory of Papua, where his movements during the next few years appear to have been quite unrestricted. There is no substance to the myth that he was 'interned' in the Trobriands.

At the age of thirty, then, Malinowski began his career as an ethnographer with five months' fieldwork among the Mailu and neighbouring peoples on the southern coast of Papua. It was a rather unpromising start. His posthumously published personal diaries depict this period as a harrowing one of recurrent sickness, lethargy and dejection. Except for a few weeks towards the end, he appears to have spent more time in the company of European residents and visitors than he did working among the Mailu (whom he found 'coarse and dull'), and it seems clear that he owed a great deal more to his missionary host, the Rev. W. J. V. Saville, than the rather perfunctory acknowledgment in his published report would suggest. *The Natives of Mailu* (1915), however, is no brief survey, but a quite solid compendium of descriptive ethnography which, while set in a conventional framework and lacking the textual richness so characteristic of his later monographs, is by no means inferior to other anthropological works of the time.

Of Malinowski's second expedition to New Guinea in 1915 – his first crucial year in the Trobriand Islands – there is unfortunately no detailed record. His choice of the Trobriands was apparently adventitious; though perhaps less so was the decision to pitch his tent in Omarakana, the 'capital' of Kiriwina. After six months he understood the language well enough to dispense with an interpreter, and thenceforth he worked entirely in the vernacular. By the end of this expedition he was a thoroughly seasoned fieldworker, and had matured into the superb ethnographer whose example was to revolutionise social anthropology.

Precisely what steps he took to achieve this maturity we do not know, but the evidence for it is plain in the celebrated *Baloma* essay he wrote in the Australian interlude of 1916. In this short monograph on the subject of Trobriand beliefs, Malinowski foreshadows in style and plan the major works which were to follow. There is the discursive form, the methodological disquisition, the weaving of ethnographic context, the illustrative use of cases, the confidential tone of the author as he builds a mosaic of interlocking detail in describing an institution. One of his favourite expository devices is to exploit the observing 'I' by self-dramatisation, to place himself squarely in the event and describe what he sees. Such devices enabled him better to convey his understanding of an unfamiliar idea or custom, and they heighten the reader's interest by their engaging effect. *Baloma* is a brilliant performance. In a judicious balance of fact, theory and viewpoint, Malinowski had found his true voice.

In September 1917 Malinowski returned to the Trobriands for his last extended period of fieldwork. This was to conclude his baptism by fire, unique documentation of which is provided by his personal diary of that year. It shows the man, bruised and wearied by the experience, but determined to complete what he'd begun, and in a far more vigorous frame of mind than he had ever known in Mailu. After his return to Australia he married, but was delayed from returning to England by ill-health. His first Trobriand epic, *Argonauts of the Western Pacific*, was published in 1922, and the same year he commenced full-time teaching at the London School of Economics where he remained until 1938. Caught in America by the outbreak of war, he was persuaded to stay as a Visiting Professor at Yale. It was there that he died in 1942, at the age of fifty-eight.

His extraordinarily productive 'London years' saw Malinowski emerge triumphant as the undisputed leader of social anthropology in Britain. From 1927 he occupied the first Chair of Anthropology in the University of London, but even before this he had established his famous teaching seminar, and had already earned a considerable popular reputation as a pundit and polemicist. Many of his students have written glowingly, if also ambivalently, of this time of intellectual ferment (e.g. see Powdermaker 1966:33–45). Malinowski's brilliant teaching was imbued with his Trobriand experiences, and work on the cycle of monographs went hand in hand with the development of his 'functionalist' viewpoint and with the vigorous publicising of the revolution in anthropology that it would bring. One of Malinowski's most eminent pupils has recalled how the typescript of *Coral Gardens* was discussed 'page by page' in the seminar of 1932–3 (Fortes 1957:157) – evidently something of an ordeal in view of Malinowski's inability to take criticism kindly. Fortes (*ibid.*) also hints that Malinowski's compulsion to present his theories and his ethnographic discoveries in the form of an assault on the *ancien régime* was as tiresome to his listeners as it is preposterous to the readers of his books. In brief, most of the Trobriand ethnography was composed while its author was strenuously engaged in asserting his academic supremacy, and whether or not the battles were more imagined than real, his ethnographic writing was vitiated by the parade of grotesque Aunt Sallys and the rustle of straw men.

Before saying any more about the shortcomings of Malinowski's ethnography, let me recapitulate the circumstances of his positive fieldwork achievement.

As early as 1913, W. H. R. Rivers had written:

The essence of intensive work . . . is limitation in extent
combined with intensity and thoroughness. A typical piece of
intensive work is one in which the worker lives for a year or
more among a community of perhaps four or five hundred
people and studies every detail of their life and culture; in
which he comes to know every member of the community
personally; in which he is not content with generalized
information, but studies every feature of life and custom in
concrete detail and by means of the vernacular language. It is
only by such work that one can realize the immense extent of
the knowledge which is now awaiting the inquirer, even in
places where the culture has already suffered much change. It
is only by such work that it is possible to discover the
incomplete and even misleading character of much of the vast
mass of survey work which forms the existing material of
anthropology (quoted by Kuper 1973:20; see also Urry 1972).

Now none of Malinowski's mentors (Westermarck, Seligman,
nor yet Rivers himself) had managed to fulfil to the letter this
prescription for first-hand, intensive research, and no one rightly
knew what its consequences would be. Until this time, most ethnographic information had been collected by amateurs – missionaries,
colonial administrators and travellers – though much 'survey work'
had been done by Rivers, Haddon, Seligman and others of their
generation. It was clear, at any rate, that academic opinion in
Britain at the time was favourably disposed to innovations in
ethnographic method, and Malinowski, through his Trobriand
fieldwork, amply provided them. It was, in short, a matter of the
right man being in the right place at the right time; though such was
the man's charismatic influence that he was able to persuade a
whole generation of his followers that 'social anthropology began
in the Trobriand Islands in 1914' (Leach 1957:124).

What were these innovations that Malinowski introduced? First
of all they comprised the necessary conditions for intensive work as
mentioned by Rivers: the anthropologist must spend a long time in
one place and remain in close contact with the people throughout,
and he must communicate with them through their own language.
Second, there were the actual strategies and techniques of data
collection, to which Malinowski attached somewhat cumbersome
labels: (1) The method of 'statistical documentation of concrete

evidence', which involved the recording of maps, censuses, genealogies, statements of norms and the observation of actual cases. The aim was to construct 'synoptic charts' which summarised the range and interconnections of customary behaviours associated with a focal institution. Such information, abstracted in a series of charts, would provide an outline of 'the organization of the tribe and the anatomy of its culture' (1922:24). (2) Another set of materials, which Malinowski called 'the imponderabilia of everyday life', should be collected 'through minute, detailed observations'. These are to flesh out the anatomy of the culture and give human sense to the tribal structure. (3) Finally, the fieldworker must accumulate a *corpus inscriptionum*, consisting of 'ethnographic statements, characteristic narratives, typical utterances, items of folk-lore and magical formulae'. These were 'documents of native mentality' which, as in historical scholarship, could be studied as texts by independent analysts. 'These three lines of approach', Malinowski asserted, 'lead to the final goal, of which an ethnographer should never lose sight. This goal is, briefly, to grasp the native's point of view, his relation to life, to realize *his* vision of *his* world' (*ibid.*:25). With this humanist credo few anthropologists would quarrel, though 'the final goal' has proved to be a good deal more elusive than Malinowski's simple directives for attaining it might suggest. None the less, a quite remarkable advance in ethnographic sophistication followed the application of these discovery procedures. Malinowski's prescriptions, as Adam Kuper has put it, 'reflect a perception of the systematic divergence between what people say about what they do, what they actually do, and what they think' (1973:30). 'Savages', Malinowski showed, could be all too human in their perverse complexity.

Now certain problems presented themselves as a direct consequence of conducting fieldwork the way Malinowski had done. They were unsought, often unarticulated, and yet quite inescapable. As far as the scientific task was concerned, there was the problem of a super-abundance of data, an extravagant wealth of detail which accumulated over the months of patient observation and questioning. Materials proliferate like thickets, and Malinowski advocated a firm hand:

> In the field one has to face a chaos of facts, some of which
> are so small that they seem insignificant; others loom so large

that they are hard to encompass with one synthetic glance. But in this crude form they are not scientific facts at all; they are absolutely elusive, and can be fixed only by interpretation, by seeing them *sub specie aeternitatis*, by grasping what is essential in them and fixing this. *Only laws and generalizations are scientific facts*, and field work consists only and exclusively in the interpretation of the chaotic social reality, in subordinating it to general rules (1916:212, original italics).

In this early formulation, Malinowski shows a sophisticated awareness of the necessarily creative role of the investigator, who deludes himself if he claims to be merely 'recording facts'. Ultimately, such views were to mature into a 'scientific theory of culture' which was rooted in the rather trite axiom that Man has biological needs which Culture satisfied (1944). This fully-fledged schema was Malinowski's contribution to Grand Theory, hatched from Durkheim but transmogrified by behaviourism into an unwieldy and essentially unilluminating bio-cultural functionalism. His earlier functionalism, however, which he had begun to articulate in the late 1920s, was of a more sociological and less pretentious variety. He seems to have discovered retrospectively that as a preliminary guide to the collection and sorting of facts according to their institutional contexts, and as a check-list of possible interconnections between institutions, elementary functionalism provides an invaluable heuristic aid. Indeed it does, as so many who have followed in the Malinowskian fieldwork tradition have found for themselves. It should be said, however, that there is no *necessary* connection between the manifold, multi-levelled ethnographic data which Malinowski's field methods produced, and the kind of laboured, holistic functionalism by which he interpreted them in his last monographs. Other scholars, including his own pupils, have re-interpreted the same data in the light of other theories – thereby paying fulsome tribute to the excellence of his ethnography in being able to do so. Malinowski's early functionalism, then, which amounted to little more than the way things hang together in a culture, can be regarded as a sort of charter for the way he wanted to present his ethnography.

III

There were other problems which arose as a consequence of intensive fieldwork by participant-observation to which Malinowski gave relatively scant attention, and for which he cannot be said to have proposed solutions. These were to do with the very immersion of the anthropologist in his tribe: heightened observer-effect, increased moral commitment, and the personal traumas of (to use a psychoanalytical concept) the countertransference of the fieldworker. Such problems, indeed, have only fairly recently been given their due as worthy of consideration, yet they are quite integral to the fact that the anthropologist is a human subject observing other human subjects, and that his presence affects their behaviour even as theirs affects his own.

In this area of humanistic concern, to which anthropologists are becoming increasingly sensitive, Malinowski made his own contribution, but it was circumscribed and it was flawed. To take first the 'vivid life' (Leach) of his ethnography which, in taking 'full account of the complexity of human nature' and seeing man 'in the round and not in the flat' (Frazer), was such a warm contrast to the dry and bloodless ethnography of his predecessors. But by the most exacting criteria his Trobrianders rarely come alive as individuals; they are more usually described in terms of generalised psychology and standardised emotions. Again, all too often he brought Trobriand Man to life only to parade him as the embodiment of a theory, and finally to kill him off as a pastiche of his own ideas. As Leach (1957:128-9) has argued, for example, Malinowski went too far in his attempt to demonstrate the 'rationality' of his Trobrianders; it was all very well to demolish the belief that primitives were pre-logical, but it was absurd to credit them with the super-rationality of scientists. More generally, anthropology may well be an art as well as a science (among other things 'the art of taking a warm interest in the particular while seeking it in the universal', as Robert Redfield (1954:11) put it in praising Malinowski), but with its vested interest in mankind's diversity, social anthropology can hardly be satisfied with facile demonstrations of the universal in the particular, and Trobriand Man could not long serve as the only paradigm for Primitive Man. Could anything be more pompous, patronising and plain silly than the opening sentence of the Author's Preface to his final monograph on the Trobrianders?

Once again I have to make my appearance as a chronicler and
spokesman of the Trobrianders, the Melanesian community so
small and lowly as to appear almost negligible – a few
thousand 'savages', practically naked, scattered over a small
flat archipelago of dead coral – and yet for many reasons so
important to the student of primitive humanity (1935(I):xix).

Consider next the somewhat incompatible demands between
scientific 'objectivity' and the personal involvement of the fieldworker's 'subjectivity'. Despite his incorrigible self-dramatisation
and his claim that 'the facts of anthropology attract me mainly as
the best means of knowing myself' (1932a:xxv), Malinowski did
not propose any theory which included the observer in its frame of
reference. This was at least partly due to his basic orientation: the
field of enquiry was wholly external to himself. He mentions the
'personal equation' of the investigator only to caution against
selectivity in observation and recording, and he counsels the
keeping of an 'ethnographic diary' of events as a corrective
measure (1922:20–1). Paradoxically, however, the field diaries
which Malinowski himself kept (1967) constitute an entirely different form of document – one which, in laying bare his prejudices,
gives the lie to his public image and puts his sincerity severely to the
test.

Malinowski valued intellectual honesty, and he could be
outrageously candid within the frame of his public image. The
'confessions of ignorance and failure' which conclude the Trobriand works (1935(I), Appendix II) amount to a remarkably self-
critical catalogue of his 'errors of omission and commission'. Yet
there is a flavour of exhibitionism about the recital, a hint of mock-
modesty to disguise a gentle boast that he could well afford, secure
in the knowledge that he had done a more thorough job of ethnography than anyone before him. Extreme candour, then, may have
been yet another of his publicity tricks. But like everyone else,
Malinowski cultivated one kind of honesty commensurate with his
public self, and nurtured another kind for his private self. It is the
hiatus between them which is revealed by the *Diary*, and is exempli-
fied by the discrepancy between the view of Malinowski as a man
who 'achieved a great measure of personal identification with the
people he lived with' (Richards 1957:17–18) and the impression
conveyed by *Diary* entries such as the following:

As for ethnology: I see the life of the natives as utterly devoid of interest or importance, something as remote from me as the life of a dog (1967:167).

In short, his much-vaunted powers of empathy are little in evidence in the figure who emerges from the *Diary* as (in Clifford Geertz's black characterisation) a 'crabbed, self-preoccupied, hypochondriacal narcissist, whose fellow-feeling for the people he lived with was limited in the extreme' (1967:12).

In Malinowski's defence, it must be said that innovating as he did the social anthropologist's role of participant-observer, he was without the psychological security afforded by existing precedents. The very ambiguity of his status and life-style was clearly unsettling. He had broken through the caste-barrier which at the time stultified understanding between Europeans and Melanesians, and he was associating with Trobrianders on approximate terms of parity (see Wax 1972). Add this 'betrayal' of White caste-solidarity to the fact that he was a Pole, an enemy alien, a pompous and condescending intellectual with a thinly-disguised antipathy towards missionaries and colonial administrators*, and we need not wonder that his only European friends appear to have been traders. On the other hand, the fact that he lived in a tent in a native village does not mean that he was warmly accepted by Trobrianders either, and his feeling that 'the native is not the natural companion of the white man' (1922:7) was probably reciprocated. A *modus vivendi* of

* With one or two exceptions (see his favourable comments on the Rev. M. Gilmour's account of the Kula, 1922:500n.), this antipathy led him to belittle and scorn their ethnographic endeavours. See, for example, his heavily patronizing and patently insincere Foreword to the Rev. W. J. V. Saville's book on the Mailu (1926), and his vituperative reply to A. G. Rentoul, a District Officer who presumed to question some of Malinowski's findings on Trobriand beliefs about conception (Rentoul 1931, 1932; Malinowski 1932c). On the other hand, he seems unaccountably to have ignored the ethnographic notes of Dr R. L. Bellamy (1908, and bibliography in Black 1957), who had been Assistant Resident Magistrate and Medical Officer on the Trobriands for a full ten years by the time of Malinowski's arrival, and who, furthermore, had excellent credentials from Malinowski's own mentor Seligman, who had quoted Bellamy extensively in his account of the Northern Massim (1910). Bellamy sheltered Malinowski on his arrival, taught him some of the language, and it was even suggested by Malinowski that they should write a joint book on 'the sociology of the Trobriand people' (Black 1957:18). Bellamy turned the offer down, however, and went off to fight in the Great War. Subsequently his friendship with Malinowski soured, and he was later to charge – somewhat obscurely – that Malinowski had undone in two years much of the work that he had accomplished in the Trobriands during his ten years as a government officer (Black 1957:18–19).

mutual tolerance was established, but Malinowski called the tune:

> In fact, as they knew that I would thrust my nose into
> everything, even where a well-mannered native would not
> dream of intruding, they finished by regarding me as part and
> parcel of their life, a necessary evil or nuisance, mitigated by
> donations of tobacco (1922:8).

Thus, while the 'ethnographer's tent' seems to have symbolised for him the breakthrough in method which he accomplished (Wax 1972; Malinowski 1922: Plate I), the breakthrough in European–native relationships remained incomplete. A tent, after all, erects and maintains more social distance than any native house.

It is only fair to point out, too, that the chronic sense of alienation which permeates the *Diary* is a common psychic experience of anthropologists in the field, and it is intensified by homesickness, nostalgia, loneliness and sexual frustration – all of which Malinowski suffered in full measure. 'Ethnological problems don't preoccupy me at all', he writes towards the end of his diary. 'At bottom I am living outside of Kiriwina, although strongly hating the niggers' (1967:264). As George Stocking has suggested in a most perceptive review of the *Diary*, Malinowski in the Trobriands invites comparison with Conrad's Mistah Kurtz in the Congo, 'alone with his instincts in the heart of darkness' (1974:283). The intense ambivalence which he displays towards his informants and their culture is a symptom of this alienation rather than proof of any character defect, and there is much evidence in the *Diary* of his moral struggle to overcome it. He oscillates between cold detachment and warm involvement, bleak despair and manic exhilaration, though it appears to have been professional ambition harnessed to an almost Calvinistic attitude to the redeeming power of hard work which 'saved' him in the end (cf. Geertz 1967). Much later, from the pinnacle of his career in London, he could look back indulgently at his ordeal and even write of himself as one 'whose heart is in Melanesia' (1932b:xxi).

Raymond Firth has declared that Malinowski's *Diary* 'cannot be ranked as more than a footnote to anthropological history' (1967:xviii). But each tradition comes to write its own history, and in the history of the 'humanist', 'confessional' genre of 'reflexive' anthropology it will surely warrant a page or two (cf. Stocking 1974). Reactions within the profession have ranged from glee at the

debunking of a myth to indignation at the indelicacy of exposing a
dead Master's private musings. There is unlikely to be consensus as
to the *Diary*'s value, or to the propriety of publishing it in the first
place, though I would incline to agree with I. M. Lewis (1968:348)
that had Malinowski lived longer, 'it would surely not have been
greatly out of character for him to have authorized publication'. As
one who relished shocking his contemporaries he could have
promoted it as the cap-stone of a career bent on creating a romantic
image of the anthropologist-as-hero; and with what disarming self-
mockery he would have nudged the pendulum (doubtless invoking
his Slavic perversity) and proclaimed the anthropologist-as-anti-
hero! Did he not preach that social reality was located somewhere
in the gap between ideal and real, between what people say they do
and what they actually do? Likewise, he would have been true to
his theories in his very human inconsistency.

   In his review of the *Diary*, Lewis (1968) asks rhetorically whether
the Trobrianders got the ethnographer they deserved. His impression is 'probably not', but whatever Malinowski's personal relations with them may have been, 'could anyone else have more
effectively trumpeted their name around the world?' (1968:349).
The implied answer is, again, 'probably not'; but no one has
thought to ask the Trobrianders whether they wanted (or still want)
their name broadcast for reasons which to them must appear
dubious. We cannot answer Lewis's question because we do not
know what Trobrianders in 1917 thought of Malinowski. There is a
tradition which recalls him as the 'Man of Songs' (Hogbin 1946),
and a recent worker on Kiriwina discovered that he was
remembered as an expert at shooing spirits away (J. W. Leach, personal communication). (Curiously enough, he mentions in his diary
an occasion when he sang the words 'Kiss my ass' to a Wagner
melody to chase away witches (1967:157).) But oral traditions are
notoriously selective, and such judgments of posterity are probably
of little significance. Until recently, the only documented response
of a Trobriander to Malinowski's writings is a complaint that he
got the ranking system wrong (Groves 1956). A somewhat different
kind of testimony comes from a Catholic missionary who spent
thirty years in the Trobriands, and whose mastery of the language
is indubitable (see Baldwin 1944–5; 1949–50). He writes, not
implausibly:

It was a surprise to me to find that Malinowski was mostly
remembered by the natives as the champion ass at asking
damnfool questions, like, do you bury the seed tuber root end
or sprout end down? Like asking, do you stand the baby or
the coffin on its head or on its feet? I preferred not to refer
to him at all with the white people who had known him. He
had made them uneasy, and they got back at him by referring
to him as the anthrofoologist and his subject anthrofoology. I
felt too that this was partly a reflection of native unease –
they did not know what he was at. Partly again because he
made of his profession a sacred cow; you had to defer,
though you did not see why; and if you were a government
official or a missionary, you did not appreciate the big stick
from one whose infallibility was no more guaranteed than
your own (Baldwin n.d.:41).

From the same source, here is a positive appraisal of Malinowski's
work:

Malinowski's research I think was as exhaustive as it could be,
short of completely absorbing the Trobriand language. I was
continually surprised on referring back to him, to find that his
enquiry had already impinged upon some discovery that I had
supposed was all my own. His analysis too was masterly. He
seems to have left nothing unexplained, and his explanations
are enlightening even to the people who live there (Baldwin
n.d.:17).

But Father Baldwin enters a caveat:

It is curious then, that this exhaustive research and patient,
wise, and honest explanation should leave a sense of
incompleteness. But it does. I feel that his material is still not
properly digested, that Malinowski would be regarded in some
ways naïve by the people he was studying. That the people he
describes would still seem somewhat foreign to the
Trobrianders themselves. I was surprised at the number of
times informants helping me with checking Malinowski would
bridle. Usually when a passage had been gone over more than
once, they would say it was not like that. They did not
quarrel with facts or explanation, only with the colouring, as
it were. The sense expressed was not the sense they had of

themselves, or of things Boyowan (Baldwin n.d.:17–18).

These opinions tend to confirm the suspicion that Malinowski's exacting goal of grasping the Trobriander's view of his own culture finally eluded him. He reproduced the outward form meticulously but, in the last analysis, was denied a vision of its inward coherence.

IV

> On the islands of the Pacific, though I was pursued by the
> products of the Standard Oil Company, weekly editions,
> cotton goods, cheap detective stories, and the internal
> combustion engine in the ubiquitous motor launch, I was still
> able with but little effort to re-live and reconstruct a type of
> human life moulded by the implements of the stone age,
> pervaded with crude beliefs and surrounded by a wide,
> uncontaminated open stretch of nature (Malinowski
> 1930:406).

Malinowski viewed the Trobriands as a natural laboratory, and his writings depict its people as dwelling in a timeless limbo – an ethnographic present innocent of colonial contamination. Although he was to deplore his neglect of the colonial impact on Trobriand culture as 'the most serious shortcoming of my whole anthropological research' (1935(I):481), one can agree with John Barnes that Malinowski 'was not much concerned with any influence his published work might have on the islanders or on the Papuan administration' (1967:195). During the 1930s, however, Malinowski had come to believe not only that anthropology should urgently concern itself with the study of social change (or 'culture contact'), but also that the uncommitted, amoral stance affected by the science of man was untenable. In a series of articles in the journal *Africa*, and in two posthumously published works, *The Dynamics of Culture Change* (1945) and *Freedom and Civilization* (1947), he edged towards a partisan view of the political and moral commitments that anthropology should assume in relation to the colonial problems and ideological crises of the era. While accepting the colonial *status quo*, he was broadly sympathetic to the stirrings of African nationalism. A 'reluctant imperialist' in Wendy James's phrase (1973), his voice was nevertheless a radical one for its time:

There is a moral obligation to every calling, even to that of a scientific specialist. The duty of the anthropologist is to be a fair and true interpreter of the Native . . .

He ought to be able to make clear to traders, missionaries, and exploiters what the Natives really need and where they suffer most under the pressure of European interference. There is no doubt that the destiny of indigenous races has been tragic in the process of contact with European invasion . . .

Shall we, therefore, mix politics with science? In one way, decidedly 'yes' . . . (1945:3–4).

But this was already too little and too late. A generation later, overtaken once more by history, by the rapid unscrambling of the colonial world in the 1960s (bringing home Lévi-Strauss's point that societies have changed more than anthropologists since the last World War), anthropology is now being accused of having been *too* political in its unwitting role as a handmaid of Imperialism. There is a painful echo of Malinowski's own words in the following quotation from John Kasaipwalova, one of the most articulate and influential Trobrianders of the present generation, who still smarts with resentment at the indignities of colonialism and the spurious identity ascribed to him by 'anthropology':

I would point to the political nature of anthropology, in that it has been concerned with data that is collected from studies of 'primitive' societies and therefore carries a biased picture to those who read it. For instance, I have many times felt very embarrassed and awkward when I meet new people and they ask me, 'Where are you from?' and I say, 'Oh, I am from the Trobriand Islands', and they reply excitedly, 'Ohhh, Malinowski, free love!!' What I am pointing out is that if we are going to depend on anthropological studies to define our history and our culture and our 'future', then we are *lost* (Kasaipwalova 1973:454).

The modern Trobriander, in short, is asserting the right to be a 'fair and true interpreter' of his own culture.

V

What of the situation in the Trobriands today? Despite the

animosity of Kasaipwalova and others towards anthropology, a number of young fieldworkers have conducted research there in recent years, and their publications will doubtless begin to appear shortly. Meanwhile, the following is a sketch based on the oral accounts of visitors to the islands, and on a handful of published sources (Beier 1975; Kasaipwalova 1975; Nisbett 1975; Powell 1976).

The year of Papua New Guinea's national independence (1975) saw the full emergence of a modernisation movement on Kiriwina. This movement, called 'Kabisawali', had simple beginnings as an economic scheme initiated in 1968 by the chief of Yalumugwa, an inland village of the Kiriwina district. Through self-imposed levies his villagers raised cash for a series of small-scale ventures. The modest success they achieved intensified the villagers' dissatisfaction with the paltry benefits they had been receiving from the Trobriand Local Government Council, which had been proclaimed in 1966. They attempted to opt out of the Council system by refusing to pay taxes, but the Australian administration responded by jailing them. Opposition to the Council and the administration quickly grew as other inland villages joined Kabisawali, and in an atmosphere of crisis exacerbated by a severe drought, the founding chief asked his sister's son and heir, John Kasaipwalova, who was then an undergraduate at the University of Papua New Guinea, to return home and become the movement's executive officer in order to deal with the increasingly complex problems of negotiation.

By 1972 the movement had grown to such an extent that it became necessary to organise an alternative local government. This was done largely along traditional lines. The highest chiefs were made ex-officio members and ceremonial heads of government; villages and village clusters elected representatives from among chiefs and commoners. If only because this political organisation was an entirely indigenous creation, it was felt to be far more responsive to local needs than the anomalous ward-system of the Council, which was based on an Australian model (Beier 1975:19-20).

With the establishment of the alternative government in 1973, conflict with the Council and the administration increased sharply. The Council continued to receive support from those coastal villages which had presumably benefited from it most, though there was also much traditional political rivalry involved (see Powell's speculative comments, 1976). A sequence of dramatic events involving crashed trucks, burnt property and unarmed clashes between rival supporters resulted in the intervention of riot police summoned from Port Moresby. The Kabisawali leadership thereupon decided to confront the Council legally by contesting the next election. It did so and won a majority of one. John Kasaipwalova was elected President, and the Council immediately voted to dissolve itself. Subsequently, the administration moved to liquidate it.

In 1974 the movement drafted a comprehensive development plan and became officially registered as the Kabisawali Village Development Corporation. In a practical implementation of its programme, it established a central buying agency for carving and artifacts and opened a shop for them in Port Moresby. It purchased a tractor for agricultural projects and a machine to help villagers make bricks from coral. By far the most ambitious plans, however, concerned the tourist trade. Since 1962 package-tours have been operating from Port Moresby. By 1970 tourism was the major source of cash for Trobrianders, and in 1971 over 2,100 tourists visited the islands – a rate of one for every seven Trobrianders per annum! (Leach, J. W. 1973:357-8). This immensely lucrative (and potentially very destructive) industry, therefore, became the prime target for Kabisawali control. The scheme includes a tourist hotel built from native materials and constructed on the model of a traditional village, regular charter flights from Port Moresby, busing facilities on Kiriwina, and the creation of a professional dance company and art centre (Beier 1975:21–4).

If such schemes succeed they will inevitably bind Trobrianders more firmly to a market economy, which will then pose even more insidious threats to the traditional culture than those experienced during the colonial era. Kabisawali appears to be alerted to this danger, and one of its principal aims is the preservation of Trobriand cultural uniqueness (Kasaipwalova 1975). There are some signs that the movement has already done much to encourage a cultural revival (see Jerry Leach's recent film *Trobriand Cricket*, and the BBC TV documentaries *The Human Conspiracy* and *The Trobriand Experiment*). In a manner which would have won the enthusiastic endorsement of Malinowski, this cultural revival was promoted by reactivating traditional stimuli to increased food production. Thus, on gaining power over the Council, Kabisawali announced a competitive gardening event, *kayasa*, in which villages vied to produce the richest harvest. The yam crop in 1974 was reportedly the best seen for a generation. The yam harvest itself has again become a significant annual event, complete with decorative competitive displays much as Malinowski witnessed them sixty years ago. The revival of festivals and *kayasa* has also brought the garden magicians back into prominence (Beier 1975:21). It must be stressed, however, that for all its emphasis on the revival of traditional forms and activities Kabisawali is not a 'revitalization movement' in the accepted sense, much less a cargo cult. Its main thrust is political, its principal goals economic, and its means thoroughly rational.

It must also be stressed that the current situation in the Trobriands is very fluid. It seethes with new ideas, but there are divided interests and many uncertainties about the future. Opponents of the Kabisawali movement have formed a rival organisation with the backing of the conservative Tabalu chiefs, and each party is engaged in trying to discredit the other. Trobriand society will surely be in ferment for some time to come (see Powell 1976).

Finally, a note on the Kula. According to the few reports available it continues to operate within and between the Trobriands and Dobu, though in somewhat modified form (Lauer 1970; Leach, J. W. 1973:359; see also the Japanese TV film shown by BBC in 1974). On this topic, let John Kasaipwalova have the last word, for although he would probably be reluctant to agree, his own view of the Kula is not too dissimilar to Malinowski's of more than fifty years ago:

> I find that in fact we have had 'development corporations' going on in the Trobriand Islands for hundreds of years before any white people came – the '*Kula* ring', as it is popularly called. And in a sense this 'development corporation' rests on the basic premise that you carry out this activity to further human happiness, so that people can be festive, they can communicate without paper; and it gives people the incentive to work and make their gardens (1973:454).

November 1976

Part one
Habitat and economy

Editor's note to part one

Sources

The following two chapters are a distillation of Malinowski's own introductory survey of Trobriand subsistence activities. The text has been assembled from *Coral Gardens and their Magic* (vol. I), pp. 6–9, 12–21, 23–34, 37–47, 50–5, 61–8, 73–83 and 181–5.

Further reading

In addition to Malinowski's other writings on the subject (see bibliography in Firth 1957a), further information on Trobriand economics is given by Austin (1945–6). Bradfield (1973) presents a useful synopsis of Malinowski's data on gardening. For further discussion of Trobriand time-reckoning see Austin (1938–9, 1949–50) and Leach (1949–50). For additional comments on and alternative interpretations of rank and chieftainship in the Trobriands see Brunton (1975), Groves (1956), Powell (1960, 1969b) and Uberoi (1962). A comparative account of subsistence gardening in Dobu can be found in Fortune (1932), and for a comprehensive study of competitive food exchange in a neighbouring Massim society see Young (1971).

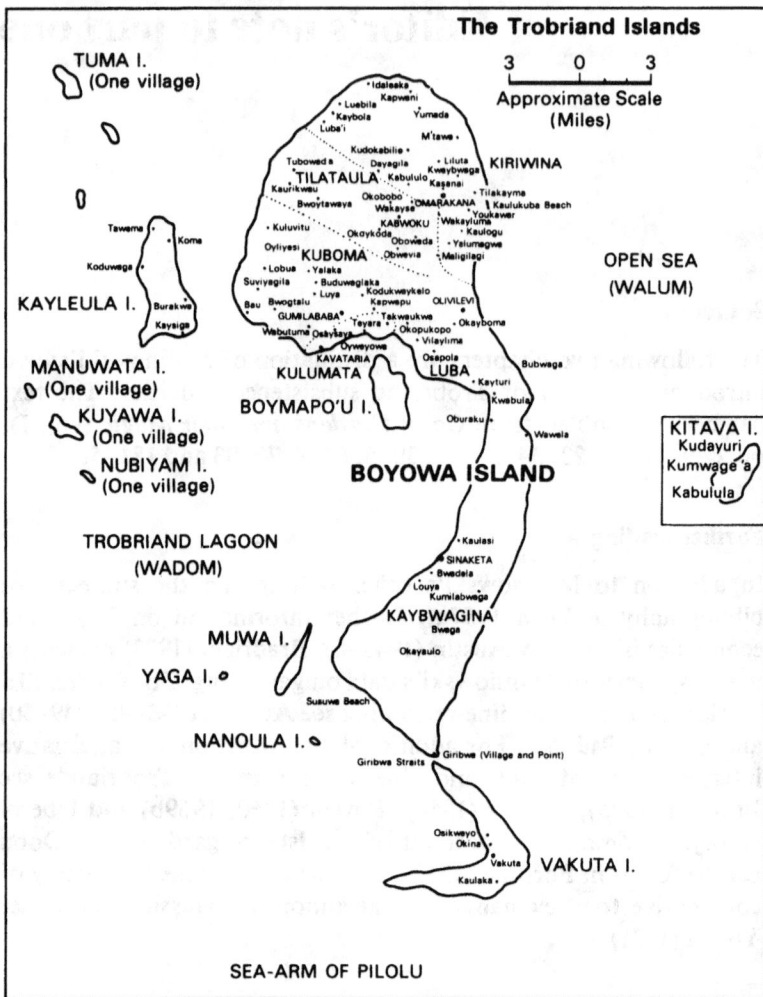

Figure 1 The Trobriand Islands

1 An outline of Trobriand economics

1 Habitat

The Trobriand archipelago which faces you on the map (Fig. 1) is a coral atoll, or more correctly a part of the Lusançay atoll. The group which concerns us consists of one big island, two of fair size – Vakuta and Kayleula – and a number of smaller ones surrounding a basin or lagoon. This latter is very shallow, parts of it are not navigable even to the native canoes, but it is crossed with deeper channels. It is open to all winds, giving no shelter whatever from the north-westerly monsoon or the strong southerly winds, and affording only a little protection near the shores of the main island from the south-easterly trade wind. To the east, at a distance of about one hundred miles, lies the second large centre of the Northern Massim culture – Woodlark Island. Between Woodlark Island and the Trobriands there is a bridge of five small islands – Kitava, Iwa, Gawa, Kwaywata and Digumenu – also inhabited by people of the same culture.

In our detailed descriptions we shall, however, dwell almost exclusively on the main island of the Trobriands, with only brief references to the contiguous areas. On this large island, called by the natives Boyowa or, after its principal province, Kiriwina, we shall find several types of scenery, soil and agriculture. The northern part, a wide circular expanse of land, harbours most of the fertile soil. Only the narrow coral ridge which runs along its northern and eastern border remains almost completely outside cultivation and is covered with patches of primeval jungle. But this never attains to full tropical luxuriance, and some economically important plants, such as the sago palm, the lawyer cane, and the bamboo, do not grow there and have to be imported as raw material from abroad. Some portions of the land in the interior are also useless because they are too swampy; while, in the west, large stretches on the coast are covered with mangrove, which grows on a brackish swamp awash at high tide. In the southern part of the island the dead coral crops up, especially at the extreme end, leaving large tracks of country uncultivable and uninhabited. The brackish swamps of the southern portion extend deeper inland and the villages are placed either on the lagoon, where fishing makes their existence possible, or on one or two fertile spots inland.

The description of the territory just given, taken in connexion with the map of the Archipelago (which shows incidentally that for a South Sea tribe the Trobriands have a very dense population), the realisation that these natives have a high level of cultural ability, of political and economic organisation – enables us roughly to assess the type of their production and industrial development. The fertile humus covering the wide expanse of dead coral lends itself obviously to an intensive cultivation of useful plants, i.e., since we are in the South Seas, of yam, taro, sweet potato, banana and coconut. The open lagoon, teeming with submarine life, would naturally invite an enterprising and intelligent population to develop effective fishing. The industrious and compact settlements would lead us to anticipate excellence in arts and crafts. Differences in habitat and opportunity might well be expected to produce special centres of industry and systems of internal trade. Again, the absence of certain indispensable raw materials – stone (dead coral is useless for any industrial purpose), clay, rattan, bamboo, sago – would suggest an extensive trade with the outside world. The absence of primeval jungle indicates that hunting cannot be of any importance and the search for wild produce can play only a subsidiary part.

This rough estimate is indeed correct almost in every essential. The Trobriander is above all a cultivator, not only by opportunity and need, but also by passion and his traditional system of values. Half of the native's working life is spent in the garden and around it centres perhaps more than half of his interests and ambitions. In gardening the natives produce much more than they actually require, and in any average year they harvest perhaps twice as much as they can eat. Nowadays this surplus is exported by Europeans to feed plantation hands in other parts of New Guinea; in olden days it was simply allowed to rot. Again, they produce this surplus in a manner which entails much more work than is strictly necessary for obtaining the crops. Much time and labour is given up to aesthetic purposes, to making the gardens tidy, clean, cleared of all débris; to building fine, solid fences; to providing specially strong and big yam-poles. All these things are to some extent required for the growth of the plant, but there can be no doubt that the natives push their conscientiousness far beyond the limits of the purely necessary. The non-utilitarian element in their garden work is still more clearly perceptible in the various tasks which they carry out entirely for the sake of ornamentation, in connexion with magical ceremonies and in obedience to tribal usage.

Fishing comes next in importance. In some villages situated on the lagoon it is the main source of sustenance and claims about half of their time and labour. But while fishing is prominent in some districts, agriculture is paramount in all. Were fishing made impossible to the Trobrianders by a natural or cultural calamity, the population as a whole would find enough sustenance from agriculture. But when the gardens fail in times of drought, famine inevitably sets in. Hunting is hardly an economic pursuit. From time to time you see a native walking out of the village spear in hand, and he tells you that perhaps he will be able to kill a small wallaby or a bush-pig. Bird-snaring has a little more importance. But every time I saw the natives eating a wild-fowl I found that it had been shot by some white trader and passed on from a distant village. Collecting of food from the bush in times of drought, the catching of crabs and molluscs in mangrove swamp and lagoon, are much more substantial contributions to the tribal larder. Transport and trade are well developed. The inland barter of fish and vegetable food is an institution which controls a great deal of their public life.

Thus, in brief, we find that the environmentalist's predictions are substantially correct. But there are a great many things referring to work and its organisation, to the production and distribution of wealth and to its consumption, which cannot be inferred from ecological indications. The environmentalist will foresee nothing of the great importance of magic and of political power in the organisation of gardening. In the distribution of produce he cannot anticipate the extremely complex way in which kinship and relationship by marriage impose obligations and place the Trobriand household economically on a two-fold foundation. Nor could he guess the intricate manner in which mother-right combined with patrilocal marriage complicates the system. The

contrivances and customs which allow these natives to accumulate
large quantities of food, and the legal system which concentrates
wealth in the hands of a few leaders who can then organise enterprises on a tribal scale, have to be observed and stated from
experience.

2 Economic provinces

A glance at the map (Fig. 1) will show that the broad expanse in the
north is thickly populated with villages scattered all over the
circular area, whereas in the south there is a collection of villages
near the western coast which run on in a continuous line to the
lagoon settlements of the north. These two constellations of
villages, the evenly distributed batch in the north and the semi-
circular belt of lagoon settlements, corresponds to the occupational
difference between agriculture and fishing. But besides these two
main distinctions, further differences can be found between every
one of the several districts – differences which are partly political,
partly sociological and partly, what is of special interest to us here,
economic.

Thus in the north we have three central provinces; Kiriwina, to
the north-east, Tilataula in the middle, and Kuboma to the south-
west. The first two depend almost exclusively on agriculture.
Kiriwina is the politically dominant, socially most exalted and
economically perhaps the richest province, and the paramount
chief of the whole area has his residence in Omarakana. The
villages at the northern end of the island count as part of Kiriwina;
and among these are Laba'i and Kaybola, the only two fishing
settlements in this district. They specialise in two types of fishing
only, shark and mullet, which though strictly seasonal have yet
some economic importance. When a large shark is caught off
Kaybola – for this is the place where shark fishing is known in
magic and practice – the whole district will have its fill of this
pungent fish. Again, when rich shoals of mullet appear at the full
moon off Laba'i, and are caught in large quantities with air-nets,
tribute will be sent to the paramount chief and to lesser chiefs, and
fish will be plentiful all over Kiriwina. There is a special magic connected with this fishing, chartered by mythological tradition and
localised ritual, and carried out by the respective headman of each
community, with taboos and ceremonial. The villages are bound to

give tribute of their catch and in turn are presented with counter-gifts from the recipient communities.

In Kiriwina most of the villages have a 'sea-front' on the eastern shore, where a large canoe for overseas trips, and several small canoes for fishing or coasting, are beached. In these villages a man would go out with his fish-hook or a group of people with a seine and make some haul on the reef. This was an amateur pursuit which enabled the villagers to obtain a little fish now and then during the calms in autumn and spring, more for pleasure of the sport and delicacy of the relish than for business. When I say amateur pursuit, I mean that there was no official magic, no season for fishing, no communal organised expeditions, no obligation to outside communities or to their own people.

The next province, Tilataula, did no fishing whatever. They would be described by a native expression meaning 'real land-lubbers'. If Kiriwina, as the brilliant, exalted, aristocratic province, might be called the Athens of the Trobriands, Tilataula, strong in military arts, hard working and sober, could be called the Sparta of the island. They themselves are proud of their agriculture and of their frequent victories over their more aristocratic but less militaristic neighbours. The chief of Kabwaku, the capital of Tilataula, used to wage war occasionally against the Paramount Chief, to whom in one way he was subject, but in another a rival and a dangerous antagonist. Economically these natives concentrate on gardening; they have no canoes either for fishing or for overseas expeditions, and they are not skilled in any art except one, the polishing of stone.

But it is only when we move further west to the district of Kuboma that we find really developed industries on that stonier soil which produces distinctly less brilliant gardens than its eastern neighbours. We might feel tempted to speak of the inhabitants of Kuboma as the industrial caste of the Trobriands; for neither in ancient Greece nor even on the Mediterranean can we find any exact parallel. They are not like Phoenicians or Jews, primarily traders, but rather industrialists and craftsmen; and, as in any strict caste system, their high manual ability does not give them rank but rather places them among the despised. This refers especially to the most admirable of all Trobriand craftsmen, the inhabitants of Bwoytalu. This village, which shares with its neighbours of Ba'u the reputation for the highest efficiency in sorcery, can certainly

show the best results in carving; it is traditionally cultivated there
and both for perfection and quantity of output is unparalleled in
the region. From time immemorial its people have been the woodworkers and carvers of eastern New Guinea. And they still turn out
wooden platters, hunting- and fishing-spears, staffs, polishing-
boards, combs, wooden hammers and bailers in large quantities,
and with a degree of geometrical and artistic perfection which any
visitor to an ethnographic museum will appreciate. They also excel
in plaited fibre work and in certain forms of basketry. During the
wet season, when some other communities are busy preparing overseas expeditions, or engaging in festivities and ceremonial distributions, or (generations ago) indulging in war, the men of Bwoytalu
will day after day sit on one of their large covered platforms,
rounding, bending, carving and polishing their masterpieces in
wood. It is a wholesale manufacture for trade and export. There is
no magic whatever connected with their work, but from childhood
skill is drilled into every individual, the knowledge of material,
ambition and a sense of value. No other community can or tries to
compete with them.

The other villages, Yalaka, Buduwaylaka and Kudukwaykela
specialise in the production of quick lime for betel chewing. The
last named village used also to produce the burnt-in designs on
decorated lime pots, which can still be admired in an ethnographic
museum and form undoubtedly one of the high-water marks of
South Sea art. Unfortunately this industry is now dead. Plain lime
pots, gaudily and as a rule vulgarly bedecked with cheap European
trade beads, have completely superseded the beautiful native
product. The inhabitants of Luya are the main producers of the
finely plaited basket work made of lalang grass, chiefly used for the
three-tiered basket, the widower's cap and small handbags. These
are traded even now all over the archipelago, indeed over the whole
Kula district. Some of the villages, notably Ba'u, Bwoytalu and
Wabutuma, also practise fishing and specialise in catching, by
means of a multi-pronged spear, that despised fish, the stingaree.

Moving in our general economic survey, we come to the lagoon
district of the north – Kulumata. In the large, compound village of
Kavataria we find again a Tabalu in residence, and in two other
neighbouring settlements chiefs of the same rank have also become
naturalised. But this district is not one political unit under the sway
of one headman as is the case with the three preceding ones.

The natives are fishermen who treat their calling as a serious and important pursuit. Since in this they are closely akin to some of the southern villages, let us cast our eye on the map again and consider the other fishing districts. There we find Luba, the complex of villages situated on what might be called the waist of the main island. Here the new capital Olivilevi, founded a few generations ago as an offshoot of Omarakana, and its neighbour Okayboma are mainly agricultural. The other villages, however, from Okopukopu down to Oburaku, depended chiefly on their fishing. Further south still and separated by a somewhat prolonged stretch of unoccupied land, we find the large village of Sinaketa surrounded by a few smaller settlements, and south of these, situated towards the eastern shore, three villages. These latter are mainly agricultural. Sinaketa, on the other hand, is an important fishing centre as well as the seat of at least one dominant industry – the production of red shell-disks used as ornaments and tokens of value.

Now concentrating our attention on the fishing villages we find that each of the coastal settlements has a type of fishing of its own. As we know, Bwoytalu and its neighbours, though they net fish, collect molluscs and catch crab, are primarily interested in the spearing of stingaree. Kavataria, the large settlement in the centre of Kulumata, has an importance specially due to the presence in their portion of the lagoon of a number of coral outcrops with cavities and shelters which afford the best opportunity for catching fish by means of a poisonous root. The coral patches are now owned individually, at times leased, and they are worked often and worked hard. The great importance of this fishing is that it is possible to make a catch in weather and under conditions in which no other type of fishing is practicable. It is remarkable that no magic whatever is now practised in connexion with this industry. By the ease of their work and their relative independence of weather, the natives of Kavataria are monopolists, in that they can provide fish when no one else can supply it. In the exchange of fish for vegetables, which plays an important rôle in Trobriand economic life, they exact about double the usual price from the other party, but in return offer punctual and reliable delivery.

The communities further east, Teyava and Osaysuya, Tukwa'ukwa and Oyweyowa, also fish, but are inferior in their effectiveness not only to Kavataria, the premier fishing centre, but

also to Oburaku and Okopukopu. The last named places have no
coral outcrops in their portion of the lagoon and all large-scale
fishing they do by nets and beating. For this they need a calm day,
favourable movements of the shoals and, of course, an organised
communal enterprise. When successful their yield is large and they
give a better measure in exchange; but their partners may very often
have to wait for a long time and even in the case of a successful
expedition the yield may be fitful. Moving further south we come
to the only village situated on the eastern shore – Wawela. The
inhabitants do some odd fishing on calm days, but their speciality is
knowledge of native astronomy and meteorology, or more
correctly, of native time-reckoning. Economically they depend on
their gardens and to a considerable extent also on the rich coconut
plantations on their beach.

The large settlement of Sinaketa, comprising some seven or eight
component villages, is important in that from here, and from the
large village of Vakuta on the adjacent island to the south, some of
the main sailing expeditions are made to the Amphletts and to
Dobu, where the ceremonial Kula exchange takes place and also
some straightforward inter-tribal trade. In olden days, and to a
certain extent even now, the natives of Sinaketa and Vakuta used
also, on their expeditions, to fish for the spondylus shell out of
which the shell-disks were manufactured. There is another industry
of the same type and that is the making of arm-shells. This was
above all the speciality of the one district not yet mentioned – the
small island of Kayleula to the west of Kuboma. To this district
also belong the smaller one-village islands of Manuwata, Kuyawa
and Nubiyam. But Kavataria, the village of the coral outcrops,
runs a near second in the production of arm-shells. The two
centres, Kavataria and the villages of Kayleula, used also to
practise a special offshoot of the Kula ring, in which the exchange
of useful industrial articles as well as foodstuffs played a greater
part than it does in the main circuit of the Kula.

One more subject must be briefly discussed here although it
stands a little outside the proper Trobriand economics. The small
pearl-shell, called by the natives *lapi*, has been fished and collected
from time immemorial, as providing the natives with the most
important edible mollusc. When in opening the shell the natives
would find a large, beautifully rounded off pearl, they would throw
it to the children to play with. Under European influence a new

industry has blossomed. By the wise legislation of the Papuan government, European traders are allowed only to purchase pearls from the natives and must not carry out or organise any diving on their own account. To five communities – Kavataria, Teyava, Tukwa'ukwa, Oburaku and Sinaketa – this has, for the last quarter of a century or so, proved what to the natives seems an incredibly large source of income. In many ways it has produced a revolution in native economics.

In spite of the fact that pearl diving opened up a prospect of untold wealth and upset the whole balance of power, it is only those communities where the *lapi* shell was fished of old which continue the industry. Neither the expert and skilled fishermen of Vakuta and Kayleula, nor the crafty and intelligent stingaree fishers of Bwoytalu, nor, least of all, any of the land-lubbers, take to pearling. Technically they could do it perfectly well, as the pursuit is simple. As regards organised effort and their ability to appreciate wealth and trade, they are all on the same level. They abstain partly because the communities in traditional possession of the industry would object and would have a moral – in native opinion also a legal – right to prevent poaching; but more because it is felt that it would be unjust as well as unseemly to encroach upon established rights.

Our survey has shown us that agriculture is not merely most important integrally, that is, for the tribe as a whole, but that everywhere it is the main food-producing activity in that everywhere it takes precedence over all other work. We have also seen that fishing, which is unknown in about half the villages, takes the second place even in those centres where it is most intensively practised. As regards industries it is important to make it quite clear that they do not play a part comparable in any way to that of agriculture or even fishing. When we speak about division of labour by districts, we do not mean anything similar to specialisation in a modern industrial community. All villages exercise every art and craft, except such as have only a local utility. Inland villages do not build canoes or make nets.

3 The village and the seasonal cycle

The visitor has to get ashore in one of the coastal villages – Sinaketa or Vakuta, if he intends starting from the south, or in Kavataria or

Tukwa'ukwa if he begins with the north. These villages – an attractive palm grove with here and there a house showing among the
trees and a few canoes drawn up on the beach, or being paddled
into the offing, do not gain by near inspection. The beach itself is
very often littered with rubbish, shells, fish-bones and, nowadays,
tins and cotton rags. European influence also shows itself in pieces
of corrugated iron disfiguring the thatch, in oil cans gradually
replacing the graceful coconut water-bottles. The coastal settlements also appear at first sight chaotic, with huts irregularly placed
and storehouses scattered among the palms without much system.
But after a close inspection of one of them, or preferably of
several, we find that in reality each coastal settlement consists of a
cluster of smaller villages. We find also that every small village has
definite constituent parts: a central public place surrounded with
one or two rings composed of stores and dwellings. Where these are
kept separate, the inner ring is formed by the storehouses and the
dwellings line the outer side of a circular street (see Fig. 2).

Walking inland we find that the villages vary in size, in structure

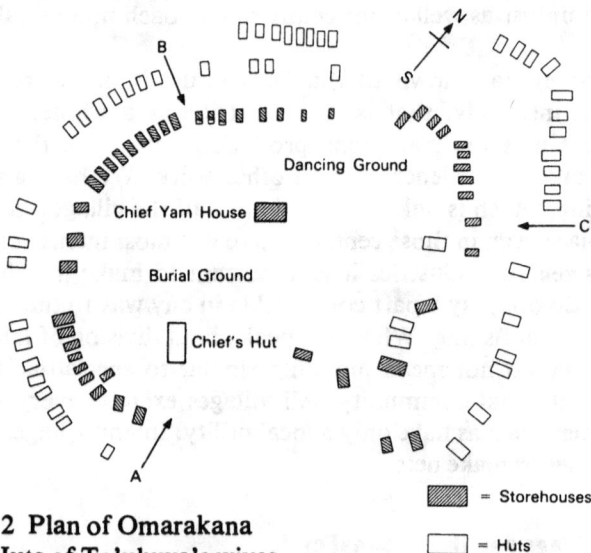

Figure 2 Plan of Omarakana
A–B Huts of To'uluwa's wives
A–C Huts occupied by Tabalu
B–C Huts of commoners

and in the degree to which the buildings are finished and decorated. If we enter one of the district capitals, say Gumilababa or better still Omarakana, we see a wide central place of a good shape, and large, well-built, and at times decorated yam-houses. But we shall also pass through small inland villages with some twenty huts and storehouses surrounding a diminutive central place; and compound settlements where several small hamlets are clustered in the same large grove. Whatever the village it is marked from a distance by a large clump of tall trees; at times this looks like a piece of untouched jungle, at times the coconut palm predominates. Such clumps of trees are sometimes found to be groves without any habitation – either sites of now deserted villages or places where the jungle is left standing because of a mythological association or some special magical taboo. Every village, whether compound or simple, whether large or small, is a unit of settlement; that is, it is surrounded by its own territory, agriculturally exploited; it has its own water-hole, fruit-trees and palm groves, and in most cases its own access to the seashore.

It is astonishing how many of the various events of public life which always happen in the central place refer to gardens, or at least involve the use of garden produce. Glancing at the Chart of Time-reckoning (Fig. 3) we see that the half to the right side of column 5 is taken up with garden activities. For even the cere-monial (col. 10) is in the first place directly dependent on harvest. The first three moons and the last three are noted in columns 1 and 10 as occupied by social, sexual and ceremonial life. If we project these entries into their actual setting in the village, they will always be framed by decorations of food: large heaps of yams on the central place, prismatic receptacles filled with produce, festoons made of coconuts and bananas, taro and yam tubers. The spirits of the deceased are greeted and gladdened at the feast of *milamala* by the sight of accumulated raw vegetables and fruit. The memory of those dead during the last year or two is celebrated with ceremonial distributions of uncooked food. In fact, no sooner have the harvest displays of yams been stacked away in the full yam-houses than these are tapped and some of the food moved again.

If during the last year no one has died in the village – that is no one of importance or rank – a dancing period is opened by a large distribution of food, followed by cooking and eating. From then on day after day the men will be dancing the whole afternoon and

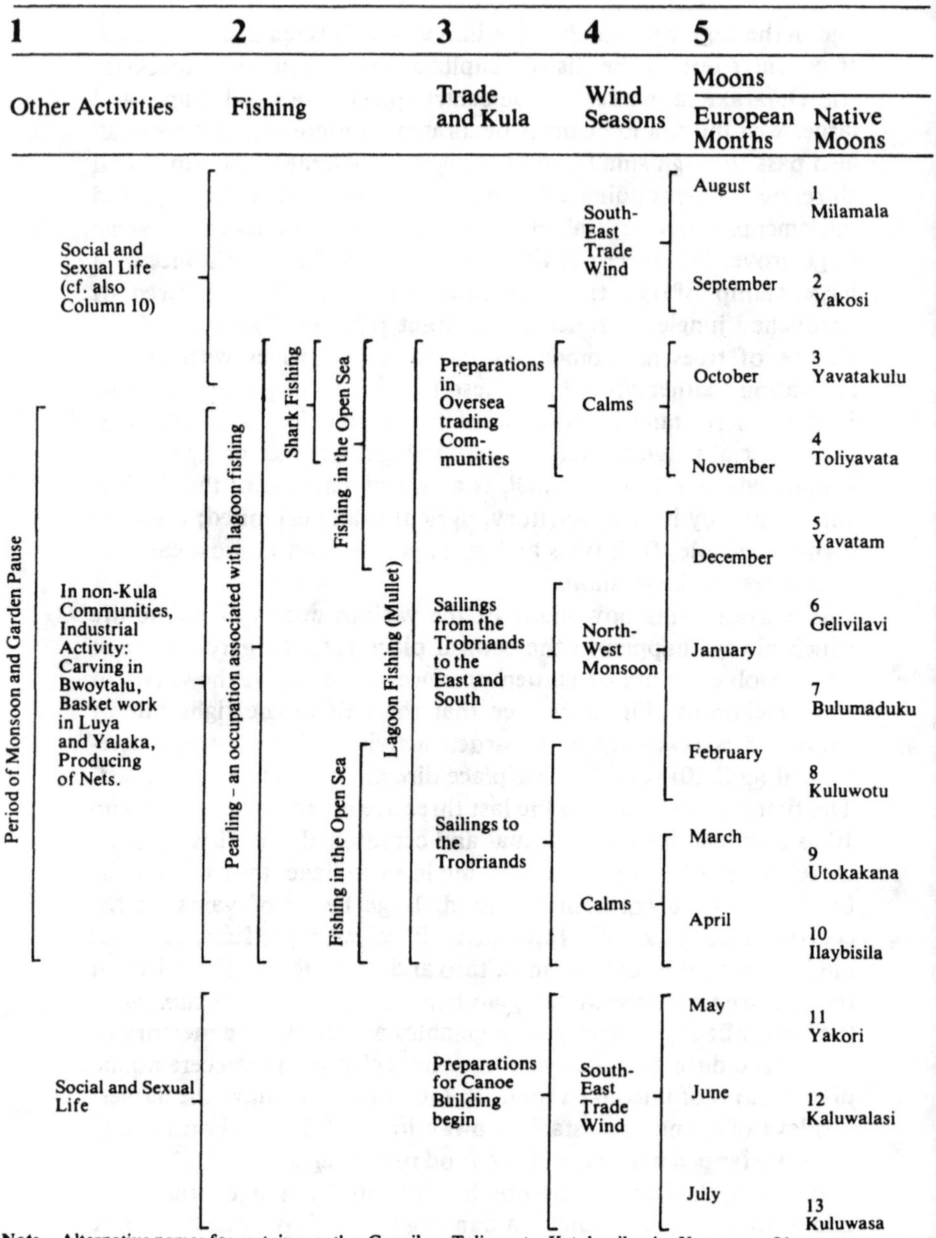

1	2	3	4	5	
				Moons	
Other Activities	Fishing	Trade and Kula	Wind Seasons	European Months	Native Moons

1 Other Activities	2 Fishing	3 Trade and Kula	4 Wind Seasons	5 European Months	5 Native Moons
Social and Sexual Life (cf. also Column 10)	*(Shark Fishing / Fishing in the Open Sea / Pearling – an occupation associated with lagoon fishing / Lagoon Fishing (Mullet) / Fishing in the Open Sea)*	Preparations in Oversea trading Communities	South-East Trade Wind	August	1 Milamala
				September	2 Yakosi
			Calms	October	3 Yavatakulu
In non-Kula Communities, Industrial Activity: Carving in Bwoytalu, Basket work in Luya and Yalaka, Producing of Nets.				November	4 Toliyavata
		Sailings from the Trobriands to the East and South	North-West Monsoon	December	5 Yavatam
				January	6 Gelivilavi
					7 Bulumaduku
		Sailings to the Trobriands	Calms	February	8 Kuluwotu
				March	9 Utokakana
				April	10 Ilaybisila
Social and Sexual Life		Preparations for Canoe Building begin	South-East Trade Wind	May	11 Yakori
				June	12 Kaluwalasi
				July	13 Kuluwasa

(Left-most bracket spanning: Period of Monsoon and Garden Pause)

Note   Alternative names for certain months: Gaygila = Toliyavat   Katubugibogi = Yavatam   Obwatayouyo = Yak

Figure 3 Chart of time-reckoning

6	7	8	9	10
Agricultural, Seasons	Kaymata (Main Gardens)	Kaymugwa (Early Gardens)	Tapopu (Taro Gardens)	Ceremonial

	Kaymata (Main Gardens)	Kaymugwa (Early Gardens)	Tapopu (Taro Gardens)	Ceremonial	
Malia	Pause in Gardening; Gabu	Sopu		Milamala in Kiriwina	Dancing; Kayasa; Ceremonial Distribution
	Koumwala and Early Planting				
				Milamala in Vakuta	
	Kamkokola and Sopu				
Geguda / Molu	Sopu and Making Fences	Isunapulo	Planting (Dry Soil)		
	Growth Magic (1); Kavatam and Weeding				
	Isunapulo		Second Cycle		
	Growth Magic (2)				
	Basi	Harvest	Isunapulo		
Matuwo			Planting (on Dumya)	Kaytubutabu Season	
	Okwala and Tum; Harvest begins				
Malia	Kayaku; Harvest continues	Kayaku; Takaywa	First Cycle	Dress in Preparation for Milamala	
	Filling the Bwayma; Vilamalia	Gabu		Milamala in Kitava	
Geguda	Yowota; Takaywa	Koumwala; Early Planting: Kuvi, Taro, etc.	Isunapulo	Milamala in Sinaketa, Luba and Western District	

evening, the women, in new and especially gaudy petticoats, will be cooking an unusual amount of food; platters of cooked food will be exchanged from one house to another and constant gifts of uncooked food will pass from hand to hand.

The dancing period, like most festivities or enterprises in the Trobriands, is punctuated by communal distributions and feasts. There is usually a specially large one at the beginning or in the middle, and several at the end. The headman of the community – whether he be also a district chief or only the local *primus inter pares* does not matter – acts throughout as master of ceremonies. He supplies the food. The members of the community by receiving it are put under an obligation to co-operate in whatever ceremonial activity is in progress: to participate in the dancing or the display of valuables, in competitive games or public singing.

If a member of the community has died during the previous year, there would be no dancing. Probably one or two ceremonial distributions of food would take place instead. Such distributions are among the most usual and characteristic ceremonial acts in the Trobriands.

They attain their most elaborate and quantitatively biggest form at mortuary commemorative feasts. Roughly speaking, the principles, sociological, economic and dogmatic, of such ceremonies are as follows. The eldest male of the deceased's kindred acts as master of the ceremony. From his kinsmen and from his wife's relatives and, if he is a notable, from those who normally give him tribute, he receives on such an occasion considerable gifts of food and to this he adds to the extent perhaps of half the contents of his storehouse. On lesser occasions all this food is then placed on the ground in circular heaps; on greater ones into prismatic receptacles. Each heap is apportioned to a person who stands in a definite social relationship to the deceased. As a rule most food is given to the deceased's children and to their kindred, for these are the people who have performed the bulk of the mortuary duties. The distribution is made by a ceremonial calling out of the name of each person as his share is allotted.

After this the gifts, which – let it be noted – consist in uncooked tubers and fruit, are put into baskets by each recipient, taken away to his own village, which is usually at a distance, and there unloaded in the house. With a few insignificant exceptions it is not put away in the storehouses, but distributed by the recipient among his kindred and relatives-in-law on both sides. Every community round the centre of distribution will be thus provided with an abundance of food which must be consumed in especially lavish meals. Plenty in the sense of glut will obtain in the district in which the mortuary distribution has been held.

I have expatiated on these facts because it is important to note that 'feasts' or 'festivities' in this part of Melanesia consist not of joint eating on a large scale, but of big agglomerations of uncooked food which are redistributed to individuals. At the same time such a redistribution does not merely mean that food changes hands, often several times, within the space of two or three days – it means also that in the whole district more food is prepared and consumed on a lavish scale. As a rule such a distribution will be accompanied by the killing of a pig or two, often as many as a dozen. Or else fish will be provided from one of the coastal villages. This again means that more tubers are consumed for, as the natives put it, 'eaten with a relish' (i.e. with fat, flesh or fish) 'the staple food slides down more easily'.

When a communal cooking of taro or yam is arranged, the food is not consumed communally; a group of men squat round a pot and each dips his shell spoon into it. The festive character of the meal does not, therefore, lie in a communal sharing of each other's company in the act of eating – the tendency is to eat in small groups, usually within the family – but much more in the common enjoyment of seeing large quantities of food accumulated and displayed. The substance of the feast consists in giving and receiving and handing on, and in satisfying the obligations of kinship by contributing first of all to the pooling and then to the redistribution of the produce.

The contemplation of agglomerated food, its handling and its movements constitute, as we have said, the substance of the collective ceremony; but the meal itself, eaten in small groups and families, or it may even be alone, forms also an essential part of this though it is never a collective act. Full satisfaction of appetite, glut and surfeit, are to the native bound up emotionally with the vision of accumulated food. They are the substance of *malia* – prosperity, fullness, satiety. The idea of 'eating till one vomits', of surfeit, of eating with the addition of meat and other relishes, is something which fits naturally into the scheme of the 'moons of plenty' which are the months of harvest.

Glancing back at our Chart (Fig. 3) on the left we find in the subsequent moons, 3, 4 and 5, such entries as preparations in sea-trading communities for overseas expeditions (col. 3), for shark fishing and fishing in the open sea (col. 2). If we watched such events as they actually happen in and around the village and on the seashore we would find that once more food is part of the ceremonial setting of canoe-making and that there are important sociological and economic implications in the presents given.

During the latter months of the monsoon season and during the calms, there would be less public display of yam food. For by that time the stores are getting low; interest in the gardens is manifested in watching the new crops and trying to estimate the chances of a 'plenty' or 'scarcity' harvest. Soon some of the early crops grow ready for harvesting. The preliminary ceremonies take place and the displays of the first fruits. And this starts the harvest which again fills the whole village with agricultural produce. Then we should see new stores and new dwellings being constructed, and gifts and counter-gifts would be exchanged: basketsful of yams, bundles of taro and bunches of banana or sugar-cane.

Taking our stand on the central place of one of the inland villages we have watched the round of the seasons. Public life consists during the early time of the year in various festivities, some of which, such as dancing, games and singing competitions, are merely framed with distributions of food. Others, such as the mortuary ceremonies, consist very largely in the handling of produce. Throughout these activities the people are busy in the evening repairing or making things or at some craft, and in the industrial centres the men work day after day on their speciality. But it can be said that throughout the year in one way or another garden produce is their mainstay, and the public display of crops forms part of all ceremonial. Small wonder, since agriculture is the dominant food-producing activity and the principal personal interest of every native.

4 The household and the daily diet

So far we have lingered on the central place and watched the events of public life. Walking from the inner to the outer ring we would have to pass between two storehouses. Facing one of these on the other side of the street we would see its owner's dwelling, where he lives with his wife and children, the rule being in the Trobriands: one living house – one family. Only seldom do remoter relatives stay with them. Usually even an old couple have a hut to themselves; a widow or widower lives alone, while bachelors share a small communal house. The house, the store, the intervening part of the street, the clear space behind where the refuse heap is to be found, all these are the domestic territory of the family. Behind the house the wife cleans and prepares the food for cooking, or works on some of her purely feminine activities, such as skirt-making, mat-sewing, or mending some domestic implement. There also small children often play. The cooking is done either in the house on the hearth stones or, when an earth oven has to be used, behind the house, or at times in front of it. The front is the social centre of family life. There in the evening they sit together, eat, and chat; there they are visited by their neighbours.

Entering the house we would find a stuffy but not offensive interior, scantily furnished and illuminated only by such light as creeps through the small door. The house is no more than an arched thatched roof placed directly on the ground. Against the walls are bunks, usually two along the back and one along the side. By spreading a few pandanus mats, these are made ready for the night. On one of those low bunks we shall watch the magician charming over his herbs and substances. Towards the free wall you invariably find the fireplace, consisting of three hearth stones – to the Trobriander in a way as to the Westerner the symbolic centre of domesticity. Here cooking is done on wet days; and on one of the stones, the garden magician will place the offering to the ancestral spirits at one of the most important ritual acts of his system. Higher up above the bunks there run one or two shelves on one of which our magician keeps the magical torches between harvest and the burning of the gardens. On the shelves you would find as a rule the cooking-pots in which food is prepared, the wooden platters from which it is eaten, and a small provision of tubers, the main supply of which is kept in the storehouse. Only when tubers are received at a ceremonial distribution will they be placed for immediate consumption within the house. Perishable vegetables, such as taro, bananas, fruit, are also kept in the house.

Following the round of daily life we would find that at the busy seasons for agriculture the family set out early for the gardens. There is no cooking of food in the morning. Some cold yams or taro are left over from the previous evening's cooking, and a meal of these is described by a special word meaning 'food left over for cold eating'. The main meal – and there is only one in the day – is prepared at sunset after the people have returned from their daily work, and consists of small yams, *taytu*, or the larger variety, *kuv*; or else of some taro, occasionally seasoned with fish or wild fowl or pork. These may be roasted on embers or boiled in a small pot or, more rarely, baked in the earth oven. During the day, whether the people be out in the gardens or return for the hot hours to the village, no cooked meal is served. Fruit, such as mangoes, bread-fruit or bananas, is eaten, or a green coconut broken, its milk drunk and its flesh eaten. Or when there is a good supply of fresh fruit, some of it may occasionally be roasted.

The large clay pots are used only for communal cooking; that is, when cooked, not raw, food is distributed. This is done in payment for communal work and sometimes it may figure as part of the gift at the other distributions already mentioned.

The natives distinguish between first 'staple food', a term which includes all agricultural produce, but refers principally to the small yams; secondly 'dainty' or 'lighter food', that is wild fruit, sugar-cane and breadfruit; and thirdly 'relish', that is all forms of protein food: pork, fowl, fish, edible grubs, and shell-fish. Though the staple food is the foundation of their prosperity, and when accumulated symbolises for them plenty, wealth and a succession of joyful tribal events, the natives show a certain lukewarmness about eating it alone. They only dimly realise that food possesses nutritive value. They know that absence of 'staple food' means famine which they profoundly dread. But the main importance of eating is that it is a lively pleasure and this is enhanced and pro-longed if some relish is added to it.

Another interesting rule of conduct towards food is founded on what might be described as the antagonism between cooking and accumulated food. Cooking, as we have seen, is always done in or around the dwelling. But in villages with an inner ring of store-houses and where these are constructed with open log-work, there is a definite taboo on cooking within this ring. Thus the chief's personal residence which always stands within the inner ring, or a bachelors' house which is also often placed there, must not be used for cooking. There is a special native word for 'dwellings where cooking is allowed'. In those villages where stores and dwellings stand side by side, the stores are invariably covered. The only open stores standing near the cooking-house are the toy stores of children.

5 Rank and chieftainship

If we walk through any local settlement in the Trobriands, we find that a village consists of a simple arithmetic sum and geometrical juxtaposition of a number of households. This again is the obvious or surface phenomenon; and here the male dominance and what might be almost described as the patriarchal principle prevails. For at the head of each village community stands the oldest male of the oldest lineage in the sub-clan of highest rank. But here also working behind the scenes is the matrilineal law, introducing another important group which is neither the village community nor the totemic clan. Descent is matrilineal; that is, every person traces his kindred, from mother to mother, to one common ancestress. The final ancestress is a person who was not born of another woman but who came on earth from underground. All the descendants from such a common ancestress form what the natives call 'kindred', but for which I shall use the term 'sub-clan'. Each of such sub-clans, of which there may be perhaps thirty or forty or fifty – I was not able to make an exhaustive list of them – belongs to one of the four dominant clans. On the surface, in conversation, even in folklore, the clan is the more apparent unit. In reality, in law and in economics, in actual behaviour and in sociological implications, the sub-clan is by far more important. As we shall see, the sub-clan is a very powerful unit in the mythological foundations of land-tenure, in the constitution of the village and in magic. The sub-clan also is the unit to which rank is attached. I have listed some ten or twelve sub-clans belonging to the Malasi clan. One of them, the one who rules in Omarakana and other capitals, is universally acknowledged as being the group of highest rank. But to the same clan belong the lowest of the low, the inhabitants of Bwoytalu and Ba'u. This clan therefore is compounded of the highest and the most despised sub-clans.

Put briefly, rank in the Trobriands consists in personal prestige and titles. A man of rank has to be addressed as chief; he is styled either *guya'u* (full chief) or *gumguya'u* (sub-chief) though the latter title would never be used as a term of address. Rank also entitles people to the wearing of certain ornaments, minutely specified and divided into at least four or five grades. Thus the Tabalu have the highest range of insignia, such sub-chiefs as Kwoynama, Burayama and Mwauri would be entitled to wear a slightly lower range of shell ornaments and decorations, the *toliwaga* of Kabwaku and their peers would have still a different insignia, slightly less aristocratic. Other sub-chiefs would have the right to certain distinctive ornaments, the commoners would have to be very soberly adorned, and the pariahs of Bwoytalu would have especially in the presence of people of higher rank, to go without any shell ornaments at all. The most poignant means of differentiation, however, refers to taboos. This is both a burden and a mark of distinction. Roughly speaking, the higher the rank, the more stringent the taboo. The disgust assumed by people of rank with regard to the 'pariahs' of Bwoytalu and Ba'u, culminates in the revulsion which the clean-eating members of a high sub-clan feel towards people who partake of such abominations as the bush-pig, the stingaree, and certain other kinds of fish eaten in Bwoytalu, but forbidden in Kiriwina. Custom here, however, is as usual very complicated and extremely contradictory. Thus the chiefs of Sinaketa eat bush-pig and stingaree and are accepted as almost equals by the chiefs of Omarakana, while the same habit in a member of the Bwoytalu sub-clan makes him profoundly disgusting.

Rank also entails a definite ceremonial, the main principle of which is that elevation must be commensurate to rank. The chief's head must not be overtopped by anybody. When commoners are moving about, he must be seated on a high platform; if he stands, they must bend. When commoners have to pass a chief who happens to be seated, the chief has to rise – an uncomfortable prerogative strictly adhered to in the Trobriands. If, for any reason, he remains seated or squatting, commoners have to creep on their bellies. I have myself witnessed all the people present in the village of Bwoytalu dropping from various elevations to the ground, as if mown down by a hurricane, at the sound of the long drawn *O guya'u!* announcing the arrival of one of my Omarakana friends who came to visit me in that village of low rank. In Omarakana also I have frequently seen people of low rank approaching the chief in a crouching position, dragging their hunting-spears behind them as was due and proper.

Bearing, therefore, in mind that, as in every human order, and especially in all primitive institutions built up on a small scale, every single rule has its many exceptions which very often contradict one another and seem to overrule the rule, it is yet possible to lay down the following essentials: chieftainship is a combination of two institutions; rank and headmanship of a village community. Each village has its headman. He is the eldest of the males in the senior lineage of the dominant sub-clan. This sounds a little complicated, but as will be seen every village consists of one or more sub-clans. Usually rank decides which of these will be dominant, and the head of it is the leader of the village community. This leader, when his village is a capital, that is, a village of high rank, is also the chief of the district and in the case of one district at least – that of Kiriwina – this man is also the paramount chief in the whole area. His writ does not extend beyond his province. On the other hand some of his economic prerogatives extend well beyond it. The recognition of his supremacy is universal and his fame runs through many archipelagoes where his language is no more spoken nor the customs and ways of his people understood. Besides this paramount chief there is the powerful headman of Kabwaku, capital of Tilataula, and the headmen of the other districts enumerated above. When I speak, therefore, about *the* chief, or *a* chief, this does not refer only to the first and foremost among them. When I speak about a minor chief or sub-chief, I usually mean either a head of a less important district or else a headman of rank whose influence does not extend beyond his own village community. By the term notables I mean the kinsmen of a chief or, in a community of low rank, the old men, especially those who either practise an important form of magic, or have acquired an outstanding position by virtue of personal skill in some industry or the knowledge of some pursuit, such as sailing, fishing, or gardening. In a village of high rank the sons of a chief, who of course under matriliny are not his kinsmen, the heads of minor sub-clans and the brothers of the chief's wives, who might be invited to reside there, belong also to the group of notables. The rank and file consists, in an aristocratic village, of the members of the lesser sub-clan, of people who reside there because they render specific services to the chief and of those who, because of the smaller importance of their mothers in the chief's polygamous household, are pushed into the background. In villages of low rank, the distinction between notable and ordinary villager depends largely on age and personal capacity.

6   The circulation of wealth

We are fully aware already that a constant flow of wealth, whether
this be agricultural produce, fish, objects of daily use or
'valuables', is characteristic of Trobriand economics, of public and
ceremonial life. The variety of types of exchange and the complexity of the transactions is so great and bewildering that it is not
easy to present the facts briefly and yet without mutilating their
reality and omitting some of their essential features.

Let us approach the matter with one or two concrete examples.
Soon after I arrived in Omarakana in 1914, the paramount chief,
To'uluwa, became aware of the need for a new three-tiered basket.
Such baskets are properly produced only in the village of Luya, as
we know. Their use to a man of high rank is double: on the one
hand their three-fold construction symbolises wealth and plenty.
But furthermore the three low cylinders can be placed one into the
other, so that only the contents of the topmost are visible. And this
is very useful, as the chief can put away into the lower compart-
ments his stores in tobacco or betel-nut. If these were exposed to
the public gaze, he would, on the principle of *noblesse oblige*, have
to distribute them among the surrounding people. The necessity for
a three-tiered basket, therefore, might have been functionally
connected with my arrival in the village, because I used to supply
the chief with about half a stick of tobacco a day, and usually with
a small bunch of betel-nut.

In order to get this basket, the chief sent one of his daughters to
Luya; she went there accompanied by her friends and carrying a
basket of yams. After having received it, a specialist from Luya
started on the three-tiered basket. Two or three weeks later he
brought the unfinished object to show it to the chief and ask him
whether he was satisfied with what was being done. He received
then another basketful of *taytu*, and a few rings of tortoiseshell.
After about a month's interval from the initial gift, he brought
the finished article and received a third basketful of yams.

This was a typical example of purchase of an article by a 'solicitary gift', a 'maintenance gift' and a 'clinching gift'. The article, it
will be noted, was made to order. This type of exchange, combined
with an order to produce and with occasional intermediary gifts, is
characteristic of a great deal of Trobriand barter. This is also the
manner in which a specialist would be invited to construct a canoe
or to carve a decorative board.

One of the main characteristics of this type of transaction is that agricultural produce always figures prominently in the soliciting gifts and in the maintenance gifts. The production of a valuable – for instance, the carving of a prow-board or of a gable-board for a storehouse or dwelling; of an ebony spatula or walking-stick – would entail the feeding of the worker by the chief or notable for whom he was producing the object.

This type of barter, therefore, is closely connected with industrial production. It consists, in fact, in giving initiative to production; in making it economically possible through the maintenance of a specialist or specialists; in reducing the need of one section to work on their gardens and allowing them to follow their craft while others produce food for them. I hardly need to repeat here that this only happens on a small scale. I have said already that everybody is a gardener in the Trobriands, and I have precisely stated in what sense we can speak about specialisation. At the same time, it is important also to make the point clear that all industries are fed by agriculture and that this feeding happens in a very direct manner.

The scheme of barter by solicitary gift and an ensuing exchange of services or goods runs right through several of their economic systems. Thus all the ceremonial gifts linked up in the vast institution of the Kula are based on the exchange of an 'opening gift' and 'return gift' with an additional play of 'solicitary gifts' of which the natives distinguish at least four classes. Then come intermediary gifts and finally a 'clinching gift'. In the exchange of fish for food there are several ways or techniques. One of them, the most ceremonial and honourable, consists in an 'opening gift' in which the agriculturalists usually, I think invariably, take the initiative. Food will be brought into the coastal village in elegantly decorated receptacles. Such an opening gift of food puts the fishermen under an obligation which cannot be waived nor subordinated to other interests to return the gift by its equivalent in fish. The fishermen have to wait for a spell of favourable weather and, having given notice to the inland villages that an expedition will take place, they go out to make the haul. The inland community then arrive on the beach about the time when the fishermen are expected back. Sometimes they have to wait for a couple of hours. The haul of fish is taken directly from the canoes where they have been already made into strings. Each man takes his strings and runs as fast as he can back to his village community.

Such ceremonial exchange of fish for vegetables is based on a permanent system of partnership, whole communities being linked up with each other, and in each community every man having his individual partner. There is a rough equivalence between the measure of food, which is the bell-shaped standard basketful, and the measure of fish, which is a string of fish some two to three kilograms in weight. Besides the ceremonial exchange, there are other forms of barter. When a rich haul in fish is anticipated, or even after it has been reported, people from inland may bring yams, taro or bananas, and exchange them directly for fish. At times, the fishermen take the initiative and ask for vegetable produce. This is especially the case when they need some taro or some yams for seed. But in such cases they will never bring their fish to the inland villages. The produce will be brought straight down to the canoes and exchanged then and there for fish. In the transfer and handling of goods, agricultural produce either takes the initiative or else is directly traded on the spot. On the whole, this system of barter is based on the obvious craving of the inland villagers for albuminous food and of the corresponding need on the coast for more agricultural crops than they can produce.

Besides the circumstantial exchange by gift and counter-gift we have already met one act in which objects are exchanged immediately – in the non-ceremonial barter of fish for food. This occurs also in the case of some of the manufactured articles. When a great number of wooden dishes or combs or lime pots or baskets and plaited armlets have been produced in one of the industrial centres the villagers will take their wares and visit places rich in agricultural produce, or fish, or possessing some of the articles imported from overseas. They show their goods and ask for what they want. They will directly mention the quantity and then bargaining will inevitably take place till both sides agree on the fair amount. On other occasions some of the seafaring people, starting on an overseas expedition, may go to an industrial community in order to acquire some goods for trade overseas. Here also 'trade with bargaining' would take place. There is a native word for 'trade with bargaining' and the forms of exchange here described have a much more definitely commercial character. At the same time, it must be remembered that in this 'trade with bargaining' the range of possible equivalents is very limited, and that the equivalence is fixed fairly narrowly by tradition. Thus a small wooden dish from Bwoytalu would be, in nine cases out of ten, exchanged for a basketful of yams. In the tenth case the wood-worker might wish to get some turtleshell ear-rings in a coastal village, or in olden days a stone blade on the eastern coast, or he might be prepared to give two wooden dishes for a small cooking-pot, usually obtainable in Kavataria or on the island of Kayleula. But the most striking feature of all trade in the Trobriands is that *de facto* in most exchanges garden produce figures as one of the elements. When the industrialists turn east to Kiriwina or Tilataula, or go south to the non-industrial parts of Kuboma or Luba, their main interest is in food. A basketful of yams is always useful and the quality of the food which can be obtained in Kiriwina is the best. And in food, especially that used for ceremonial purposes and gifts, size and quality count for very much.

Again, when the members of an overseas trading community, let us say, Sinaketa or Vakuta, prepare for their expeditions, and visit, as we have seen, the industrial centres, they may take, as well as their garden produce, coconut and betel-nut, certain articles from overseas which they have kept for this purpose from a previous expedition. But food always preponderates. For while food is always welcome and always fetches its price, the exchange value of any other article depends very much on whether it is wanted by one or other of the potential purchasers at that moment. There is an interesting counterpart to this in modern conditions, when among all the European importations there is one and one only which can be used as an almost universal medium of exchange. This is trade tobacco. But even this has its quantitative limits; that is, the purchasing power of this narcotic will not increase in direct ratio to its quantity. When it is a matter of exercising a powerful economic incentive, only native objects of value can be used. But in matters of small exchange, that is in everything which an ethnographer might need from a native, either as specimens or services, tobacco has become now universal currency. The white traders, who as we know are mainly after pearls, find it necessary to keep in their stores an assortment of other goods: steel blades for axe or adze, knives, belts, mirrors, calico, hurricane-lamps, kerosene, rice and sugar. When a native needs one of these articles, he wants that and nothing else. The trader who lacks it is at a disadvantage. But if the trader has to take the initiative – unless it is the matter of a very large pearl – he can best obtain the native's commercial response with tobacco.

In this tobacco has completely paralleled, though not replaced, the one and only article which, under the old conditions, approached currency – a basketful of *taytu*, the staple variety of yam. Yams measured by basketsful constitute always the initial or solicitary gift. They figure as maintenance gift in what might be called feeding or financing the work of a specialist. Large quantities of yams are indispensable for the starting and carrying on of any tribal enterprise. In ordinary barter, a basketful of yams is the only commercial unit which functions as a measure of value. A basket of yams has another equivalent in a bundle of taro. But there are two differences between taro and yams. Firstly taro ripens in small quantities throughout the seasons, so that there is always a steady supply but never any great abundance; and secondly it does not keep. Thus, though a bunch of taro is technically equivalent to a basket of yams, it never attains anything like the importance of the latter. But in neither case would it be correct to speak about food being currency, still less money. As a rule, in every type of article exchanged, there is a limited range of counter-articles, and there is a specific measure of equivalence established. Sometimes this can be reduced to and expressed in basketsful of yams. At times, however, it would be impossible to do so. Thus while a small wooden dish is worth a basketful of yams in Kiriwina, and eight coconuts in some of the southern villages, this does not establish the equivalence of eight coconuts to one basketful of yams. There are communities which would exchange one basketful of yams for four coconuts and others where sixteen coconuts would be readily offered. Again, in some of the more traditionally fixed forms of exchange we might find that a large valuable object, such as a ceremonial axe-blade, a string of shell-disks, or a pair of large arm-shells, has cost a man some one hundred basketsful of yams; but if you wanted to purchase a valuable with tobacco you would have to pay perhaps a thousand or two thousand sticks, that is about ten or twenty times its price in yams. In fact it would be very doubtful whether you could make this exchange at all, except on the very rare occasion when the person in possession of the valuable needs a large quantity of tobacco for a distribution. The explanation of this lies in the fact that the first transaction, that of valuable for yams, conforms to the traditional obligatory type of exchange. In the selling of a valuable for tobacco, the native's greed or his need of smoking supplies for a large ceremonial distribution would supply the incentive. In other words, there is no regular market, hence no prices, hence no established mechanism of exchange, hence no room for currency – still less for money.

In brief, it would be as incorrect to speak about currency or money or a medium of exchange in the Trobriands as it would be to apply to their economics the concept of capital and interest, or imagine that they have specialisation of industry and labour comparable to ours, or to imply that their trade is based on a system of markets where haggling determines the price. There is nothing of the sort in the Trobriands, and the paramount part played in their exchanges by agricultural produce has been clearly defined.

We have looked at matters from the point of view of the industrialist who offers his wares to members of neighbouring communities. The average man in an agricultural district – and in a way he is a 'standard Trobriander' – produces enough vegetable food for his household; though actually he only keeps half of it, giving the other half to his sister's household and receiving a corresponding amount from his wife's brother. Therefore of garden produce he has as much as he needs. The only things which he must obtain by exchange are some of the raw materials not to be found in his district, protein food in the form of fish, which is a very welcome addition to his overwhelmingly starchy diet; and finally articles of some special kind or excellence. Now for every one of these things he is able to pay in food. Occasionally, when trading with his western neighbours, he may be asked for a finished or unfinished piece of stone (this refers to olden days); or when trading eastwards, he may offer a cooking-pot, some rattan or feathers, or some other importation from the d'Entrecasteaux Archipelago. We see therefore that both the industrialist and the agriculturalist are mostly driven to exchange manufactures for food, and only very seldom and in so far as they act as middlemen are other objects introduced into the exchange.

There is one more actor in this game whom we have to consider. How does the movement of wealth and the forms of exchange look from the point of view of a chief or of an important headman? As we shall see, the chief through his plurality of wives is able to accumulate a considerable proportion of agricultural produce. In addition to this, he also receives tribute from his subjects. He has also a number of important economic monopolies. Thus in Kiriwina, the paramount chief is the titular owner of all the coconut and betel-nut palms in the district, which means in practice that he is given annually a small proportion of the nuts from each palm – enough to make his quota mount to the large figure of several thousand nuts per annum. He also is the only person who is allowed to keep pigs within the whole district of Kiriwina. This means again that every pig in the district is 'apportioned' to an individual who on the killing has to give part of it to the chief. In reality pigs used to be killed almost exclusively in the chief's village, some part of them left there, and only what remained taken to the home of the actual keeper. A chief of minor rank, an important headman, enjoys similar privileges within his own village.

But the real importance of this lies in the fact that the chief on the one hand has the power to accumulate agricultural produce and to control the livestock and the palms of the district, while on the other hand, he is the one who has both the right and duty to use this accumulated wealth effectively. At the chief's bidding, objects of wealth are produced, canoes constructed, large storehouses and dwellings built. Again he is the organiser of big enterprises. Finally the wealth which he accumulates, or such wealth as is produced by means of this accumulated food, he can use to organise war, to pay a sorcerer for killing a man by witchcraft, or even to pay a man for spearing an offender. The actual way in which a chief in the Trobriands exercises his power is largely economic. For every service received he has to pay, and the wherewithal for these payments he obtains through the duty of most of his subjects to produce for him. Yet in the long run, all the wealth accumulated by him flows back to his subjects. This pooling and reapportionment, however, is not a mere idle play of changing hands. In the course of it some wealth becomes transformed into more permanent objects, and again a great many events and institutions in tribal life are organised by this process of concentration and redistribution. It is this process which allows of such industrial specialisation as exists. It is this process also which makes wealth an instrument of political organisation.

2 Gardening

1 The seasonal rhythm

The cultivation of gardens gives the full rhythm and measure of the seasonal sequence in the year. The chart of native time-reckoning (Fig. 3) brings out clearly the dependence of the gardening cycle on the seasons, and of the various phases of tribal life on gardening. To the natives the annual revolution of the seasons is defined by the cycle of agricultural activities. Even the name for 'year' is *taytu*, a small species of yam, which is the staple crop of the district.

Again the year is subdivided for them into the season when the gardens are unripe (*geguda*) and into that when they begin to mature (*matuwo*). Within both subdivisions there are periods of intensive and exacting labour and times when work can be slackened; but, during the time that gardening is really important and the whole community are busy at it, nothing else is allowed to interfere with this work. (See cols 1–3, which show only such tribal activities, during moons 2, 3 and 4, as can be fitted in with agriculture.) If the crops are not ready, the overseas expeditions, Kula (col. 3) which have such a fascination for the Trobriander, are postponed, until all that can be done by man is finished. Sex interest, dancing, festivities are made subordinate to agriculture; even warfare (as far as I was able to ascertain, for it has been completely suppressed) was not allowed to break out during the three moons (2, 3 and 4, cols 1 and 10) of intensive work after the gardens had been burnt and the clearing, planting, fencing and erection of supports were in progress. The festive, ceremonial and love-making season falls between harvest and this period of work, while fighting and sailing take place during the slack time of gardening.

The correlation of the season of rejoicing and dancing, or else of mortuary festivities and distributions with its phase of garden work is shown on our chart. It is not very easy, however, to express it clearly there because, in the first place, the central moon of ceremonial life, *milamala*, varies according to four districts. In the second place, when the festive season is extended by agreement, the gardens are started later. Thus, though there is no confusion in the seasonal correlation, the exact adjustment is fluid. Roughly speaking, the longest time between harvest and the new gardens is about four moons, while it may, on occasion, extend only over two.

Gardening seasons thus constitute the real measure of time. The native who wishes to define a period or to place an event will always co-ordinate it with the most important, the most rigidly maintained, and the most characteristic index of that period; that is, with the concurrent gardening activity. He will say: this happened *o takaywa*, during the cutting of the scrub; *wa gabu*, in the burning, the period when the cut and dried scrub is being burnt; *wa sopu*, in planting time; *o pwakova*, during weeding; *wa basi*, during the removal of the surplus tubers; *o kopo'i*, during the preliminary taking out of taro and yams; *o tayoyuwa*, during the harvest proper.

Gardening activities are correlated with the sequence of moons, for which the natives also have names. Thus the moon of *milamala* or festive period, in which the spirits of the departed visit their native villages, usually coincides with the pause between the cutting and burning. This correlation is shown in column 5 of our chart. Here we find the thirteen names for native moons which correspond, not rigidly, but with a high degree of approximation, to our counting of months within the year. Since the prevailing winds (col. 4) fit precisely into our calendar, the correspondence of columns 4 and 5 is close. Column 6 shows the native distinction between the seasons of plenty and hunger (*malia* and *molu*), indicating the supply of crops, and the seasons of ripe and unripe (*matuwo* and *geguda*) gardens which marks the development of the crops. Garden activities (cols 7, 8 and 9) are through this correlated to moons and seasons, though this correlation may, as we know, vary within a moon or even more.

But it is the gardening activities that really matter and that determine the sequence of time – the moons have a subordinate importance. When precision in dating is required, the natives have to refer coming events to such and such a moon, and such and such a day within a moon, and for this purpose their lunar calendar is necessary. But even then they usually have first to place the moon within the gardening activities to which it belongs and then only use the moon names as a means of more detailed and precise definition.

The chronological sequence of the years is also defined by gardening activities. The natives have a name for every *kwabila* (field, or division of garden land) and since the gardens are made successively on such fields they are able to associate a past event with the name of the two or three fields which were put under cultivation in that year. Thus when they are asked about a past date, they will enumerate the names of the sites on which gardens have been made in each of the preceding years, till they arrive at the right combination of names and thus they are able to count the years for several decades back.

Let us now follow the seasonal round of garden work. This falls into four main divisions. First comes the preparing of the soil by cutting down the scrub and burning it after it has dried. The second stage consists in clearing the soil, planting, erecting the yam supports, and making the fence. The third stage has for the most part to be left to nature; the seeds sprout, the vines climb upwards round the supports, the taro plants develop their big leaves and their roots; while human intervention is confined to weeding, which is done by women, and a preliminary pruning or thinning out of the tubers and training of vines by the men. Meanwhile the magician is at work, casting spells favourable to growth. Finally, after the crops have matured, we come to the last stage, the harvest. Apart from the magic of growth just mentioned, each new type of work is inaugurated by a magical rite, and these form a series which correspond to the sequence of practical activities.

Garden work is never done in heavy rain or in windy and what to the natives would be cold weather. During the intolerably hot hours of the day, at the season of calms, the gardeners usually return home or rest in the shade. Whether for communal or individual or family work, the farmers generally go early to the gardens, return between ten and eleven to the village, and then start out again, perhaps after a light meal and a siesta, to work from about three or four o'clock till nightfall. Since some of the gardens directly adjoin the village and the most distant are not more than half an hour's walk away, there is no difficulty in interrupting and resuming work at the convenience of the moment.

The technical efficiency of the work is great. This is the more remarkable because the outfit of the Trobriand farmer is of the most rudimentary nature. It consists of a digging-stick (*dayma*), an axe (*kema*), an adze (*ligogu*) and, last but not least, of the human hand, which in many of their activities serves as an implement and often comes into actual contact with the soil. The digging-stick is used for turning up the soil at planting and thinning, at harvest and weeding. Axe and adze play an important part in the cutting of the scrub, the thinning out of the tubers and at harvesting. Skill with the hand is important during clearing, planting, weeding, thinning and at harvesting. These then are the tasks and the tools of a 'good gardener' (*tokwaybagula*) – one of the proudest titles which a Trobriander can enjoy.

But besides hard work, and a technical skill based on a sound knowledge of the soil and its properties, of the weather and its vicissitudes, of the nature of crops and the need of intelligent adaptation to the soil, another element enters into Trobriand gardening which, to the natives, is as essential to success as husbandry. This is magic.

2 The garden magician

Garden magic (*megwa towosi* or simply *towosi*) is in the Trobriands a public and official service. It is performed by the garden magician, also called *towosi*, for the benefit of the community. Everybody has to take part in some of the ceremonial and have the rest performed on his account. Everybody also has to contribute to certain payments for magic. The magic being done for each village community as a whole, every village and at times every subdivision of a village has its own *towosi* (garden magician) and its own system of *towosi* magic, and this is perhaps the main expression of village unity.

Magic and practical work are, in native ideas, inseparable from each other, though they are not confused. Garden magic and garden work run in one intertwined series of consecutive effort, form one continuous story.

To the natives, magic is as indispensable to the success of gardens as competent and effective husbandry. It is essential to the fertility of the soil: 'The garden magician utters magic by mouth; the magical virtue enters the soil'. Magic is to them an almost natural element in the growth of the gardens. I have often been asked: 'What is the magic which is done in your country over your gardens – is it like ours or is it different?' They did not seem at all to approve of our ways as I described them, saying that we either do not perform any magic at all, or else let our 'misinaris' do the magic wholesale in the *bwala tapwaroro* – the house of the divine service. They doubted whether our yams could 'sprout' properly, 'rise up in foliage' and 'swell'.

The round of gardening opens with a conference, summoned by the chief and held in front of the magician's house, to decide where the gardens are going to be made, who will cultivate such and such a plot, and when the work will be started. Directly in connexion with this, the magician prepares for the first big ceremony, which is to inaugurate the whole gardening sequence, while the villagers procure a quantity of special food, usually fish, to be offered as a ceremonial payment to the magician. A small portion of this gift is exposed in the evening to the ancestral spirits, sacrificially and with an invocation; the bulk is eaten by the magician and his kinsmen. Then he utters a lengthy spell over certain leaves which will be used on the morrow. Next morning the magician and the men of the village go to the gardens and the inaugural ceremony takes place. The *towosi* strikes the ground and rubs it with the charmed leaves – acts which symbolise in speech and sentiment the garden magic as a whole. This rite officially opens the season's gardening as well as its first stage: the cutting of the scrub. Thereafter each stage of practical work is ushered in by the appropriate ceremony. After the cut scrub is sufficiently dried, he imposes a taboo on garden work, ritually burns the refuse, and introduces the planting of certain minor crops by a series of ceremonies extending over a few days. Later on, a sequence of rites inaugurate successively the main planting of yams, the erection of vine supports, weeding, preliminary thinning out, and finally of harvesting. At the same time in a parallel sequence of rites and spells, the garden magician assists the growth of the crops. He helps the plants to sprout, to burst into leaf, to climb; he makes their roots bud, develop and swell; and he produces the rich garlands of exuberant foliage which intertwine among the vine supports.

Each rite is first performed on one of the standard magical plots, the *leywota*. This is important from the practical point of view, because the men who cultivate these plots are bound to keep time with the rhythm of magical ritual and not lag behind. At the same time they must also be worked with special care. They are scrupulously cleared and cleaned, perfect seed tubers are selected, and since they are always made on good soil, they represent not only a very high standard of garden work but also of gardening success. Thus, in punctuality, quality and finish of work, and in perfection of results, these plots set a definite pattern to all the others, and this excellence is mainly attributed to the influence of magic.

The *towosi* or garden magician is an hereditary official of every village community. As a matter of fact, the position of *towosi* coincides with that of the chief or the head-man, if not in identity of person, at least in the principle of lineage. In native mythology and legal theory, it is always the head of the kinship group owning a village who is the garden magician. This man, however, frequently delegates his duties to his younger brother, his matrilineal nephew, or his son. Such handing over of the office of garden magician was especially frequent in the lineage of the paramount chiefs of Omarakana, on whom the duties of charming the gardens weighed too heavily.

The mythological system of the Trobrianders establishes a very close connexion between the soil and human beings. The origins of humanity are in the soil; the first ancestors of each local group or sub-clan – for these two are identical – are always said to have emerged from a certain spot, carrying their garden magic with them. It is the spot from which they emerged which is usually, though not always, the sub-clan's soil, the territory to which it has an hereditary right. This hereditary ownership of the soil – mythological, legal, moral and economic – is vested in the head-man; and it is in virtue of these combined claims that he exercises the function of garden magician. 'I strike the ground,' as I was told by Bagido'u, the proudest garden magician of the island, 'because I am the owner of the soil.' The first person meant, 'I, as the representative of my sub-clan and my lineage.'

The traditional filiation of garden magic is kept alive by every officiating magician. In some of the spells he has to repeat the whole series of the names of those who have wielded the magic before him. At one or two stages of his magic, he offers a ceremonial oblation, consisting of a minute portion of cooked food taken from the substantial present he has received, to the spirits of his predecessor. Such presents from the community are the expression of their gratitude and their submission to him rather than a commercial gift. They are the recognition of his services, and in this spirit they are offered to him and to his forerunners. This ritual offering of food, which is an integral part of the magical proceedings, is called *ula'ula*.

The members of the community, however, usually offer the magician other presents as well. At the beginning of the gardening cycle he is usually given small gifts of food, such as coconuts or bananas; or else he may accept a bunch of betel-nut or such objects of daily use as baskets, axes, mats, spears or cooking-pots. This type of gift, called *sousula*, is meant to repay him for the hardships undergone in the exercise of his calling.

Again from time to time the magician receives a present of valuables called *sibugibogi*: a large ceremonial axe-blade, belts or ornaments of shell-disks or a pair of arm-shells. This gift is usually offered after a bad season to propitiate him, or else at an especially good harvest to express gratitude.

In the carrying out of his duties, the magician is usually helped by some younger men: his younger brothers and his sisters' sons are his natural successors, whom he will have in due course to instruct in magic, teaching them the spells, telling them the substances to be used, advising them how to carry out the ritual and what personal observances they have to keep. Of this instruction, the most difficult is the learning of the formulae. Even this, however, does not require much special training, for garden magic is a public ceremonial, the spells are heard often by everybody, while the ritual is well known and anyone is able to tell you exactly what observances the magician has to keep. Those who have to inherit garden magic and practise it, and are therefore more interested in it, will be acquainted with every detail early in their life. They are the magician's natural help-mates and acolytes. Whenever the ceremony is cumbersome, they take part in it; or they repeat on other garden plots the rite which the chief magician performs on the standard plots. And they assist him often in the collecting of ingredients or preparing of magical mixtures and structures.

Besides these, he has non-official helpers among the younger people and children, who carry some of his paraphernalia, assist him in putting up certain magical signs and do other such minor services.

I have just mentioned the magician's taboos. These consist

almost exclusively in the abstention from certain foods. In no circumstances may he touch the meat of certain animals and fish, or eat certain vegetables. Generally these are sympathetically connected with the substances which he uses in his ritual or with the aims of his magic. The magician is also not allowed to partake of the new crops until after the performance of a special ceremony, which consists as a rule in an offering to the ancestral spirits. A third type of abstention is the fast which he has to keep on the days on which he performs any ceremony.

From all this it can be seen that a garden magician's office in the Trobriands is no sinecure. Not only does he have to carry out a series of inaugural rites, following closely the practical work of the gardens, not only does he stimulate the growth of the plants in his spells of encouragement; but he also has to observe a system of by no means easy abstentions and fasts, and last, but not least, to carry out a considerable amount of practical work and control.

The garden magician is regarded by the community as the garden expert. He, together perhaps with his elder kinsman, the chief, decides what fields are to be cultivated in a given year. Later on, at each stage, he has to find out how the work in the gardens stands; how the crops are sprouting, budding, ripening, and then he has to give the initiative to the next stage. He must watch the weather and the state of the cut scrub before the burning. He has to see whether the gardens are sufficiently advanced before he performs the planting magic, and so at every stage. And when he finds that people are lagging behind, or that some of them, by neglecting a communal duty, such as the fencing of the garden plots, are endangering the interests of the whole community, it is his function to upbraid the culprits and induce them to mend their ways and to work energetically.

Thus the *towosi* exercises not merely an indirect influence on garden work, by giving the initiative and inaugurating the successive stages, by imposing taboos, and by setting the pace, but he also directly supervises a number of activities. In order to do this he has constantly to visit the gardens, survey the work, discover shortcomings, and last but not least, note any special excellencies. For public praise from the *towosi* is a highly appreciated reward and a great stimulus to the perfect gardener, the *tokwaybagula*.

The natives are deeply convinced that through his magic the *towosi* controls the forces of fertility, and in virtue of this they are prepared to admit that he should also control the work of man. And let us remember, his magical power, his expert knowledge and his traditional filiation to his magical ancestors are reinforced by the fact that he is the head-man, or, in a community of rank, a chief of high lineage, or a nephew or younger brother of such. When the office is in the hands of the chief's son, he again only holds it as the delegate of the rightful head of the community. Furthermore, the acts of magic are an organising influence in communal life: firstly because they punctuate the progress of activities at regular intervals and impose a series of taboo days or rest periods; and secondly because each rite must be fully performed on the standard plots, and these plots must be perfectly prepared for it, whereby a model is established for the whole village. Magic therefore is not merely a mental force, making for a more highly organised attitude of mind in each individual, it is also a social force, closely connected with the economic organisation of garden work.

3 The mythology of gardening

To each village community this magic, as already mentioned, is a very precious possession and a symbol of its social integrity as well as of its standing in the tribal hierarchy. A village of high rank always leads in gardening. This is natural because the most noble sub-clans have settled in the most fertile territory – that of Kiriwina. The renown of this district, especially for its gardening excellence, extends over the whole area of the Northern Massim. The first evening on which I arrived at the village of Dikoyas in Woodlark Island, some eighty miles from the paramount chief's capital, I was told, in glowing language, about the wealth of Kiriwina, and that the culture hero, Tudava, who gave gardens and taught gardening to all men in and around Woodlark Island, had come out of the soil in Kiriwina; also that Kiriwina was the first island to exist, and the first where gardens had been made. Thus, more than a year before I came to Kiriwina by a very roundabout way of several thousand miles, I was made to feel that agriculture originated in the Trobriands; that gardening, the knowledge of how to do things, the knowledge of proper conduct, of totemic origins and the totemic identity of man, had spread from Kiriwina, eastwards and southwards; that Kiriwina still remained the most fertile, wealthy, and aristocratic place in the world.

The legend of Tudava is known all over the district of the Northern Massim. Everywhere in Woodlark Island, in the d'Entrecasteaux Archipelago, in the Amphletts, in the Marshall Bennett group, stories are told of how the culture hero was a native of Kiriwina, and was the first to institute gardening and garden magic. In one version of the legend, also obtained in Woodlark Island, I was told that Tudava was the first man to come out of the ground in Kiriwina. After him the other men came out. As each man emerged, Tudava gave him his totem. When he first came out, there was no land except Kiriwina. He threw a large stone into the sea and there arose the island of Kitava. Then he went there and threw other stones, and the islands of Iwa, Kwayawata, and Digumenu came into being. Then he made the district of Madawa (part of Woodlark Island), then the rest of Woodlark Island, and Suloga where the big stone quarries are. Then he came to Nada or Nadili (Laughlan Islands) where some people had been before him, for these islands already existed. The other islands which were made by Tudava were all peopled by men from Kiriwina, who came over in canoes. When he went to the Laughlans, the people wanted to kill him, so he went away.

In Kiriwina itself, of course, his story is told – or rather a great many stories, for there is a whole cycle of Tudava myths, legends and even fairy-tales. But remarkably enough that part of the legend which expresses so tellingly the gardening supremacy of Kiriwina over the outlying districts is not known in Kiriwina itself.

The reason for this apparent anomaly is, I think, that the Trobrianders, notably those of Kiriwina and Tilataula, take their supremacy in agriculture for granted. They have good reason for doing so, and no one ever challenges their claim. They have tangible evidence of their competence and wealth. It is obvious to everyone, whether he be a native of Kiriwina or a visitor from some neighbouring village, a Kula partner from Kitava or Woodlark Island, the Amphletts or Dobu, that the storehouses of Kiriwina are unparalleled, their gardens are the biggest and best in the district, and the total amount of yams harvested there yearly the greatest. In short, the Kiriwinian does not need to tell a story about his past wealth; he can point to the present with pride and assurance. Still less does he need to justify his poverty as do some natives; he does not suffer from it.

With all this it would be incorrect to assume that there is no mythological foundation to gardening in Kiriwina. In the first place they have a brief mythology which merely asserts that the local or naturalised sub-clan whose ancestors emerged from a given territory controls the magic of fertility of that territory. Such brief mythological affirmations define traditionally and legally safeguard the claims of the sub-clan to their lands.

In the second place there exists an ever growing and constantly renewed tradition of good gardening. This consists of the stories told about the achievements of one village or another; of the accounts of specially glorious harvests; of the results of institutionalised food competitions, in which one village is 'beaten' by another. But all this is more a glorification of the present than a reference to miracles in the past. To a certain extent the historical records of occasional famines, offset by accounts of plenty, function in the same way.

To return to the wider cycle of myths, the gist of the stories about the origins of gardening is an explanation of the excellence of some places and the poverty of others. They contain a legendary charter of gardening in general and of the differences in local fertility and custom. In most of them we have a moral reason for Tudava's preference for certain islands: where he was well received their gardens blossomed, yams swelled inside the fertile ground, taro flourished, and garlands of *taytu* shaded the soil with foliage, and so they continue till the present day. Where the inhabitants threatened and drove him off, there the soil remained barren or swampy, good only for coconut palms and wild fruits of the bush, the two commodities which will grow anywhere and everywhere on these islands. The main island of the Trobriands, notably the district of Kiriwina where gardens originate and whence Tudava went off on his wanderings, has always remained the supreme centre of gardening.

4 Magic and work

In order to appreciate this mythological cycle of ideas, we must keep in mind the relation of magic to practical work as this is conceived by the natives. The short myths of first emergence have in the Trobriands a very close connexion with magic, since this latter has always been brought by the ancestors from underground.

The gift of fertility bestowed by the mythical founders and wielders of magic on the richest districts of that region is without exception conceived in a two-fold manner, magical and natural. The natives realise that on sandy, brackish and stony soil neither yams nor taro, and still less *taytu*, could ever grow. If you ask whether one could start any plantation or garden on the precipitous slopes of the Amphletts, on the barren sands of the Laughlans or on the windswept, brine-drenched fragments of the Lusançay atoll, they will answer, no, and explain why most plants cannot thrive there in perfectly reasonable, almost scientific language.

At the same time they attribute the supreme fertility of some districts, the prosperity which dwells there permanently and the beautiful expanse of successful gardens to the superiority of one magical system over another. Thus from native commentaries on the above myths, it becomes clear that the culture hero is, on the one hand, always supposed to bestow fertile soil, sound seedlings, instruction in gardening skill, the knowledge of how to handle crops and protect them from blights and other dangers; and, on the other hand, it is understood that he brings with him a powerful system of magic. The two ways, the way of magic and the way of garden work – *megwa la keda, bagula la keda* – are inseparable. They are never confused, nor is one of them ever allowed to supersede the other. The natives will never try to clean the soil by magic, to erect a fence or yam support by a rite. They know quite well that they have to do it by hand and in the sweat of their brow. They also know that no work can be skimped without danger to the crops, nor do they ever assume that by an overdose of magic you can make good any deficiencies in work.

Moreover, they are able to express this knowledge clearly and to formulate it in a number of principles and causal relations. They have a sound knowledge of the soil and of the crops; in fact they distinguish between six or seven types of soil and know well which variety of crop is best adapted to swampy, heavy soil, to black humus, and to the light and stony ground of the dry regions.

As to the varieties of yam, taro and *taytu*, they have literally hundreds of names for each of them. Some names distinguish what might be properly regarded as real botanical varieties, others describe characteristics of size, shape, perfection and so on. The natives will explain intelligently why it is necessary to have the soil well cleared and weeded. They have got a clear theory as to why *taytu* must be planted rather deeply and covered with a hillock. They have clever devices for keeping off pigs, and whenever their fence is temporarily damaged they will put sharp pointed stakes on the other side of it, so that tHe pigs are caught in jumping over the fences. They have several types of scarecrow and bird rattle. All these practical devices they handle rationally and according to sound empirical rules.

Nor does this distinction between work and magic remain implicit and unexpressed. I was always able to ask whether it was the way of magic or of gardening, and received unambiguous answers very early in my work. I was told, for instance, that the large, bulky structures, the *kamkokola*, were matters of magic: '*Megwa wala; gala tuwayle si koni wa bagula* – only magic; no other task [is incidental] to them in the garden.' I was told also that the spirit houses (*si bwala baloma*), the miniature fences, the tufts of grass bound rouṅd the *kavatam* (yam support) and certain horizontal sticks placed on the *kamkokola* were all purely magical. It was, on the other hand, explained to me that ashes fertilise the ground; that deep planting is advisable in dry seasons; that stones must be removed from the soil; that weeds choke the crop, and so on. To the natives, therefore, the aims of magic are different from the aims of work. They know quite well what effects can be produced by careful tilling of the soil and these effects they try to produce by competent and industrious labour. They equally know that certain evils, such as pests, blights, bush-pigs, drought or rain, cannot be overcome by human work however hard and consistent. They see also that, at times and in a mysterious way, gardens thrive in spite of all anticipations to the contrary, or else that, in a fairly good season favoured by good work, the gardens do not give the results they should. Any unaccountable good luck over and above what is due the natives attribute to magic; exactly as they attribute unexpected and undeserved bad luck to black magic or to some deficiency in the carrying out of their own magic.

Briefly, magic, performed officially by the garden magician under ceremonial conditions, by means of rite and spell and with the observance of taboos, forms a special department. Practical husbandry, on the other hand, carried out by each one with the aid of his hands and common sense, and based on the recognition of the causal relation between effort and achievement, constitutes another department. Magic is based on myth, practical work on empirical theory. The former aims at forestalling unaccountable mishaps and procuring undeserved good luck, the latter supplies what human effort is known naturally to bring about. The first one is a sociological prerogative of the leader, the *towosi*; the second is the economic duty of every member of the community.

I have so far spoken exclusively of public magic and, when making clear the distinction between magic and work, I referred only to the rites and spells of the public garden magician, the *towosi*. It will be well to state here at once that private garden magic exists in the Trobriands. Private magic is performed chiefly over seed yams at the time of planting, and over the digging-stick and axe at the time of the thinning of the tubers. It consists of simple spells directly chanted over the object to be charmed. It never integrates with the work in the gardens as public garden magic does.

Another form of garden magic which must be mentioned here is the evil and malicious magic, *bulubwalata*, which is supposed to be carried out by neighbours in order to injure the garden. Unfortunately I only got on the track of this towards the end of my stay in the Trobriands, and, as in most cases of black magic, it would have required a long time and a great deal of patience to make sure whether it even exists. It would have taken even longer to obtain details of it, and I was not successful in either task. My impression is that *bulubwalata* is a mere myth as far as the gardens are concerned; that people are suspected of doing it but that they never live up to the suspicion; that unskilful and unsuccessful gardeners would impute it to neighbours of their own village or some more distant place, and that these would return the suspicion and the ill-will.

The true black magic of the gardens is the magic of rain and drought, the magic which regulates the conditions of fertility. This is not a surreptitious form of sorcery, however: it remains in the hands of the chief; he wields it openly and officially as an expression of his anger and as a means of collective punishment and enforcement of his will. The wielding of rain and drought magic is, as a matter of fact, one of the most dreaded and coveted privileges of the paramount chief of Omarakana.

Turning now to the practical side: garden work is done in the Trobriands by everybody, man and woman, chief and commoner, chief's principal wife, chief's own sister, as well as the humblest spinster. Nor is the garden magician excluded from work unless, as was the case with Bagido'u, the garden magician of Omarakana, he is ill. He will work on quite as many garden plots as everyone else, he will carry out all the activities with the same vigour and he will not be able to shuffle any of his burdens on to another man. The garden magician and the chief were indeed always expected to be specially effective gardeners.

The most important distinction is that between a man's and woman's part in gardening. A woman never gardens in her own right. She is never styled 'owner of a garden' or 'owner of a plot'. She never works independently but must always have a male for whom and with whom she works the soil, and this refers also to women of the highest rank whose husbands are necessarily of a lower rank than themselves. An unmarried girl will simply assist her mother. On marriage she works on her husband's garden land. The family, that is husband, wife and their children, is the smallest co-operative unit in Trobriand gardening. Between them they cultivate the several plots allocated to them at the garden council. In this joint work there is a regular division of labour. The man cuts the scrub; man and woman clear the ground and prepare it for planting; the man does the planting; the woman weeds. The man has to train the vines and to thin out the roots; while finally harvesting is done by men and women together. The renown of good gardening, the praise and other emoluments of ambition go to the man and not to the women. She only shares in them vicariously. It is rather the quantity of produce which a woman receives for her household from her brother that redounds to her credit.

Certain complications arise, however, from the fact that work is done differently by an unmarried man or woman; that the sharing of garden work between a chief and one of his several wives cannot be done on the same principle as between a monogamous couple. When in olden days the paramount chief had some fifty wives and plots to correspond, he could only do roughly one-fiftieth of the male's share for each. It will be best to take one type of status after another and see how the rights to a garden, the work in the garden, and co-operation appear:

(1) A bachelor or widower has to do all the work for himself, including weeding which, however, might be done by some related woman out of kindness. (2) An ordinary man with one wife and perhaps with children will do only the male's work, assisted by his

sons, as long as these are small, while his wife and daughters carry out the female part. The grown-up sons may take up their own plots in the father's community if they continue to reside there for some time, or else they make their own gardens in their maternal community after they have moved there. (3) The head-man or notable with two or more wives will usually have as many times the normal portion of plots as he has wives. On this greater number of plots he is not able to do all the work himself. On the other hand, through his rank he can command and pay for communal work at cutting and planting. Such a man again would usually retain his sons for a longer time in the village, and these also would assist him, each working on his mother's portion. (4) The paramount chief with a large compound establishment of some forty to sixty wives (at the time of my stay in the Trobriands they were reduced to fourteen) would cultivate some two or three plots for each wife. Obviously his own share in the work would amount to very little. As far as I can judge, he would work with one or two, or at the most three wives. The rest of the work would be done partly by the sons of each wife, partly by communal labour. At cutting and at the planting of the main crops, communal labour would invariably be used.

5   Display and competitive exchange

The gardens are, in a way, a work of art. Exactly as a native will take an artist's delight in constructing a canoe or a house, perfect in shape, decoration and finish, and the whole community will glory in such an achievement, exactly thus will he go about the laying out and developing of his garden. He and his kinsmen and his fellow-villagers as well, will be proud of the splendid results of his labours.

A considerable amount of energy is spent on purely aesthetic effects, to make the garden look clean, showy and dainty. The ground before planting is cleared of stones, sticks and débris, with a meticulousness far beyond what would be strictly necessary on purely technical grounds. The cleared soil is divided into neat rectangles about 4 to 10 metres long, and 2 to 5 metres broad, by means of sticks laid on the ground. These rectangles have little practical purpose, but much value is attached to the propor-tions and quality of the sticks which mark their boundaries. There are the purely magical constructions already mentioned, the *kamkokola*, and much effort is expended to make them look imposing. Pride is taken in selecting strong, stout and straight poles as supports for the yam vine. During all the successive stages of the work, visits are exchanged and mutual admiration and appreciation of the aesthetic qualities of the gardens are a constant feature of village life.

Accumulated food is to them a good thing – its absence is not only something to be dreaded, but something to be ashamed of. There is no greater insult than to tell a man that he has no food, *gala kam*, 'no food thine'; or that he is hungry, *kam molu*, 'thy hunger'. No one would ever ask for food, or eat in a strange place, or accept food unless in obedience to traditional usage. The giving of food is an act of superiority; and generosity is the highest of privileges, as well as an appreciated virtue.

Food, as we know, is used in the production of other utilities and its accumulation in the hands of the chiefs makes possible certain enterprises on a tribal scale. In connexion with this it is important to remember that the glory of gardening, the renown which attaches to a *tokwaybagula* (efficient husbandman) is always subordinate to the rules which make accumulation of food a privilege of rank. You may earn the reputation of a good gardener, but you must devote your energies to contributing to the yam-houses of the chiefs or head-men. No commoner must become too rich or work for anyone else but those really in power. Ill-health or even death by sorcery rather than renown would then reward his labours.

The under-current of malice, suspicion and envy which accompanies the display of food and the show of praise and admiration, may lead to bitter personal animosity, which in the Trobriands usually ends in attempts to kill by witchcraft. When this happens between people belonging to two different communities, the quarrel may be taken up by their fellow-kinsmen and fellow-villagers. Then there comes into play the contest of wealth, the comparison of the respective harvest yields, which is called *buritila'ulo*.

The *buritila'ulo* is one of the most characteristic examples of the double-edged nature of gift among the Trobrianders. On the one hand it is a present given with the grandiloquent yet calculating generosity which the natives affect on such an occasion, and received with the vigilant and grudging scrutiny which is always ready to perceive meanness. Thus marked as a gift, the *buritila'ulo* is a mutual pitting of economic resources in which each of the opposing sides means to score, to show that it is the richer, the superior and the more powerful. For the same present will have to be returned immediately in exactly the same quantity and quality. If the repayment is too small, its inadequacy will be thrown into the face of the givers. If the return be too generous, this will be taken as an insult to the recipients.

The *buritila'ulo* occurs only at harvest and only in connexion with quarrels about food. Were a man, contrary to the established code of manners, to criticise the quality of another man's harvest yield, the latter would naturally reply with invective. It is characteristic of a Trobriander, if told that he has got bad yams, to reply almost automatically: 'It is you who have bad yams.' When such an argument starts, it is quite obvious where it will lead. The insult: *gala kam* 'no food thine', 'thou hast no food', is inevitable sooner or later, and this leads to a stream of mutual abuse of that type which cannot pass without serious consequences. Usually the quarrel degenerates into an immediate fight on the spot. This, however, may not go very far if there are persons of authority, a headman or a man of rank, present. These might intervene and then the matter would be sooner or later put to the arbitrament of competitive food exchange, *buritila'ulo*.

Now the principles underlying a *buritila'ulo* are in brief the following: Community A, which is either worsted in the quarrel, or which received an injury, or which is first severely taunted, issues the challenge. This community then has to muster all the yams possible, for the *buritila'ulo* is invariably carried out in terms of *kuvi*, large yams, and never in *taytu*. All the yams which community A can muster will be accumulated, carried over to community B, displayed there, ceremonially given, and then community B will make a return gift. If the return is made in exactly the same quantity, all comes to a happy ending; otherwise, as said already, further trouble will arise.

Let us start with the preparations. All the large yams have to be taken out of the *bwayma* (storehouses) and displayed in heaps in the village. The long yams called *kwibanena* are then sandwiched between two sticks and ornamented with pandanus streamers and dabs of white paint. Then as much sugar-cane and betel-nut as possible is accumulated. Only these two products may be used besides the large yams. The contributions in yams have to be made exclusively from the villagers' own produce. No one from the outside is allowed to contribute to the joint store. There is no *dodige bwala*, that is helping out by relatives-in-law, as at ordinary displays or distributions. On the other hand every man has to give all the yams he possesses. Each man carefully counts his contribution and keeps a rough tally of the size of each tuber. The long yams are measured by sticks of equivalent length, one stick for each yam. The round yams are measured by means of string, knots being made to indicate their size. Each owner keeps this private tally of yams so that he can claim back his share and neither more nor less from the common pool of the return gift.

Then the natives have to make an approximate computation of the cubic capacity necessary to contain their accumulated yams. They go to the bush and collect a few stout poles and some sticks. With these they roughly construct a crate (called *liku*) and fill it with the yams to test its capacity. Then they take it to pieces again, and the whole village (A) starts on the work of transporting the yams and the component parts of the crate to the challenged village (B). Here the yams are deposited on the *baku* while the crate is reconstructed, this time more solidly, because it will have to be carried bodily by the men of village B back to village A.

When the crate is finished, each man places his contribution into it. The long tubers, each tied between two sticks, as well as pieces of sugar-cane and bunches of betel-nut are put on top.

Then comes the actual transaction. First of all the exact measurements of the crate are taken. Community B will have to return the same crate, in no way changed, to community A, and fill it exactly to the same height. In order to ensure against any fraud and have a clear standard of measurement, a number of sticks are cut on which the length, width and height of the *liku* are recorded. Then the size and quality of the most important of the gifts, the long yams, is measured. Community B have by this time prepared their *kaydavi*, that is their yams tied between sticks, and for each *kaydavi* brought to them by A, they check off a corresponding *kaydavi*, which, however, they do not yet present. Then the number of bunches of betel-nut is ascertained and their size roughly estimated and recorded. The contents of the *liku* are now distributed; each man in community B receives his share in exchange for an exactly corresponding contribution to the return gift from his own storehouse. Next day the *liku* is transported bodily to village A where it was first built. Some twenty men were necessary to lift and transport it on the occasion when I was present. The rest of the villagers, men, women and children, were busy carrying the yams. Arrived at village A, the proceedings of the previous day are exactly repeated, only now the transfer is from community B to community A.

And now comes the dramatic moment. Community B have been straining all their resources not only to repay the full quantity of yams but to provide a surplus. The strict return measure is called *kalamelu*, which might perhaps be translated 'its equivalent', 'the equivalent of the gift received'. If they can offer an extra quantity, this will be put on the ground and declared to be *kalamata* 'its eye'. The word 'eye' is here used in the figurative sense of something which is ahead of, which overtakes, goes beyond.

Now such a surplus gift would not be offered in a very friendly spirit. Community B would boast of having given it. They would also immediately clamour for a repayment of it. But since community A have strained all their resources for their original gift, they cannot repay. They would have recourse to argument, they would say that the surplus was not a real surplus but due to the fact that the *kalamelu* was not honestly and fully meted out. A quarrel will break out again and another fight arise from the *buritila'ulo*.

Since, however, community B, by supposition the richer one, would also be stronger, the people of A would obviously be beaten on every point. But two communities practising a *buritila'ulo* against each other are not essentially hostile, so the fight would probably have no very serious consequences. I was told, however, that in old days, especially when the *buritila'ulo* was not between two adjoining communities normally friendly, but between two communities who, though not on terms of recurrent warfare might yet fight if occasion arose, a serious regulated combat might follow.

Part two

Kinship, marriage and land

Editor's note to part two

Sources

Chapter 3, 4 and 5 have been compiled almost exclusively from *The Sexual Life of Savages* (3rd edn, 1932), pp. 416–26, 431–51 (chapter 3); 140–50, 152–7, 164–8, 170–7 (chapter 4); and 68–83, 93–101, 103–8, 121–37 (chapter 5). Section 6 of chapter 5 was abstracted from pp. 206–10 and 191–2 of *Coral Gardens* (vol. I), and the whole of chapter 6 from the same work: pp. 335–44, 348, 350–64 and 368–9.

Further reading

More or less systematic and more or less radical re-interpretations of Malinowski's data on Trobriand clanship and marriage (including the significance of *urigibu*) have been offered by: Fortes (1957), Leach (1958), Lounsbury (1965), Montague (1971), Powell (1960, 1969a, 1969b), Robinson (1962), Sider (1967) and Sloan (1974). The issue of the Trobriander's alleged ignorance of physiological paternity has been particularly controversial: see Austin (1934–5), Leach (1967), Montague (1971), Rentoul (1931, 1932) and Spiro (1968). The phenomenon of 'adolescent sterility' is discussed by Chowning (1969). In the light of their own field researches in the Trobriands, Powell (1969a, 1969b) and Weiner (1976) present fresh perspectives on various aspects of kinship and marriage.

3   Exogamy and incest

1   Clanship

The totemic organization of the natives is simple and symmetrical in its general outline. Humanity is divided into four clans (*kumila*). Totemic nature is conceived to be as deeply ingrained in the substance of the individual as sex, colour, and stature. It can never be changed, and it transcends individual life, for it is carried over into the next world, and brought back unchanged into this one when the spirit returns by reincarnation. This fourfold totemic division is thought to be universal, embracing every section of mankind. The natives of neighbouring areas, where there are more than four clans, are invariably and readily made to conform to the fourfold scheme by allocating several of the alien clans to each one of the four Trobriand divisions. For such subordination of minor groups to the larger divisions there is a pattern in Trobriand culture, since each of their big totemic clans comprises smaller groups called *dala*, or, as we shall call them, 'sub-clans'.

The sub-clans are at least as important as the clans, for the members of the same sub-clan regard themselves as real kindred, claim the same rank, and form the local unit in Trobriand society. Each local community is composed of people belonging to one sub-clan, who have joint rights to the village site, to the surrounding garden-lands, and to a number of local privileges. Large villages are compounded of several minor local units, but each unit has its own compact site within the village and owns a large contiguous area of garden-land. There are even different terms to denote membership within the sub-clan and membership in the clan. People of the same sub-clan are real kinsmen, and call one another *veyogu*, my kinsman. But a man will only apply this term loosely and metaphorically to one who, though a member of the same clan, belongs to a different sub-clan, and will, if questioned directly, inform you that the other man is only pseudo-kindred, using the deprecatory term *kakaveyogu* (my spurious kinsman).

Each of the four clans has its own name: Malasi, Lukuba, Lukwasisiga, Lukulabuta. Such a clan name is used by a man or a woman as a definition of his or of her social identity: 'My name is so-and-so, and I am a Malasi.' When a man says *Tomalasi yaygu*, he gives a sociological definition of his place within the universal fourfold division of mankind, and he also thereby settles his associations in any community to which he has recently arrived. To a native this statement indicates a number of personal characteristics as well, or at least potentialities: such as magical knowledge, citizenship (when the sub-clan is also mentioned), moral and intellectual propensities, historical antecedents, relation to certain animals and plants and also an indication of rank. Thus the Malasi claim primacy among other totemic divisions, though this is only very grudgingly granted by members of other clans.

The Malasi have, however, a good piece of heraldic evidence in their favour. Near the village of Laba'i, on the northern shore of the main island, there is a spot called Obukula, which is marked by a coral outcrop. Obukula is, in fact, a 'hole' (*dubwadebula*), or 'house' (*bwala*); that is to say, one of the points from which the first ancestors of a lineage emerged. For before they appeared on this earth, human beings led a subterranean existence similar in all respects to life in surface Trobriand villages and organized on the same social pattern. They dwelt in identical local communities, were divided into clans and sub-clans, were grouped into districts, and lived as good a family life as do present-day natives. They also owned property – that is *gugu'a*, the workaday implements and chattels, and *vaygu'a*, 'valuables', and houses, canoes, and land. They practised arts and crafts and possessed specific magic.

Now, when they decided to come up to the surface of the earth, they collected all their belongings and emerged in the locality of which they wanted to take possession. The spot of their emergence is usually marked by a grotto, a large boulder, a pool, the head of a tidal creek, or merely a large stone in the village centre or street. In this way they established the traditional claim to ownership of the 'hole' and its surroundings; that is, of the village site, which often lies immediately round the hole, of the adjoining lands, and of the economic privileges and pursuits associated with the locality. It is the rule in Trobriand mythology that, originally, only one couple emerged from each such 'hole', a brother and a sister; she to start the lineage, he to protect her and look after her affairs. Thus the rule is: one clan, one village, one portion of garden-land, one system of gardening and fishing magic, one pair of brother and sister ancestors, one rank and one pedigree. This latter can never be really traced, but it is firmly believed to go back to the original woman who came out of the hole.

To this 'one-hole-one-line-one-sub-clan' rule there is only one exception, the hole of Obukula already mentioned. In this case we have one hole for the four main clans; we have ancestors who are defined not by sub-clan but by their clan identity; and we have an act of emergence which established not a special form of citizenship and ownership, not privileges for one sub-clan, but the respective position of the four clans in the scale of rank.

The myth of the hole of Obukula runs thus. First the representative of the Lukulabuta, its totemic animal the *Kaylavasi* (iguana or giant lizard), came to the surface, scratching away the earth as these animals will do. He ran up a tree and from this point of vantage waited for what should follow. Nor did he have to wait long. Through the hole he had made scrambled the dog, the animal of the Lukuba clan, who, the second on the scene, obtained the highest rank for the time being. His glory was short-lived, however, for soon afterwards came the pig: that noble animal, very close to man himself in rank, and representative of the Malasi. The last to appear was the animal of the Lukwasisiga clan, variously described as the snake, the opposum, or the crocodile. The myths disagree as to its identity and indeed this ambiguous animal plays the least important part in the story and in Trobriand totemism.

The pig and the dog played together; and the dog, running through the bush, saw the fruit of a plant called *noku*. This is considered by the natives a very inferior form of nourishment, and although it is not specifically forbidden to any clan or person, it is eaten only in times of greatest dearth and famine. The dog smelt it, licked it, and ate it. The pig seized his opportunity, and then and there laid down the charter of his rank, saying: 'Thou eatest *noku*, thou eatest excrement; thou art a low bred commoner. Henceforth I shall be the *guya'u*, the chief.' From this incident dates the Malasi claim to rank higher than the other clans, and one of their sub-clans, the Tabalu, have, indeed, the highest position; they are the real chiefs, acknowledged to be of supreme rank, not by the

Trobriands only, but by the adjoining areas as well.

Thus do the natives account for the difference in rank. The partaking of unclean food – the most important criterion of social inferiority – caused the downfall of the Lukuba, and the rise of the Malasi. But it must be remembered that this latter clan includes besides the highest sub-clan (the Tabalu), that one which is most despised, associated with the village of Bwoytalu. No respectable Lukuba man would marry a Malasi woman from that village; no Tabalu would claim kinship with anyone of its inhabitants, and he takes it very badly when it is pointed out that they are his *kakaveyola* (pseudo-kindred).

Thus in respect of rank, it is the sub-clan rather than the clan that matters, and this holds good with regard to local rights and privileges. In a village community which belongs to the Lukwasisiga of the Kwaynama sub-clan, only members of the latter are citizens. Others of the Lukwasisiga clan, who do not belong to that sub-clan are no more at home there than the Malasi or the Lukuba would be. The clan, therefore, is primarily a social category rather than a group, a category into which a number of animals, plants, and other natural objects are placed. But the totemic nature of a clan is not of great importance, and its religious significance is very much overshadowed by its social functions. The clan as a whole is only to be seen at work in certain big ceremonies, when all the sub-clans of the Malasi or Lukuba or Lukwasisiga or Lukulabuta act together and support one another.

2 Clan exogamy

The real importance of the clan in native imagination and society is illustrated by an interesting linguistic distinction. The native word for 'friend' is *lubaygu*, signifying 'the man with whom I associate from choice, because I like him'. But this word may only be applied to a man's friend from another clan, and it is not only incorrect, but even improper, to use it of a kinsman. Thus a twofold scheme in the relations between men is clearly defined linguistically by the two words for friend, one meaning 'friend within the barrier', the other 'friend across the barrier'. This distinction shows how strong is the idea of clanship; it also corresponds to the classificatory use of kinship terms, and to the whole scheme of native relationship.

Needless to say, the same distinction is made when speaking or thinking of the relation between a man and a woman. The word *lubaygu*, meaning here 'sweetheart or lover', can never be applied to a woman of the same clan. In this context it is even more incompatible with the concept of *veyola* (kinship, that is the sameness of substance) than in the relation between two men. Women of the same clan can only be described as sisters. Women of other clans are described by the generic term *tabu-*. The primary meaning of this word is 'father's sister'. It also embraces 'father's sister's daughter' or 'paternal cross-cousin', or, by extension, 'all the women of the father's clan'; and, in its widest sense, 'all the women not of the same clan'.

In this, its most extensive application, the word stands for 'lawful woman', 'woman with whom intercourse is possible'. For such a woman the term *lubaygu* ('my sweetheart') may be correctly used; but this term is absolutely incompatible with the kinship designation, *luguta*, my sister. This linguistic use embodies, therefore, the rule of exogamy, and to a large extent it expresses the ideas underlying this. Two people of the opposite sex and standing in the relation of brother and sister in the widest sense, that is belonging to the same clan, must neither marry nor cohabit, nor even show any sexual interest in one another. The native word for clan incest or breach of exogamy is *suvasova*.

The expressions *tosuvasova yoku* (thou incest committer), *kaysuvasova kwim* (thou incestuous penis), *kwaysuvasova wim* (thou incestuous cunnus) fall into the category of insults or accusations. They can, however, be used either lightly and without offence, or seriously as statements of fact with even tragic consequences. This double use of the expression corresponds to a deep-lying moral distinction between degrees of exogamous breach; a distinction which is not easily grasped save after prolonged field-work, as it is overlaid by an official and indoctrinated theory which the natives invariably retail to the unwary ethnographer.

If you inquire from intelligent and *bona fide* informants into the various aspects of exogamy and clan organization point by point, and make a composite picture from their various statements, you will necessarily arrive at the conclusion that marriage and sex intercourse within the clan are neither allowed nor ever practised and that they do not even constitute a serious temptation to the natives. Marriage, anyone will tell you, is quite impossible between men and women of the same clan; nor does it ever happen. As to intercourse, this would be most improper and would be censured by an indignant public opinion. A couple guilty of such an act would, if discovered, incur the anger of the whole community; they would be deeply mortified and terribly ashamed. And to the question: 'What would they do on discovery?' the invariable answer is that they would commit suicide by jumping from a coconut palm. This well-known method of escaping from an unpleasant situation is called *lo'u*.

'What would happen if they were not discovered?' To this the usual answer is that a breach of exogamy entails by itself an unpleasant though not necessarily fatal disease. A swelling of the belly heralds the oncoming of this retributive ailment. Soon the skin becomes white, and then breaks out into small sores which grow gradually bigger, while the man fades away in a wasting sickness. A little insect, somewhat like a small spider or a fly, is to be found in such a diseased organism. This insect is spontaneously generated by the actual breach of exogamy. As the natives put it: 'We find maggots in a corpse. How do they come? *Ivagi wala* – it just makes them. In the same way the insect is made in the body of the *tosu-vasova* (exogamy breaker). This insect wriggles round like a small snake; it goes round and round; it makes the eyes swollen, the face swollen, the belly swollen, like in *popoma* (dropsy, or any other pronounced bodily swelling), or in *kavatokulo* (wasting disease).' And examples are readily given of people who have had or are going through a similar disease.

Thus the native statements supply us with a consistent theory of incest and exogamy, which could be summarised so far by a conscientious ethnographer somewhat as follows: 'Exogamy is an absolute taboo for the natives, both as regards marriage and sexual intercourse; there is a strong moral disapproval of it which would provoke the anger of the community against delinquents and drive them, on discovery, to suicide. There is also a supernatural sanction against it, a dreadful disease culminating in death. Hence exogamy is strictly kept and breaches never occur.'

To substantiate this statement an ethnographer would adduce linguistic testimony: there is only one word for the breach of exogamy, *suvasova*, whether this be incest with the nearest relative or merely intercourse with a woman of the same clan. The linguistic usage is, moreover, the typical expression of clan solidarity, of the so-called spontaneous obedience to law and custom. Clan solidarity is also expressed in the unity of names, in the unity of totemic animals, and in the many other forms of totemic identification. And, as an additional proof of its reality, there is the classificatory use of kinship terms.

And yet we have already had indications that neither the solidarity of clanship, nor the classificatory nature of kinship, nor the completeness of the exogamous taboo are absolutely maintained in real life. Not only does there exist a long scale of penalties and blame inflicted for the various degrees of exogamous breach, but marriages within the same clan are not unknown and even the most flagrant transgressions of the taboo allow of customary evasions and adjustments.

What I wish to make clear, by confronting the gist of native statements with the results of direct observation, is that there is a serious discrepancy between the two. The statements contain the ideal of tribal morality; observation shows us how far real behaviour conforms to it. The statements show us the polished surface of custom which is invariably presented to the inquisitive stranger; direct knowledge of native life reveals the underlying strata of human conduct, moulded, it is true, by the rigid surface of custom, but still more deeply influenced by the smouldering fires of human nature. The smoothness and uniformity, which the mere verbal statements suggest as the only shape of human conduct, disappears with a better knowledge of cultural reality.

The fact is that the breach of exogamy within the clan, intrigues with what the natives call *kakaveyola* (kindred-in-clan or pseudo-kindred), though officially forbidden, ruled to be improper, and surrounded by supernatural sanctions, is yet everywhere committed. There is no moral indignation or horror about it, but the transgression encroaches upon an important institution, and cannot be officially regarded as permissible.

Marriages – as distinct from intrigues – *within the clan* are definitely regarded as a serious breach of the rule. The one or two cases on record show that natives will not actively interfere with them, once they are contracted. But I found that it was not proper to mention the incestuousness of a marriage to any of the people concerned nor yet speak about it in the presence of their near relatives. Even general allusions to incest and exogamy have to be carefully avoided in the presence of such transgressors. As to the supernatural sanctions, prophylactic magic performed over wild ginger root wrapped up in leaves, over water warmed by heated stones, and over dry banana leaf, is well-nigh universally known and is used very freely.

Thus the rule of exogamy, far from being uniform and wholesale in its application, works differently with regard to marriage and to sexual intercourse; is allowed certain latitudes by public opinion and permits of evasions of the supernatural sanctions. All this had to be stated in detail to give a clear idea of the mechanism of exogamy.

There is also an interesting difference in stringency according to the clans in which it happens. Of the four totemic divisions, the Malasi have the reputation of being the most persistent exogamy breakers and committers of incest. All the incestuous marriages on record have happened within this clan; and I was told that this was not an accident but that only the Malasi and no other clan will tolerate such marriages. The myth of incest is associated with the Malasi, and so also is the magic of love and the magic to frustrate incest disease.

Far more stringently are the rules of exogamy obeyed when the two people concerned belong, not only to the same clan, but to the same sub-clan (*dala*). Such people are called real kinsmen (*veyola mokita*, or simply *veyola*) in contradistinction to *kakaveyola*. Between such people a much greater secrecy is observed when incest is committed; there is no jauntiness or covert boasting, and marriage is impossible.

A still higher degree of stringency obtains when we come to kinship traceable in actual genealogy. Incest with a mother's sister's daughter is a real crime, and it may lead to consequences as serious as suicide. Incest with the own sister is a dreadful crime to the natives. Yet even here it would not be correct to assume an absolutely smooth and secure working of tribal law, because cases of breach of the rule occur in reality as well as in folk-lore

Thus the uniformity of the rules and the simplicity of the sanctions by which they are enforced is shown to be a surface phenomenon, below which run the complex currents and undercurrents which form the true course of tribal life. On the surface we have one word, *suvasova*, one clan kinship, one punishment, one sense of right and wrong. In reality we have the distinction between marriage and mere intercourse, between clan and sub-clan (*kakaveyola* and *veyola*), between genealogical kinship and mere community of sub-clan, between the own sister and the classificatory sisters. We have also to distinguish between direct enforcement by public opinion and by supernatural sanctions, neither of which work in a simple or infallible manner.

3 Sex prohibitions

All the sociological divisions, local communities, clans, sub-clans, and classificatory kinship groups of the Trobrianders are rooted in the family. Only by studying the formation of the earliest bonds between parent and child, by following the gradual growth and development of these, and their ever-widening extension into bonds of local grouping and clanship, can we grasp the kinship system of the natives (see the Table).

Table of relationship terms

A   Kinship terms

1   *Tabu(gu)* Grandparent, grandchild; father's sister, father's sister's daughter.
2   *Ina(gu)* Mother, mother's sister; mother's clanswoman.
3   *Tama(gu)* Father, father's brother; father's clansman; father's sister's son.
4   *Kada(gu)* Mother's brother and, reciprocally, sister's son and sister's daughter.
5   *Lu(gu)ta* Sister (man speaking), brother (woman speaking); woman of same clan and generation (man speaking), man of same clan and generation (woman speaking).
6   *Tuwa(gu)* Elder brother (man speaking), elder sister (woman speaking); clansman of same generation but older (man speaking), clanswoman of same generation but older (woman speaking).
7   *Bwada(gu)* Younger brother (man speaking), younger sister (woman speaking); clansman of same generation but younger (man speaking), clanswoman of same generation but younger (woman speaking).
8   *Latu(gu)* Child, male or female.

B   Marriage relationships

9   *(Ulo)mwala* Husband.
10   *(Ulo)kwava* Wife.

C   Relationships-in-law

11   *Yawa(gu)* Father-in-law, mother-in-law.
12   *Lubou(gu)* Wife's brother, sister's husband.
13   *Iva(gu)ta* Husband's sister, brother's wife.
14   *Tuwa(gu)* Wife's elder sister, husband's elder brother.
15   *Bwada(gu)* Wife's younger sister, husband's younger brother.

I. Terms of Kinship

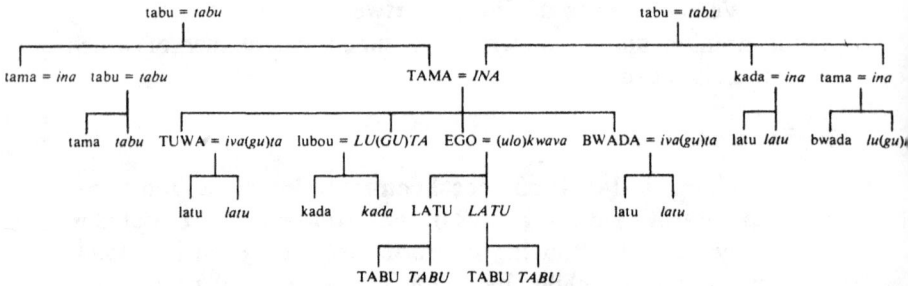

II. Relationships-in-law (Man Speaking)

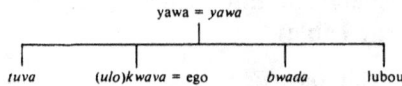

III. Relationships-in-law (Woman Speaking)

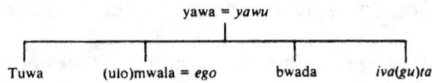

Figure 4   Genealogical diagram of relationship

In the annexed genealogical diagram we find, printed in capital letters, the few words which furnish the key to the whole terminology of kinship and form the foundation both of the sociological system within the native culture and of its linguistic expression. These are the words used to designate the inmates of the household, the words which convey the dominant interests and emotions of childhood. They denote those relationships which are the starting point of all the social bonds of later life.

Take, to begin with, the word *inagu*, my mother, which is the first to be uttered by a child in the Trobriands as everywhere else.*

* In the genealogical diagram the terms are given, without possessive pronouns; in the Table with the affixed particle of the first person (*gu*). This particle is usually suffixed to the end of the root (*inagu*, 'my mother', *tamagu*, 'my father', etc.), but it is infixed in two terms *lu-gu-ta* and *iva-gu-ta*. The second person is designated by the particle *m* or *mu*; *tamam*, 'thy father', *lumuta*, 'thy sister'; the third pers. sing. by the particle *la*, and so on. In actual speech the root is never used alone. The abstract meaning is conveyed by using the word with the third person singular suffix. *Inala* means 'mother' as well as 'his mother'. All male terms are in roman types; the female in italic. Terms for the nearest family relationship are printed in capitals.

The term correlated to it is *latugu*, by which the mother designates her own child. These are the two terms of the mother-to-child relationship on which the whole system of native kinship organisation rests. (In our diagram, Ego is addressed by his mother, *latugu*, and, later, he in turn uses this word to his own offspring as indicated there.) Apart from the intense emotional interest taken by the mother in her child, and the response of the infant to the maternal organism – both these elements being physiological and universal in all human societies – the relation in the Trobriands is sociologically defined by a number of ritual observances, beginning with pregnancy and leading the woman into those various duties and taboos of early maternity which isolate mother and child into a small group of two, intimately bound up in each other. The father, *tama*, not regarded as of the same bodily substance, stands, nevertheless, in a close emotional, legal, and economic relation to the child.

When the child grows up, it gains a gradual independence. Weaning takes place and the child is surrounded by the tender cares of the mother and father, constantly carried and watched over, until it passes to freedom and independence almost at a single stride. Children suffer very little interference from their parents in the matter of sexual freedom, and in this respect the interests of the child are naturally directed away from home and find an easy outlet among his playmates of the same age.

The removal of a child out of his family is due to yet another factor, which becomes increasingly prominent and which will colour the future sexual life of the individual. This is the supreme taboo of the Trobriander; the prohibition of any erotic or even of any tender dealings between brother and sister. This taboo is the prototype of all that is ethically wrong and horrible to the native. It is the first moral rule seriously impressed in the individual's life, and the only one which is enforced to the full by all the machinery of social and moral sanctions. It is so deeply engrained in the structure of native tradition that every individual is kept permanently alive to it.

The relation between brother and sister is denoted by the term *luguta*. This term means 'sister' when uttered by a male, and 'brother' when spoken by a female. In its wider meaning it designates a person of the opposite sex and of the forbidden class, that is, of the same sub-clan or clan as Ego. In its widest and metaphorical sense it is used for any tabooed person or thing. As a metaphor the word 'sister' (*luguta*) is frequently used in magical formulae when such things as a blight or a disease are to be exorcised.

The term *luguta* is used only with regard to the tabooed relationship, since children of the same parents and of the same sex use different kinship designations (*tuwagu, bwadagu*) to describe each other; *tuwagu* meaning 'my elder brother' (man speaking) and 'my elder sister' (woman speaking); and *bwadagu* 'my younger brother' (man speaking) and 'my younger sister' (woman speaking).

Round the word *luguta* a new order of ideas and moral rules begins to grow up at an early stage of the individual's life history. The child, accustomed to little or no interference with most of its whims or wishes, receives a real shock when suddenly it is roughly handled, seriously reprimanded and punished whenever it makes any friendly, affectionate, or even playful advances to the other small being constantly about in the same household. Above all, the child experiences an emotional shock when it becomes aware of the expression of horror and anguish on the faces of its elders when they correct it. This emotional contagion, this perception of moral reactions in the social environment is perhaps the most powerful factor in a native community by which norms and values are imposed on an individual's character.

The circumstantial arrangements and set customs which preclude any possibility of intimate contact between brother and sister are also, of course, very important. Brother and sister are definitely forbidden to take part at the same time in any childish sexual games, or even in any form of play. And this is not only a rule laid down by elders, but it is also a convention rigorously observed by the children themselves.

When a boy grows up and there is a sister of his living in the parental house, he has to sleep in the bachelors' hut (*bukumatula*). In her love affairs, the girl must most rigorously avoid any possibility of being seen by the brother. When, on certain occasions, brother and sister have to appear in the same company – when they travel in the same canoe, for instance, or participate in a domestic meeting – a rigidity of behaviour and a sobriety in conversation falls upon all those present. No cheerful company, no festive entertainment, therefore, is allowed to include brother and sister, since their simultaneous presence would throw a blight on pleasure and would chill gaiety.

Although, in a matrilineal society, the brother is the guardian of his sister, although she has to bend down when he approaches, to obey his commands and to regard him as the head of the family, he never has any concern in his sister's love affairs, nor in her prospective marriage. After she is married, however, he becomes the head of her family in more than a metaphorical sense. He is called by his sister's children *kadagu* (my maternal uncle), and as such exercises great influence, especially over the boys.

The careful avoidance by a man of any knowledge about his sister's amorous prospects is, I am certain, not only an ideal but also a fact. I was over and over again assured that no man has the slightest inkling as to whom his sister is going to marry, although this is the common knowledge of everyone else. And I know that nothing remotely touching upon the subject would be uttered within earshot of him. I was told that if a man came by chance upon his sister and her sweetheart while they were making love, all three would have to commit *lo'u* (suicide by jumping from a coconut palm). This is obviously an exaggeration which expresses the ideal and not the reality: if such a mishap occurred the brother would most likely pretend to himself, and to them, that he had seen nothing, and would discreetly disappear. But I know that considerable care is taken to preclude any such possibility, and no one would dream of mentioning the subject in the presence of the brother.

Brother and sister thus grow up in a strange sort of domestic proximity: in close contact, and yet without any personal or intimate communication; near to each other in space, near by rules of kinship and common interest; and yet, as regards personality, always hidden and mysterious. They must not even look at each other, they must never exchange any light remarks, never share their feelings and ideas. And as age advances and the other sex becomes more and more associated with love-making, the brother and sister taboo becomes increasingly stringent. Thus, to repeat, the sister remains for her brother the centre of all that is sexually forbidden – its very symbol; the prototype of all unlawful sexual tendencies within the same generation and the foundation of prohibited degrees of kinship and relationship, though the taboo loses force as its application is extended.

The nearest female of the previous generation, the mother, is also surrounded by a taboo, which is coloured, however, by a

somewhat different emotional reaction. Incest with her is regarded
with real horror, but both the mechanism by which this taboo is
brought home and the way in which it is regarded are essentially
distinct from the brother–sister taboo. The mother stands in a close
bodily relation to her child in its earliest years, and from this
position she recedes, though only gradually, as he grows up.
Weaning takes place late, and children, both male and female, are
allowed to cuddle in their mother's arms and to embrace her
whenever they like.

When a small boy begins his playful sexual approaches to small
girls, this does not in any way disturb his relationship to the
mother, nor has he to keep any special secrecy on the subject. He
does not, by preference, discuss these matters with his parents, but
there is no taboo against his doing so. When he is older and carries
on more serious intrigues, he might, in certain circumstances, even
be allowed to sleep with his sweetheart in his parents' house. Thus
the relation to the mother and the sexual relation are kept distinct
and allowed to run side by side. The ideas and feelings centring
upon sex on the one hand, and maternal tenderness on the other,
are differentiated naturally and easily, without being separated by a
rigid taboo.

The maternal grandmother and her grandson are also sexually
forbidden to each other, but there is no horror about this relationship, such incest appearing as a merely ridiculous possibility.
Sexual intercourse with an old woman is regarded as something
indecorous, ludicrous, and unaesthetic; and this is the light in
which any suggestion of grandson–grandmother incest is looked
upon. But such a lapse from good morals and manners does not
loom largely in fantasies, folk-lore or tribal morals. These two call
each other by the reciprocal term *tabugu*, which also has the wider
meaning of 'grandparent', 'grandchild', and wider yet, 'ancestor',
'descendant'.

So far we have discussed individual kinship in the female line and
within the household: between mother and child, brother and
sister, and, going beyond the household, the relation with the
grandmother. I have intentionally and carefully distinguished this
from so-called classificatory kinship ties; for the mixing up of the
individual and the 'classificatory' relation, kept apart by the
natives in law, custom, and idea, has been a most misleading and
dangerous cause of error in anthropology, vitiating both observa-

tion and theory on social organisation and kinship. Looking back to our diagram, and carrying the genealogy beyond the family circle, we can see that certain terms from within the circle are repeated outside it. In the life history of the individual most people who come into contact with the growing child are, in one way or another, partially assimilated or compared to the child's primary relatives within the household and the terms used for parents, brothers, and sisters are gradually extended. The first person from the larger world to enter into the circle of kinsmen is the mother's sister, who, although she is called by the same term as the own mother, *inagu*, is very definitely distinguished from her. The word *inagu* extended to the mother's sister is, from the outset given an entirely different meaning – something like 'second mother' or 'subsidiary mother'. When the mother's sister is a member of the same village community, she is a very frequent visitor within the household; she replaces the mother in certain functions or at certain times, she tends the child, and shows it a considerable amount of devotion. The child is taught by its elders to extend the term *inagu* to her, and this extension is made natural and plausible to the child by the considerable similarity between its relations to mother and mother's sister.

But there can be no doubt that the new use of the word remains always what it is, an extension and a metaphor. In its second sense *inagu* is used with a different feeling-tone; and there are circumlocutions, grammatical usages, and lexicographical indices which differentiate the secondary from the primary meaning.

The same gradual extension, and corresponding change in emotional content, takes place with regard to other terms, and the word *luguta*, used to the mother's sister's daughter, conveys to the boy only an attenuated and diluted idea of sisterhood. The own sister remains a prototype of the new relation, and the taboo observed towards the own sister has also to be kept with regard to the secondary sister, but the distinction between the two taboos and the two relations is well marked. The real sister lives in the same house; for her the boy, as her future guardian, feels a direct responsibility; she remains the object on which the first and only serious prohibition has been brought home to him. The secondary sister lives in another house or even village; there are no duties or responsibilities towards her and the prohibition with regard to her is a weakened extension of the primary taboo. Thus the own sister and the first maternal cousin appear in an entirely different light, not only as regards the degree, but as regards the fundamental quality of the relation. Incest with the first maternal cousin is regarded as wrong, but not horrible; as daring and dangerous, but not abominable. The early feeling for this distinction becomes, later on, crystallized in the doctrine of tribal law. The man knows and recognises that *luguta* (1) is a person to whom he owes a great many duties, whom he has partly to support after her marriage and with regard to whom he has to observe the supreme taboo. *Luguta* (2) has no specific claims on him, he is not her real guardian nor head of her household after marriage, and the sexual taboo does not operate with anything like the same stringency.

When we pass from the 'secondary' relations, denoted by the terms *inagu* (2) and *luguta* (2) to more distant relatives, the intimacy of the bond and the stringency of the taboo falls off rapidly. Taking the relation of *luguta* as an example: if a boy and girl can be traced to a common great-grandmother in the mother line, they are *luguta*. But the taboo would be much weaker. Beyond this it would be difficult even to index the term, as the relationship ceases to be traceable by pedigree. It would be just that of real kinship within the same sub-clan: *luguta, veyogu mokita – dalemasi taytanidesi* ('sister mine, kinswoman mine truly – sub-clan our identical').

When we go beyond the sub-clan to the clan (*kumila*), the relation becomes less intimate once more and the taboo less stringent: *luguta wala, kakaveyogy – kama kumila taytanidesi* ('just my sister, my pseudo-kinswoman – mine and her clan identical'). This defines the word *luguta* in its fully extended, that is truly classificatory sense. It means, as we know already, one of those women with whom sex intercourse is legally forbidden, but with whom it may be indulged. The widest meaning of the word *luguta* is thus profoundly different from *luguta* (1), the carrier of the supreme taboo.

Thus, starting from the individual relationships within the household and following the kinship extensions in the life history of the individual, we have arrived at the same results as in our discussion of clanship and the general prohibitions of exogamy and incest. The word *luguta* is one term of a dichotomy separating women into 'forbidden' and 'lawful'.

The other term *tabugu* ('lawful woman') also originates within the family and is extended thence. To follow this process we must turn to the other side of the pedigree and examine the paternal relations.

The most important person on the father's side is obviously the father himself. Here we meet the second fundamental fact in household morality: though the father is not a kinsman of his children, sexual intercourse between father and daughter, though it occurs, is not only illegal and improper, but it is viewed with definite moral repugnance. Marriage between father and daughter is not allowed nor even imaginable to the native.

It is consistent with native theory that, morally, the natives do not distinguish between a man's real daughter and his stepdaughter, and have no special term for the latter relationship. For since his relation to the child is determined through the mother and since incest is prohibited because of her, it is equally wrong to have intercourse with any of her offspring, whether of the present or of a previous marriage.

It must be clearly understood that, although father to daughter incest is regarded as bad, it is not described by the word *suvasova* (clan exogamy or incest), nor does any disease follow upon it; and the whole ideology underlying this taboo is different from that of *suvasova*.

The anomalous extension of the word for father (*tama*) to the father's sister's son is important, for it demonstrates the influence which language has upon customs and ideas. Marriage and intercourse with the male paternal first cousin is not strictly forbidden, but it is regarded somewhat askance. It is perhaps least censured among the Malasi of Kiriwina; and natives from other districts, who lose no opportunity of slandering their neighbours when a difference in custom allows of it, speak derisively of the people of Kiriwina 'who marry their fathers and sleep with them'.

A man is not allowed to have intercourse with his daughter because she is his wife's nearest kinswoman; therefore we might expect to find that the wife's other near female kindred are also tabooed. This is actually the case. A strong taboo is placed on a wife's sisters, whom, strangely enough, the man calls by the same two names (according to age) which he applies to his elder and younger brothers and which a woman uses to her elder and younger sisters: *tuwagu* and *bwadagu*. Thus here a man uses towards persons of the opposite sex names which indicate identity of sex. Analogously a woman addresses these same two terms to her husband's elder and younger brothers, with whom sexual intercourse is forbidden. There are a few recorded cases of this rule's transgression. Here, again, although the word *suvasova* is not applied to the taboo, the natives feel strongly against intercourse with a wife's sister, who, after marriage, becomes to him somewhat like his own sister. A man must also abstain from intercourse with his wife's mother, but otherwise no taboo of avoidance exists.

By careful inquiry of several informants and by direct observation, I have compiled the following table of sex taboos in order of stringency. It is meant rather to facilitate a survey of the whole subject than to establish any rigid gradations.

1. By far the most stringent is the prohibition on brother–sister incest; it is the core of the *suvasova* taboo, and is of very rare occurrence either in reality or legend.

2. Incest with the mother is regarded as unnatural and unthinkable; there are no cases on record; it is an important form of *suvasova*; it is not spoken of with the same abhorrence as brother–sister incest.

3. Sexual intercourse with the own daughter is not called *suvasova*; it is not sanctioned by supernatural penalties; it is felt to be extremely bad; there are several cases on record.

4. Intercourse with the mother's sister's daughter is a form of *suvasova*; it is of rare occurrence; it is regarded as very bad and always kept secret; on discovery it is severely penalized.

5. Intercourse with the wife's sister is not a form of *suvasova*, but it is considered bad; marriage, whether in the form of polygamy or with a deceased wife's sister, is strongly disapproved of, but it does occur, while intrigues are not infrequent.

6. Intercourse with the mother-in-law or with the brother's wife is not proper, though it is not *suvasova*, and it probably occurs but infrequently.

7. Intercourse with the 'classificatory' *luguta* (my sister) is *suvasova*: it is prohibited by legal doctrine and sanctioned by supernatural penalties; it is, however, frequently practised, and is, so to speak, at a premium.

One important relationship still remains, that called *tabugu*, father's sister, or father's sister's daughter, which has already been mentioned as the opposite category, correlated with that of *luguta*, sister (man speaking). The father's sister is the prototype of the lawful, and even sexually recommended woman; that is, in the theory of native tradition, for, in reality, it is her daughter that really plays this part.

To the father's sister exactly the opposite attitude with regard to sexual behaviour is sanctioned and approved, to that which must be adopted towards the sister. Sexual intercourse with the father's own sister is emphatically right and proper. 'It is very well when the boy copulates with his father's sister.' The natives are never tired of repeating this moral maxim, and they use, in this context, the coarse term *kayta*, instead of the polite circumlocution *masisi deli* (sleep together), or *mwoyki* (come to, visit). Her presence always carries with it the suggestion of licence, of indecent jokes and improper stories. In bawdy ditties, the refrain: *deli sidayse, deli tabumayase* (with our companions, with our paternal aunts) is of frequent occurrence. The paternal aunt and the sister must never be in the same company, since the first relaxes the bonds of propriety and the second constrains them.

Sexual intercourse, however, between a man and his paternal aunt, is important theoretically, symbolically and verbally rather than in actual life. She represents to him the class of lawful women and sexual freedom in general. She might be used to advise or even to procure for him; with herself, however, sexual intercourse is not frequently practised. She belongs to a previous generation, and, as a rule, what remains of her sexual endowment is not attractive. But whenever she and her nephews desire it, they are allowed to sleep together, preserving only a certain decorum when she is married. Marriage with the paternal aunt, though permissible and even desirable, seems never to occur: it was impossible for me to find a single instance of it among living people or in historical tradition.

The real practical substitute for his paternal aunt, the boy finds in her daughter. The two are regarded by tradition as specially suited for intercourse and for marriage. They are often engaged to each other by infant betrothal. The natives will say that the paternal cross-cousin should be the first person, if age allows, with whom a boy should copulate.

The term, however, soon becomes extended to other girls belonging to the same sub-clan and clan. Finally by an extension which goes beyond the usual limits of classificatory terminology, it becomes synonymous with 'all women not of the same clan as the sister'. It should be realized that the ordinary extensions of classificatory terminology go only to the limits of the clan. The widest sense in which the word for mother is used embraces all the women of the mother's clan. But the word *tabugu*, in its meaning of 'lawful woman', extends over three clans, and embraces roughly three-quarters of female humanity, in contrast to the one-quarter which are forbidden.

4 Dogmas of procreation and paternity

1 Physiological beliefs

The natives have a practical acquaintance with the main features of the human anatomy, and an extensive vocabulary for the various parts of the human body and for the internal organs. They often cut up pigs and other animals, while the custom of *post mortem* dissection of corpses, and visits among their overseas cannibal neighbours supply them with an exact knowledge of the homologies of the human and animal organism. Their physiological theories, on the other hand, are remarkably defective; there are many notable gaps in their knowledge about the functions of the most important organs, side by side with some fantastic and strange ideas.

Their understanding of sexual anatomy is, on the whole, limited in comparison with what they know about other parts of the human body. Considering the great interest which they take in this matter, the distinctions which they make are superficial and rough, and their terminology meagre. They distinguish and name the following parts: vagina (*wila*), clitoris (*kasesa*), penis (*kwila*), testes (*puwala*). They have no words to describe the *mons veneris* as a whole, nor the *labia majora* and *minora*. The *glans penis* they describe as the 'point' of the penis (*matala kwila*) and the prepuce as the skin of the penis (*kanivinela kwila*). The internal female organs are called generically *bam*, and this comprises the uterus and the placenta. There is no special word for the ovaries.

Their physiological views are crude. The organs of sex serve for excretion and for pleasure. The excretive urinary processes are not associated with the kidneys. A narrow duct (*wotuna*) leads from the stomach directly to the bladder, from which it passes through the male and female genitals. Through this canal the water which we drink passes slowly till it is expelled, and on its way it becomes dis-coloured and sullied in the stomach by contact with excrement. For

96

food begins to be changed into excrement in the stomach.

Their ideas about the sexual functions of the genitals are more complex and systematic, and present a sort of psycho-physiological theory. The eyes are the seat of desire and lust (*magila kayta*, literally 'desire of copulation'). They are the basis or cause (*u'ula*) of sexual passion. From the eyes, desire is carried to the brain by means of the *wotuna* (literally, tendril or creeper; in the anatomical context, vein, nerve, duct, or sinew), and thence spreads all over the body to the belly, the arms, the legs, until it finally concentrates in the kidneys. The kidneys are considered the main or middle part or trunk (*tapwana*) of the system. From them, other ducts (*wotuna*) lead to the male organ. This is the tip or point (*matala*, literally eye) of the whole system. Thus, when the eyes see an object of desire they 'wake up', communicate the impulse to the kidneys, which transmit it to the penis and cause an erection. Hence the eyes are the primary motive of all sexual excitement: they are 'the things of copulation'; they are 'that which makes us desire to copulate'. In proof of this the natives say: 'A man with his eyes closed will have no erection'; though they qualify this statement by admitting that the olfactory sense can sometimes replace the eyes, for 'when a woman discards her grass petticoat in the dark, desire may be aroused'.

The process of sexual excitement in the female is analogous. Thus the eyes, the kidneys and the sexual organs are united by the same system of *wotuna* (communicating ducts). The eyes give the alarm, which passes through the body, takes possession of the kidneys, and produces sexual excitation of the clitoris. Both the male and female discharge are called by the same name (*momona* or *momola*), and they ascribe to both the same origin in the kidneys, and the same function, which has nothing to do with generation, but is concerned with lubricating the membrane and increasing pleasure.

The drawing of a parallel between the two sexes is consistent. The indication of the three cardinal points of the sexual system is sound, and characteristic of native canons of classification. In many subjects they distinguish these three elements: the *u'ula*, the *tapwana*, and the *matala*. The image is derived from a tree or a pillar or a spear: *u'ula* – in its literal sense the foot of the tree, the base, the foundation – has come, by extension, to mean cause, origin, source of strength; *tapwana*, the middle part of the trunk, also means the trunk itself, the main body of any elongated object, the length of a road; *matala* – originally eye, or point (as in a spear) and sometimes replaced by the word *dogina* or *dabwana*, the tip of a tree or the top of any high object – stands for the highest part, or, in more abstract metaphor, the final word, the highest expression.

Very remarkable is their entire ignorance of the physiological function of the testes. They are not aware that anything is produced in this organ, and leading questions as to whether the male fluid (*momona*) has not its source there are answered emphatically in the negative. 'See, women have no testes and yet they produce *momona*.' This part of the male body is said to be only an ornamental appendage (*katububula*). 'Indeed, how ugly would a penis look without the testes,' a native aesthete will exclaim. The testes serve 'to make it look proper' (*bwoyna*).

Love or affection (*yobwayli*) has its seat in the intestines, in the skin of the belly, and of the arms, and only to a lesser extent in those springs of desire, the eyes. Hence, we like to look at those of whom we are fond, such as our children, our friends, or our parents, but when this love is strong we want to hug them.

Menstruation the Trobrianders regard as a phenomenon connected with pregnancy in a vague manner: 'the flow comes, it trickles, it trickles, it ebbs – it is over.' They denote it simply by the word blood, *buyavi*, but with a characteristic grammatical peculiarity. While ordinary bodily blood is always mentioned with the pronoun of nearest possession, which is affixed to all the parts of a human body, menstruous blood is spoken of with the same possessive pronouns as are used for ornamentation and articles of apparel (second nearest possession). Thus *buyavigu*, 'blood-mine' ('part of me – blood'), means bodily blood coming from a cut or haemorrhage; *agu buyavi*, 'my blood' ('belonging to me – blood'), means menstruous blood.

There is no pronounced masculine dislike or dread of menstruous blood. A man will not cohabit with his wife or sweetheart during her monthly period, but he will remain in the same hut and participate in the same food, and only refrains from sleeping in the same bed. Women, during menstruation, wash themselves daily, for purposes of cleanliness, in the same large water hole from which the whole village draws its drinking water, and in which, also, males occasionally take a bath. There are no special ablutions ceremonially carried out at the end of the period, nor is any rite

performed when a girl menstruates for the first time. The women
have no special way of dressing during menstruation, except that at
times they wear a longer skirt, and there is no particular modesty
on the subject between the sexes.

2 Reincarnation

The relation between menstruous blood and the formation of the
foetus has been observed and recognized by the natives, but their
ideas about it are extremely vague. Such as they are, they are so
mixed up with beliefs about the incarnation of spiritual beings, that
physiological process and spiritual agencies will have to be considered together in this account.

The spirit after death moves to Tuma, the Island of the Dead,
where he leads a pleasant existence analogous to the terrestrial life –
only much happier. Whenever the spirit (*baloma*) sees that bodily
hair is covering his skin, that the skin itself is getting loose and
wrinkled, and that his head is turning grey, he simply sloughs his
covering and appears fresh and young, with black locks and
smooth hairless skin.

But when a spirit becomes tired of constant rejuvenation, when
he has led a long existence 'underneath' as the natives call it, he
may want to return to earth again; and then he leaps back in age
and becomes a small pre-born infant. Some of my informants
pointed out that in Tuma, as on earth, there are plenty of sorcerers.
Black magic is frequently practised, and can reach a spirit and
make him weak, sick and tired of life; then, and then only, will he
go back to the beginnings of his existence and change into a spirit-
child. To kill a spirit by black magic or accident is quite impossible;
his end will always mean merely a new beginning.

These rejuvenated spirits, these little pre-incarnated babies or
spirit-children, are the only source from which humanity draws its
new supplies of life. A pre-born infant finds its way back to the
Trobriands and into the womb of some woman, but always of a
woman who belongs to the same clan and sub-clan as the spirit
child itself. Exactly how it travels from Tuma to Boyowa, how it
enters the body of its mother, and how there the physiological processes of gestation combine with the spirit activity, are questions on
which native belief is not altogether consistent. But that all spirits
have ultimately to end their life in Tuma and turn into unborn

infants; that every child born in this world has first come into existence (*ibubuli*) in Tuma through the metamorphosis of a spirit; that
the only reason and real cause of every birth is spirit activity, are
facts known to everybody and firmly believed by all.

The rejuvenation process is associated in a general way with sea-
water. In the myth which describes how humanity lost the privilege
of regaining youth at will, the scene of the last rejuvenation is laid
on the seashore in one of the lagoon inlets. In the first account of
rejuvenation which I obtained in Omarakana, I was told that the
spirit 'goes to the beach and bathes in the salt water'. Tomwaya
Lakwabulo the Seer, who in his trances often goes to Tuma and has
frequent intercourse with the spirits, told me: 'The *baloma* go to a
spring called *sopiwina* [literally "washing water"]; it lies on the
beach. There they wash their skin with brackish water. They
become *to'ulatile* (young men).' Likewise in the final rejuvenation,
which makes them return to the infant state, the spirits have to
bathe in salt water, and, when they become babies again, they go
into the sea and drift. They are always spoken of as floating on
drift-logs, or on the leaves, boughs, dead seaweed, sea-scum, and
the other light substances which litter the surface of the sea.
Tomwaya Lakwabulo says that they float all the time around the
shores of Tuma, wailing *wa, wa, wa*. 'At night I hear their wailing.
I ask, "What is it?" "Oh, children; the tide brings them, they
come."' The spirits in Tuma can see these pre-incarnated infants,
and so can Tomwaya Lakwabulo when he descends into the spirit
world. But to ordinary people they are invisible. At times, however,
fishermen from the northern villages of Kaybola and Lu'ebila,
when they go far out into the sea after shark, will hear the wailing –
wa, wa, wa – in the sighing of the wind and the waves.

Tomwaya Lakwabulo and other informants maintain that such
spirit children never float far away from Tuma. They are transported to the Trobriands by the help of another spirit. Tomwaya
Lakwabulo gives the following account. 'A child floats on a drift
log. A spirit sees it is good-looking. She takes it. She is the spirit of
the mother or of the father of the pregnant woman (*nasusuma*).
Then she puts it on the head, in the hair, of the pregnant woman,
who suffers headache, vomits, and has an ache in the belly. Then
the child comes down into the belly, and she is really pregnant. She
says: "Already it [the child] has found me; already they [the spirits]
have brought me the child."' In this account we find two leading

ideas: the active intervention of another spirit – the one who some-how conveys the child back to the Trobriands and gives it to the mother – and the insertion of it through the head, with which (not in the statement quoted, but usually) is associated the idea of an effusion of blood, first to the head and then into the abdomen.

As to how the transportation is actually accomplished opinions vary: there are natives who imagine that the older spirit either carries the baby in some sort of receptacle – a plaited coconut basket or a wooden dish – or else simply in her arms. Others say candidly that they do not know. But the active control of another spirit is essentially important. When natives say that the children are 'given by a *baloma*', that 'a *baloma* is the real cause of child-birth', they refer always to this controlling spirit (as we might call it), and not to the spirit baby itself. This controlling spirit usually appears in a dream to the woman about to be pregnant.

Frequently a woman will tell her husband who it was that brought the baby to her. And the tradition of this spiritual god-father or godmother is preserved. Thus the present chief of Omarakana knows that it was Bugwabwaga, one of his predecessors in office, who gave him to his mother. My best friend, Tokulubakiki, was a gift to his mother from her *kadala*, mother's brother. Tokulubakiki's wife received her eldest daughter from her mother's spirit. Usually it is some maternal relative of the prospective mother who bestows the gift; but it may be her father, as in Tomwaya Lakwabulo's statement.

The physiological theory associated with this belief has already been touched on. The spirit-child is laid by the bringer on the woman's head. Blood from her body rushes there, and on this tide of blood the baby gradually descends until it settles in the womb. The blood helps to build the body of the child – it nourishes it. That is the reason why, when a woman becomes pregnant, her menstru-ous flow stops. A woman will see that her menstruation has stopped. She will wait one, two, three moons, and then she will know for certain that she is pregnant. A much less authoritative belief maintains that the baby is inserted *per vaginam*.

Another version of the story of reincarnation ascribes more initiative to the pre-incarnated infant. It is supposed to be able to float of its own will towards the Trobriands. There it remains, probably in company with others, drifting about the shores of the island, awaiting its chance to enter the body of a woman while she

bathes. Certain observances kept by girls in coastal villages are
evidence that the belief has vitality. The spirit children are
imagined, as around Tuma, to be attached to drift logs, scum,
leaves, and branches, or else to the small stones on the bottom of
the sea. Whenever, through wind and tide, much débris accumulates near the shore, the girls will not enter the water for fear they
might conceive. Again, in the villages on the northern coast, there
is a custom of filling a wooden baler with water from the sea which
is then left overnight in the hut of a woman who wishes to conceive,
on the chance that a spirit-child might have been caught in the baler
and transfer itself during the night into the woman. But even in this
case, the woman is said to be visited in her dream by the spirit of
some deceased maternal relative, so that a controlling spirit is still
essential to conception. It is important to note that the water must
always be fetched by her brother or by her mother's brother; that
is, by a maternal kinsman.

The chief points in which this belief differs from the one first
described are that the pre-incarnated spirit child is endowed with
more spontaneity – it can float across the sea and enter the bathing
woman without help – and that its entry is effected *per vaginam*, or
else through the skin of the abdomen if conception takes place in
the hut. I found this belief prevalent in the northern part of the
island, and especially in its coastal villages.

It is important, however, that, in all principal points, the various
versions and descriptions agree, overlap and fortify one another;
and we are left with a composite picture which, though blurred in
some of its details, presents a strong outline when viewed from a
distance. Thus all spirits rejuvenate; all children are incarnated
spirits; the identity of sub-clan is preserved throughout the cycle;
the real cause of childbirth is the spirit initiative from Tuma.

3   Conception

The correlation of the mystical with the physiological aspects in
pregnancy belief – of the origin of the child in Tuma and its journey
to the Trobriands with the subsequent processes in the maternal
body, the welling up of the blood from the abdomen to the head
and down again from the head to the womb – provides a co-ordin-
ated and self-contained, though not always consistent, theory of
the origin of human life. It also gives a good theoretical foundation

for matriliny; for the whole process of introducing new life into a community lies between the spirit world and the female organism. There is no room for any sort of physical paternity.

But there is another condition considered by the natives indispensable for conception and childbirth, which complicates their theory and blurs the clear outline of their belief. This condition is related to sexual intercourse, and brings us face to face with the difficult and delicate question: are the natives really entirely ignorant of physiological fatherhood? Is it not rather a fact of which they are more or less aware, though it may be overlaid and distorted by mythological and animistic beliefs? Is it not an instance of empirical knowledge possessed by a backward community, but never formulated because it is too obvious to need explicit statement, whereas the traditional legend which is the basis of their social structure is carefully expressed as a part of the body of authoritative dogma? The facts which I am about to adduce contain an unambiguous and decisive answer to these questions. I shall not anticipate the conclusion, which, indeed, as we shall see, will be drawn by the natives themselves.

A virgin cannot conceive.

Tradition, diffuse folk-lore, certain aspects of custom and customary behaviour, teach the natives this simple physiological truth. They have no doubt about it, and it will be seen from what follows that they can formulate it tersely and clearly.

This statement was volunteered by Niyova, a sound informant in Oburaku: 'A virgin does not conceive, because there is no way for the children to go, for that woman to conceive. When the orifice is wide open, the spirits are aware, they give the child.' This is quite clear; but during the same sitting, the same informant had previously given me a detailed description of how the spirit lays the child on the woman's head. The words of Niyova, here quoted verbatim, imply an insertion *per vaginam*. Ibena, a clever old man of Kasana'i, gave me a similar explanation – in fact, it was he who first made it clear to me that virginity mechanically impedes spirit impregnation. His method of explanation was graphic. Holding out his closed fist, he asked: 'Can anything enter?' then, opening it, he continued: 'Now, of course, it is easy. Thus it is that a *bulabola* (large orifice) conceives easily, and a *nakapatu* (small or closed entrance, a virgin) cannot do it.'

I have quoted these two statements *in extenso*, as they are telling and characteristic; but they are not isolated. I received a great number of similar declarations, all expressing the view that the way must be open for the child, but this need not necessarily be brought about by sexual intercourse. The point is quite clear. The vagina must be opened to remove the physiological obstacle, called simply *kalapatu* (her tightness). Once this has been done, in the normal way by sexual intercourse, there is no need for male and female to come together in order to produce a child.

Considering that there are no virgins in the villages – for every female child begins her sexual life very early – we may wonder how the natives arrived at this *conditio sine qua non*. Again, since they have got so far, it may appear difficult to see why they have not advanced just a little further and grasped the fertilizing virtue of seminal fluid. Nevertheless, there are many facts to prove that they have not made this advance: as certainly as they know the necessity of a mechanical opening of the vagina, so they do not know the generative power of the male discharge. It was in discussing the mythological tales of mankind's beginnings on earth and fantastic legends of distant lands, to the account of which I shall now proceed, that I was made aware of this subtle yet all-important distinction between mechanical dilation and physiological fertilization; and was thus enabled to place native belief regarding procreation in its proper perspective.

According to native tradition, mankind originated from underground, whence a couple, a brother and a sister, emerged at different specified places. According to certain legends, only women appeared at first. Some of my commentators insisted upon this version: 'You see, we are so many on the earth because many women came first. Had there been many men, we would be few.' Now, whether accompanied by her brother or not, the primeval woman is always imagined to bear children without the intervention of a husband or of any other male partner; but not without the vagina being opened by some means. In some of the traditions this is mentioned explicitly. Thus on the island of Vakuta there is a myth which describes how an ancestress of one of the sub-clans exposed her body to falling rain, and thus mechanically lost her virginity. In the most important Trobriand myth, a woman, called Mitigis or Bolutukwa, mother of the legendary hero Tudava, lives quite alone in a grotto on the seashore. One day she falls asleep in her rocky dwelling, reclining under a dripping stalactite. The drops of water pierce her vagina, and thus deprive her of virginity. Hence her second name, Bolutukwa: *bo*, female, prefix, *litukwa*, dripping water. In other myths of origin the means of piercing the hymen are not mentioned, but it is often explicitly stated that the ancestress was without a man, and could, therefore, have no sexual intercourse. When asked in so many words how it was that they bore children without a man, the natives would mention, more or less coarsely or jestingly, some means of perforation which they could easily have used, and it was clear that no more was necessary.

Moving into another mythological dimension – into present-day legends of countries far to the north – we find the marvellous land of Kaytalugi, peopled exclusively by sexually rabid women. They are so brutally profligate that their excesses kill every man thrown by chance upon their shores, and even their own male children never attain maturity before they are sexually done to death. Yet these women are very prolific, producing many children, male and female. If a native is asked how this can be, how these females become pregnant if there are no men, he simply cannot understand such an absurd question. These women, he will say, destroy their virginity in all sorts of ways if they cannot get hold of a man to torture to death. And they have got their own *baloma*, of course, to give them children.

I have adduced these mythical instances first, for they clearly demonstrate the native point of view; the need for perforation, and the absence of any idea concerning the fertilizing value of the semen. But there are some convincing present-day instances which show that the natives believe that a girl can be with child without previous sexual intercourse. Thus, there are some women so ugly and repulsive that no one believes that they can ever have had intercourse (save, of course, for those few who know better, but who are very careful to keep silent from shame). There is Tilapo'i, now an old woman, who was famous for her hideousness in youth. She has become blind, was always almost an idiot, and had a repulsive face and deformed body. Her unattractiveness was so notorious that she became the subject of a saying: *kwoy Tilapo'i* ('have connection with Tilapo'i'), a form of abuse used in mild chaff. Altogether she is an infinite source and pivot of all kinds of matrimonial and obscene jokes, all based on the presumed impossibility of being Tilapo'i's lover or prospective husband. I was assured, over and over again, that no one ever could have had connection with her. Yet this woman has had a child, as the natives would triumphantly point out, when I tried to persuade them that only by intercourse can children be produced.

Their attitude to their own children also bears witness to their ignorance of any causal relation between congress and the ensuing pregnancy. A man whose wife has conceived during his absence will cheerfully accept the fact and the child, and he will see no reason at all for suspecting her of adultery. One of my informants told me that after over a year's absence he returned to find a newly-born child at home. He volunteered this statement as an illustration and final proof of the truth that sexual intercourse has nothing to do with conception. And it must be remembered that no native would ever discuss any subject in which the slightest suspicion of his wife's fidelity could be involved. In general, no allusion is ever made to her sexual life, past or present. Her pregnancy and child-birth are, on the other hand, freely discussed.

Thus of children born by a married woman, her husband is the father *ex officio*, but for an unmarried mother, there is 'no father to the child'. The father is defined socially, and in order that there may be fatherhood there must be marriage.

4 Illegitimacy

Since there is so much sexual freedom, must there not be a great number of children born out of wedlock? If this is not so, what means of prevention do the natives possess? If it is so, how do they deal with the problem, what is the position of illegitimate children?

As to the first question, it is very remarkable to note that illegitimate children are rare. The girls seem to remain sterile throughout their period of licence, which begins when they are small children and continues until they marry; when they are married they conceive and breed, sometimes quite prolifically. I express myself cautiously about the number of illegitimate children, for in most cases there are special difficulties even in ascertaining the fact. To have prenuptial children is, by an arbitrary ruling of doctrine and custom, considered reprehensible. Thus, out of delicacy towards people present, out of family interest or local pride, the existence of such children is invariably concealed. Such children are often adopted by some relative, and the elasticity of kinship terms makes it very difficult to distinguish between actual and adopted children.

If a married man says: 'This is my child', it may quite easily be his wife's sister's illegitimate baby. So that only an approximate estimate can be made even in a community with which one is very well acquainted. I was able to find roughly a dozen illegitimate children recorded genealogically in the Trobriands, or about one per cent.

Thus we are faced with the question: Why are there so few illegitimate children? On this subject I can only speak tentatively, and I feel that my information is perhaps not quite as full as it might have been, had I concentrated more attention upon it. One thing I can say with complete confidence: no preventive means of any description are known, nor the slightest idea of them entertained. This, of course, is quite natural. Since the procreative power of seminal fluid is not known, since it is considered not only innocuous but beneficient, there is no reason why the natives should interfere with its free arrival into the parts which it is meant to lubricate. Indeed, any suggestions of neo-Malthusian appliances makes them shudder or laugh according to their mood or temperament. They never practise *coitus interruptus*, and still less have any notion about chemical or mechanical preventives.

But though I am quite certain on this point, I cannot speak with the same conviction about abortion, though probably it is not practised to any large extent. I may say at once that the natives, when discussing these matters, feel neither fear nor constraint, so there can be no question of any difficulties in finding out the state of affairs because of reticence or concealment. My informants told me that a magic exists to bring about premature birth, but I was not able either to obtain instances in which it was performed, nor to find out the spells or rites made use of. Some of the herbs employed in this magic were mentioned to me, but I am certain that none of them possess any physiological properties. Abortion by mechanical means seems, in fine, the only effective method practised to check the increase of population, and there is no doubt that even this is not used on a large scale.

So the problem remains. Can there be any physiological law which makes conception less likely when women begin their sexual life young, lead it indefatigably, and mix their lovers freely? This, of course, cannot be answered here, as it is a purely biological question; but some such solution of the difficulty seems to me the only one, unless I have missed some very important ethnological clue.

Fecundity in unmarried girls is discreditable; sterility in married women is unfortunate. The same term *nakarige* (*na*, female prefix, *karige*, to die) is used of a childless woman as of a barren sow. But this condition brings no shame on the person concerned, and does not detract from the social status of such a woman. The oldest wife of To'uluwa, Bokuyoba, has no children, yet she ranks first among the wives as is the due of her age. Nor is the word *nakarige* considered to be indelicate; a sterile woman will use it when speaking of herself, and others will apply it to her in her presence. But fertility in married women is considered a good thing. Primarily it affects her maternal kinsmen, and is a matter of great importance to them. 'The kinsmen rejoice, for their bodies become stronger when one of their sisters or nieces has plenty of children.' The wording of this statement expresses the interesting conception of collective clan unity, of the members being not only of the same flesh, but almost forming one body.

Returning again to the main trend of our argument, it must be noted that the scorn and disapproval levelled at illegitimacy is highly significant sociologically. Let us realize once more this interesting and strange constellation of facts: physical fatherhood is unknown; yet fatherhood in a social sense is considered necessary and the 'fatherless child' is regarded as something anomalous, contrary to the normal course of events, and hence reprehensible. What does this mean? Public opinion, based on tradition and custom, declares that a woman must not become a mother before she marries, though she may enjoy as much sexual liberty as she likes within lawful bounds. This means that a mother needs a defender and provider of economic necessities. She has one natural master and protector in her brother, but he is not in a position to look after her in all matters where she needs a guardian. According to native ideas, a woman who is pregnant must, at a certain stage, abstain from all intercourse and 'turn her mind away from men'. She then needs a man who will take over all sexual rights in regard to her, abstain from exercising even his own privileges from a certain moment, guard her from any interference, and control her own behaviour. All this the brother cannot do, for, owing to the strict brother–sister taboo, he must scrupulously avoid even the thought of anything which is concerned with his sister's sex. Again, there is the need for a man to keep guard over her during childbirth, and 'to receive the child into his arms', as the natives put it. Later it is the duty of this man to share in all the tender cares bestowed on the child.

Thus the part played by the husband is strictly defined by custom and is considered socially indispensable. A woman with a child and no husband is an incomplete and anomalous group. The family, consisting of husband, wife, and children, is the standard set down by tribal law, which also defines the functions of its component parts. It is therefore not right that one of the members of this group should be missing.

Thus, though the natives are ignorant of any physiological need for a male in the constitution of the family, they regard him as indispensable socially. This is very important. Paternity, unknown in the full biological meaning so familiar to us, is yet maintained by a social dogma which declares: 'Every family must have a father; a woman must marry before she may have children; there must be a male to every household.'

The institution of the individual family is thus firmly established on a strong feeling of its necessity, quite compatible with an absolute ignorance of its biological foundations. The sociological rôle of the father is established and defined without any recognition of his physiological nature.

5 Sociological paternity

The interesting duality between matrilineal and patriarchal influences, represented by the mother's brother and the father respectively, is one of the Leitmotivs of the first act of Trobriand tribal life. Here we have come to the very core of the problem: for we see within this social scheme, with its rigid brother–sister taboo and its ignorance of physical fatherhood, two natural spheres of influence to be exercised over a woman by a man: the one, that of sex, from which the brother is absolutely debarred and where the husband's influence is paramount; the other, that in which the natural interests of blood relationship can be safeguarded properly only by one who is of the same blood. This is the sphere of the woman's brother.

By the brother's inability to control or to approach, even as a distant spectator, the principal theme in a woman's life – her sex – a wide breach is left in the system of matriliny. Through this breach the husband enters into the closed circle of family and household, and once there makes himself thoroughly at home. To his children he becomes bound by the strongest ties of personal attachment, over his wife he assumes exclusive sexual rights, and shares with her the greater part of domestic and economic concerns.

On the apparently unpropitious soil of strict matriliny, with its denial of any paternal bond through procreation and its declaration of the father's extraneousness to progeny, there spring up certain beliefs, ideas and customary rules, which smuggle extreme patrilineal principles into the stronghold of mother-right. One of these ideas is of the kind which figures so largely in sensational amateur records of savage life, and it strikes us at first as savage indeed, so lop-sided, distorted and quaint does it appear. I refer to their idea about the similarity between parents and offspring. That this is a favourite topic of nursery gossip in civilized communities needs no special comment. In a matrilineal society, such as the Trobriands, where all maternal relatives are considered to be of the 'same body', and the father to be a 'stranger', we would have no doubt in anticipating that facial and bodily similarity would be traced in the mother's family alone. The contrary is the case, however, and this is affirmed with extremely strong social emphasis. Not only is it a household dogma, so to speak, that a child never resembles its mother, or any of its brothers and sisters, or any of its maternal kinsmen, but it is extremely bad form and a great offence to hint at any such similarity. To resemble one's father, on the other hand, is the natural, right, and proper thing for a man or woman to do.

I found that everyone in the Trobriands will, in the teeth of all the evidence, stoutly deny that similarity can exist between matrilineal kinsmen. The Trobrianders maintain that mention of such likenesses can only be made to insult a man. It is, in fact, a technical phrase in serious bad language to say *migim lumuta*, 'Thy face thy sister's', which, by the way, is the worst combination of kinship similarity. This expression is considered quite as bad as 'have intercourse with thy sister'! But, according to a Trobriander, no sane and decent man can possibly entertain in a sober dispassionate mood such an outrageous thought as that anyone should in the slightest degree resemble his sister.

Still more remarkable is the counterpart to this social dogma; namely, that every child resembles its father. Such similarity is always assumed and affirmed to exist. Where it is really found, even to a small degree, constant attention is drawn to it as to a thing which is nice, good and right. It was often pointed out to me how strongly one or other of the sons of To'uluwa, the chief of Omarakana, resembled his father, and the old man was especially proud of the more or less imaginary resemblance between himself and his youngest son, Dipapa. Especially were the five favourite sons of himself and Kadamwasila each said to be exactly like his father. When I pointed out that this similarity to the father implied similarity to each other, such a heresy was indignantly repudiated. There are also definite customs which embody this dogma of patrilineal similarity. Thus, after a man's death, his kinsmen and friends will come from time to time to visit his children in order to 'see his face in theirs'. They will give them presents, and sit looking at them and wailing. This is said to soothe their insides because they have seen once more the likeness of the dead.

How do the natives reconcile the inconsistency of this dogma with the matrilineal system? When questioned they will say: 'Yes, maternal kinsmen are the same flesh, but similar faces they have not.' When you inquire again why it is that people resemble their father, who is a stranger and has nothing to do with the formation of their body, they have a stereotyped answer: 'It coagulates the face of the child; for always he lies with her, they sit together.' The expression *kuli*, to coagulate, to mould, was used over and over again in the answers which I received. This is a statement of the social doctrine concerning the influence of the father over the physique of the child, and not merely the personal opinion of my informants. One of my informants explained it to me more exactly, turning his open hands to me palm upwards: 'Put some soft mash (*sesa*) on it, and it will mould like the hand. In the same manner, the husband remains with the woman and the child is moulded.' Another man told me: 'Always we give food from our hand to the child to eat, we give fruit and dainties, we give betel nuts. This makes the child as it is.'

Thus we see that an artificial physical link between father and child has been introduced, and that on one important point it has overshadowed the matrilineal bond. For physical resemblance is a very strong emotional tie between two people, and its strength is hardly reduced by its being ascribed, not to a physiological, but to a sociological cause – that of continued association between husband and wife.

5 Marriage

1 Preliminaries to marriage

The first thing to be realized is that the Trobriander has no full status in social life until he is married. A bachelor has no household of his own, and is debarred from many privileges. There are, in fact, no unmarried men of mature age, except idiots, incurable invalids, old widowers and albinos. Several men were widowed during my stay in the Islands, and others were deserted by their wives. The former remarried almost as soon as their mourning was over, the latter as soon as their attempts at reconciliation had proved fruitless.

The same applies to women. Provided she is at all sexually tolerable, a widow or divorcee will not have long to wait. Once released from mourning, a widow again becomes marriageable. She may sometimes delay a little, in order to enjoy the sexual freedom of her unmarried state, but such conduct will ultimately draw on her the censure of public opinion, and a growing reputation for 'immorality', that is disregard of tribal usage, will force her to choose a new mate.

Another very important reason for marriage, from the man's point of view, is economic advantage. Marriage brings with it a considerable yearly tribute in staple food, given to the husband by the wife's family. This obligation is perhaps the most important factor in the whole social mechanism of Trobriand society. On it, through the institution of rank and through his privilege of polygamy, rests the authority of the chief, and his power to finance all ceremonial enterprises and festivities. Thus a man, especially if he be of rank and importance, is compelled to marry, for, apart from the fact that his economic position is strengthened by the income received from his wife's family, he only obtains his full social status by entering the group of *tovavaygile* (married men).

There is, further, the natural inclination of a man past his first youth to have a house and a household of his own. The services rendered by a woman to her husband are naturally attractive to a man of such an age; his craving for domesticity has developed, while his desire for change and amorous adventure has died down. Moreover, a household means children, and the Trobriander has a natural longing for these. Although not considered of his own body nor as continuing his line, they yet give him that tender companionship for which, when he reaches twenty-five or thirty, he begins to crave. He has become used, it should be remembered, to playing with his sister's children and with those of other relatives or neighbours.

These are the reasons – social, economic, practical and sentimental – which urge a man towards marriage. And last, though not least, personal devotion to a woman and the promise of prolonged companionship with one to whom he is attached, and with whom he has sexually lived, prompt him to make certain of her by means of a permanent tie, which shall be binding under tribal law.

The woman, who has no economic inducement to marry, and who gains less in comfort and social status than the man, is mainly influenced by personal affection and the desire to have children in wedlock.

This personal motive comes out very strongly in the course of love affairs which do not run smoothly, and brings us from the reasons for marriage in general to the motives which govern the individual's particular choice.

In this matter it must first be realized that the choice is limited from the outset. A number of girls are excluded completely from a man's matrimonial horizon, namely those who belong to the same totemic class. Furthermore, there are certain endogamous restrictions, though these are by no means so precisely defined as those imposed by exogamy. Endogamy enjoins marriage within the same political area, that is within some ten to twelve villages of the same district. The rigidity of this rule depends very much on the particular district. For instance, one area in the north-west corner of the island is absolutely endogamous, for its inhabitants are so despised by the other Islanders that the latter would not dream either of marrying or of having sexual relations within it. Again, the members of the most aristocratic province of Kiriwina seldom marry outside their own district, except into the neighbouring

island of Kitava, or into certain eminent families from one or two
outside villages.

Even within this limited geographical area, there are further
restrictions on the choice of a mate, and these are due to rank.
Thus, members of the highest sub-clan, the Tabalu, and more
especially their women, would not marry into a sub-clan of very
low caste, and a certain correspondence in nobility is considered
desirable even in marriage between less important people.

It follows that choice must be made from among persons who are
not of the same clan, who are not widely different in rank, who
reside within the convenient geographical area, and who are of a
suitable age. In this limited field, however, there is still sufficient
freedom of selection to allow of *mariages d'amour, de raison, et de
convenance.*

Permanent liaisons which are on the point of ripening into
marriage become known and are talked about in the village, and
now the girl's family, who, so far, have taken no interest in her love
affairs, who have, indeed, kept ostentatiously aloof, must face the
fact about to be accomplished, and make up their minds whether or
no they will approve it. The man's family, on the other hand, need
show little interest in a matter in which they have practically no say.
A man is almost entirely independent with regard to matrimony,
and his marriage, which will be a matter of constant and considerable effort and worry to his wife's family, will continue to lie completely outside the sphere of his own people's concerns.

It is remarkable that, of all the girl's family, the person who has
most to say about her marriage, although legally he is not reckoned
as her kinsman (*veyola*), is her father. I was astonished when this
information was given to me early in the course of my field work,
but it was fully confirmed later on by observation. This para-
doxical state of affairs becomes less incomprehensible, however, if
we bring it into relation with certain rules of morals and etiquette,
and with the economic aspect of marriage. One would naturally
expect a girl's brothers and maternal kinsmen to take the most
important part in deliberations concerning her marriage, but the
strict taboo which rules that the brother must have nothing at all to
do with the love affairs of his sister, and her other maternal kinsmen but little, debars them from any control over her matrimonial
plans.

Thus, although her mother's brother is her legal guardian, and her own brothers will in the future occupy the same position with regard to her own household, they must all remain passive until the marriage is an accomplished fact. The father, say the natives, acts in this matter as the spokesman of the mother, who is the proper person to deliberate upon her daughter's love intrigues and marriage. It will also be seen that the father is closely concerned in the work of his sons from the economic standpoint, and that, after the marriage of their sister, these will have to divide the fruits of their labour between her and their mother, instead of, as previously, giving them all to the parental household. When two lovers have decided on marriage, the young man becomes assiduous in his attentions to his sweetheart's family, and perhaps her father will, on his own initiative, say: 'You sleep with my child: very well, marry her.' As a matter of fact, if the family are well disposed to the youth, they will always take this initiative either by such a direct declaration or else by asking him for small gifts, an equally unambiguous indication that he is accepted.

When the family are definitely opposed to the match and give no sign of goodwill, the boy may take the initiative and plead on his own behalf. If he is refused it may be either because he is of too low a rank, or because he is notoriously lazy, and would be too great a drag on his future relatives-in-law, or else because the girl is intended for someone else. After such a refusal, the pair may relinquish their plans, or, if they are strong enough to fight the matter out, they may try to bring about their marriage in the teeth of opposition. If they decide to do this, the bride stays in her lover's house (that is, in his parents' house), as if she were really married, and the news is spread abroad that the man is attempting to wed her in spite of her people. Sometimes the two actually elope and go to another village in the hope of impressing and mortifying their hard-hearted opponents. In any case, they stay indoors all day, and do not eat any food to see if this will soften the hearts of her family. This abstention from the common meal, which constitutes a definite declaration of marriage, shows that they are still waiting for her family's consent.

In the meantime, the boy's father or maternal uncle may go as an ambassador to the girl's family and offer them a gift of high value to melt their resistance. Under this combined pressure the latter may give in, and send the customary present to the young couple. If, on the other hand, they do not relent, they repair in great numbers to the spot where the girl stays with the youth and 'pull her back', a customary and technical expression, but one which also indicates what actually occurs. The boy's relatives and friends may possibly oppose the 'pulling back', and then a scuffle will ensue. But the girl's people always have the whip hand, for, as long as they withhold their consent, nobody can force them to supply the pair with food, and without this the household is soon dissolved in the natural course.

When the parents are well disposed and signify their pleasure in the match by asking the intended for a small present, the engaged couple must still wait for a little in order to give necessary time for the preparations. But one day the girl instead of returning in the morning to her parents' house, will remain with her husband, take her meals in the house of his parents and accompany him throughout the day. The word goes round: 'Isepuna is already married to Kalogusa.' Such proceedings constitute the act of marriage. There is no other rite, no other ceremony to mark the beginnings of wedlock. From the morning on which she has remained with the bridegroom, the girl is married to him, provided, of course, the consent of the parents has been given. Without this, as we have seen, the act constitutes only an attempt at marriage. Though utterly simple, this act of remaining with the man, of openly sharing a meal with him, and of staying under his roof, has a legally binding force. It is the conventional public declaration of marriage. It has serious consequences, for it changes the life of the two concerned, and it imposes considerable obligations on the girl's family, obligations associated in turn with counter-obligations on the part of the bridegroom.

2 Marriage gifts

This simple declaration of marriage is followed by that exchange of gifts which is so typical of any social transaction in the Trobriands. Each gift is definite in nature and quantity, each has to take its proper place in a series and each is reciprocated by some corresponding contribution. The subjoined table will help to make clear the description which follows it.

The girl's family have to make the first offering to signify their consent to the marriage. Since their agreement is absolutely essential, this gift, in conjunction with the public declaration of the union of the partners, constitutes marriage. It is a small gift, a little

cooked food brought in baskets and offered by the girl's father to
the boy's parents. It is set down in front of their house with the
words *kam katuvila*, 'thy *katuvila* gift'. It must be given on the day
on which the two remain together, or on the morning of the next
day. As we have seen, when the consent of the girl's family is doubtful the two partners often abstain from food till this gift is
brought.

Marriage gifts

I G—B	1	*Katuvila*: cooked yams, brought in baskets by the girl's parents to the boy's family.
	2	*Pepe'i*: several baskets of uncooked yams, one given by each of the girl's relatives to the boy's parents.
	3	*Kaykaboma*: cooked vegetables, each member of the girl's family bringing one platter to the boy's house.
II B—G	4	*Mapula kaykaboma*: repayment of gift (3), given in exactly the same form and material by the boy's relatives to the girl's family.
	5	*Takwalela pepe'i*: valuables given by the boy's father in repayment of gift (2) to the girl's father.
III G—B	6	*Vilakuria*: a large quantity of yam-food offered at the first harvest after the marriage to the boy by the girl's family.
IV B—G	7	*Saykwala*: gift of fish brought by the boy to his wife's father in repayment of (6).
	8	*Takwalela vilakuria*: a gift of valuables handed by the boy's father to the girl's father in payment of (6).

G—B (girl to boy), gifts from the girl's family); B—G, return gifts from
the boy's relatives to the girl's.

Soon afterwards, usually on the same day, the girl's relatives
bring a bigger present. Her father, her maternal uncle, and her
brothers who now for the first time emerge from the inaction
imposed on them by the specific brother–sister taboo, each bring a
basket of uncooked yam food, and offer it to the boy's parents.
This gift is called *pepe'i*. But even this is not enough. A third
offering of food is brought to the boy's parents, cooked this time
and carried on large platters. This gift is called *kaykaboma*.

The boy's family must not delay long before they reciprocate.
The last gift, cooked food on trays, is returned almost immediately
and in exactly the same form as it was received. A more important
gift follows. The boy's father has already prepared certain
valuables of the *vaygu'a* type, that is to say, large, polished axe-

blades of green stone, necklaces of polished spondylus shell discs, and armlets made of the *conus* shell; also, when the second gift of uncooked food was brought to him by the girl's family, he made a small distribution of it among his own relatives, and they in turn now bring him other valuables to add to his own. All these he presents to the girl's family; he has kept the baskets in which the food was brought to him; he puts the valuables into these, and they are carried by himself and his family to the girl's house. This gift is called *takwalela pepe'i* or 'repayment in valuables of the *pepe'i* gift'.

The reader is perhaps weary of all these petty details, but this meticulous absorption in small gifts and counter-gifts is highly characteristic of the Trobrianders. They are inclined to boast of their own gifts, with which they are entirely satisfied, while disputing the value and even quarrelling over what they themselves receive, but they regard these details as most important and observe them scrupulously. In the exchange of marriage gifts, as a rule, they are less cantankerous than on other occasions, and a more generous and friendly spirit prevails. After the *takwalela pepe'i* there is a long pause in the exchange of gifts, which lasts until the next harvest. During this time and while the couple's own dwelling is being built, the wife usually remains with her husband in his father's house. At harvest time they will receive the first substantial gift due from the girl's family, and of this they will themselves make a distribution by way of payment to those who have helped in the building of their new home.

To resume, then, the girl's family give a present of considerable value at the next harvest, and from then on at every harvest they will have to help the new household with a substantial contribution of fresh yams. The first present of this sort, however, has a special name (*vilakuria*), and is surrounded by a ceremonial of its own. Prism-shaped receptacles (*pwata'i*) are constructed of poles, in front of the young couple's yam-house, and the girl's family, after selecting a large quantity, a hundred, two hundred, or even three hundred basketfuls of the best yams, arrange them in these receptacles with a great amount of ceremony and display.

This gift also must be repaid without any too great delay. Fish is considered a proper counter-offering. In a coastal village, the husband will embark with his friends on a fishing expedition. If he lives inland, he has to purchase the fish in one of the coastal villages, paying for them in yams.

1 The ethnographer talking to Togugu'a, a sorcerer of some repute and a good informant, who is wearing a full wig and holding a lime gourd and spatula

2 An offering of cooked food is exposed to the spirits for some time in the garden. The magician, with the ceremonial axe on his arm, is seen squatting to the right. In the forefront, a big bundle of leaves which he will presently charm over (see ch. 2)

3 Ceremonial distribution of food (see ch. 2)

4 The *urigubu* in the village. The carriers arrange the yams into a conical heap in front of the store-house, to which they will be transferred after a time (see ch. 5)

5 Canoe under sail. This illustrates the rigging, the tilt of the canoe—the raised outrigger—and the carrying capacity of a canoe. This one is well in the water, with a crew of eighteen men (see chs 7 and 8)

6 Two women adorned with necklaces. This shows the manner in which a *soulava* is worn, when used as a decoration (see chs 7 and 8)

7 The personal share of To'uluwa from the haul of arm-shells brought from Kitava to Omarakana in October 1915 (see ch. 8)

8 Bringing in a *soulava*. The party, the second man blowing the conch-shell and the leader carrying the necklace on a stick, approach the chief's house (see ch. 8)

9 Offering the *soulava*. The necklace is thrust on its stick into the chief's house. Plates 8 and 9 both represent an act of purely domestic Kula; one of the sons of To'uluwa offering his father a necklace, hence the scanty attendance of the general public (see ch. 8)

The fish is laid in front of the girl's parents' house, with the words '*Kam saykwala*' (thy *saykwala* gift). Sometimes, if the young husband is very rich, or else if he and his family were not able previously to repay the *pepe'i* present, a gift of *vaygu'a* (valuables) will be given at this point in answer to the first harvest offering. This is called *takwalela vilakuria* (repayment by valuables of the *vilakuria* present), and closes the series of initial marriage gifts.

This series of gifts appears at first sight unnecessarily complicated. But, if we examine it more closely, we find that it represents a continuous story, and is no mere disconnected jumble of incident. In the first place it expresses the leading principle in the economic relation which will subsequently obtain for the whole duration of the marriage: that the girl's family provide the newly-established household with food, being occasionally repaid with valuables. The small initial gifts (1, 2, and 3), express the consent of the girl's family, and are a sort of earnest of their future and more considerable contributions. The return offering of food (4), made immediately by the boy's family, is a characteristically Trobriand answer to a compliment. And the only really substantial gifts from the bridegroom's family to the bride's (5, or 8, or both) exert a definitely binding force on the husband, for if the marriage be dissolved, he does not recover them save in exceptional cases. They are about equivalent in value to all the other first year's gifts put together. But this present from the husband must emphatically not be considered as purchase money for the bride. This idea is utterly opposed both to the native point of view and to the facts of the case. Marriage is meant to confer substantial material benefits on the man. These he repays at rare intervals with a gift of valuables, and it is such a gift that he has to offer at the moment of marriage. It is an anticipation of the benefits to follow, and by no means a price paid for the bride.

It may be mentioned that not all of this series of gifts are equally indispensable. Of the first three, only one (either 1 or 2) must be given at all costs. Of the rest, 6 and 7 are never omitted, while either 5 or 8 are absolutely obligatory.

3 Infant betrothal and cross-cousin marriage

There is another way of arranging marriages in the Trobriands beside the ordinary method of courtship, and in many respects the two are in sharp contrast to each other. Normal marriage is brought about by free choice, by trial, and by the gradual strengthening of bonds which assume a legal obligation only after marriage. In marriage by infant betrothal, a binding agreement is made by the parents in the children's infancy; the boy and girl grow up into the relationship, and find themselves bound to each other before they have had an opportunity to choose for themselves.

The great importance of this second type of marriage lies in the fact that infant betrothal is always associated with cross-cousin marriage. The two people who, according to native ideas, are most suited for marriage with each other – a man's son and the daughter of his sister – are betrothed in infancy. When the father's sister's daughter is too old to be betrothed to her male infant cousin, her daughter may replace her. By the native legal system the two are equivalent, for the purposes of this marriage.

The significance of this institution can only be understood if we return to a consideration of the compromise between father-love and matriliny. Cross-cousin marriage is an arrangement whereby both tribal law, which enjoins matrilineal succession, and the promptings of paternal love, which incline the father to bestow all possible privileges on his son, find equitable adjustment and adequate satisfaction.

Let us take a concrete instance. A chief, a village headman – or, indeed, any man of rank, wealth, and power, will give to a favourite son all that he can safely alienate from his heirs; some plots in the village lands, privileges in fishing and hunting, some of the hereditary magic, a position in the Kula exchange, a privileged place in the canoe and precedence in dancing. Often the son becomes in some sort his father's lieutenant, performing magic instead of him, leading the men in tribal council, and displaying his personal charm and influence on all those occasions when a man may win the much-coveted *butura* (renown). As examples of this tendency, which I have found in every community where there was a chief of outstanding influence, we may take the arrogant Namwana Guya'u, before his banishment the leading figure in the village life of Omarakana. Again, in the sister village of Kasana'i, the chief's son Kayla'i, a modest and good-natured fellow, wielded the power of thunder and sunshine in virtue of the supreme system of weather-magic which his father had imparted to him. And the coastal villages of Kavataria, Sinaketa, Tukwa'ukwa, each had its leader in a son of the chief. But such privileged positions are invidious and insecure, even while they last; as the rightful heirs and owners in matriliny resent being pushed aside during the lifetime of the chief; and, in any case, all such benefits cease with the father's death. There is only one way by which the chief can establish his son permanently in the village with rights of full citizenship for himself and his progeny, and secure possession of all the gifts until death; and that is by contracting the son in paternal cross-cousin marriage, marriage with his sister's daughter or with this daughter's daughter. Figure 5 will help to make the genealogy of the relation clear.

Our diagrammatical chief has a sister; and she has a son, the chief's heir and successor, and a daughter, the chief's niece by his sister, a girl who will continue the aristocratic line. The husband of this girl will enjoy a very privileged position, into which he will step on the day of his marriage. By native law and custom he will have a definite claim on his wife's brother or brothers and other male relatives, who will be obliged to give him annual tribute of food, and

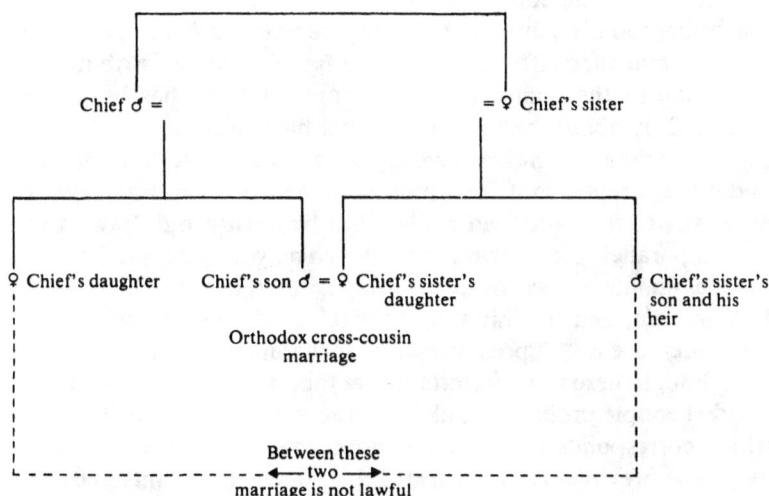

Figure 5   Diagrammatic genealogy of cross-cousin marriage

will be considered his *ex-officio* allies, friends, and helpers. He also acquires the right to live in the village if he choose, and to participate in tribal affairs and in magic. It is clear, therefore, that he will occupy practically the same position as that enjoyed by the chief's son during his father's lifetime, and from which he is ousted by the rightful heir at his father's death. This type of marriage differs from the ordinary one also in that the husband comes to live in his wife's community. Cross-cousin marriage is thus matrilocal in contradistinction to the ordinary patrilocal usage.

The obvious and natural solution, therefore, of the chief's difficulty is to marry his son to his niece or grand-niece. Usually all parties benefit by the transaction. The chief and his son get what they want; the chief's niece marries the most influential man in the village, and in so doing confirms this influence; and an alliance is established between the son of the chief and his lawful heirs which frustrates the potential rivalry between them. The girl's brother cannot oppose the marriage, because of the taboo; nor, as it is contracted in the chief's son's infancy, would he normally be in a position to do so.

4 Husband and wife

We left the young couple starting their common life in the hut of the bridegroom's parents; here they remain until the protracted series of marriage gifts and counter-gifts, and the redistribution of every one of these among more distant relatives, has been completed. Only about the time of the next harvest do they build their own home; until then they have to spend a protracted 'honeymoon' under the parental roof. This must seem a most unsatisfactory state of affairs to the European reader. But he must avoid drawing too close a parallel to our own conditions. The young people have left the passionate stages of their life together behind them in the *bukumatula*, and the initial months of matrimony, on which they now enter, are not of predominantly sexual interest to them.

Although there is no definite sexual taboo at this time, the newly-wedded couple probably think less of love-making during the stage which corresponds to our honeymoon than they have done for a long time previously. I have heard this statement volunteered: 'We feel ashamed in the house of our mother and father. In the *bukumatula* a man has intercourse with his sweetheart before they marry. Afterwards they sleep on the same bunk in the parental house, but they do not take off their garments.' The young couple suffer from the embarrassment of new conditions. The earlier nights of marriage are a natural period of abstinence.

It must be remembered that it is impossible to get direct information from any man concerning his own conjugal life; for in this matter a very strict etiquette has to be observed. In speaking to a husband the slightest allusion to this must be avoided. Nor is any reference allowed to their common sexual past, nor to the woman's previous love adventures with other men. It would be an unpardonable breach of etiquette were you to mention, even unwittingly and in passing, the good looks of a wife to her husband: the man would walk away and not come near you for a long time. The Trobriander's grossest and most unpardonable form of swearing or insult is *Kwoy um kwava* (copulate with thy wife). It leads to murder, sorcery, or suicide.

There is an interesting and, indeed, startling contrast between the free and easy manner which normally obtains between husband and wife, and their rigid propriety in matters of sex, their restraint of any gesture which might suggest the tender relation between them. When they walk, they never take hands or put their arms about each other in the way, called *kaypapa*, which is permitted to lovers and to friends of the same sex. Ordinarily a married couple walk one behind the other in single file. On public and festival occasions they usually separate, the wife joining a group of other women, the husband going with the men. You will never surprise an exchange of tender looks, loving smiles, or amorous banter between a husband and wife in the Trobriands.

This punctilio does not preclude good-humoured familiarity in other respects. Husband and wife may talk and exchange banter in public as long as any allusion to sex is rigidly excluded. Generally speaking, husband and wife remain on excellent terms, and show a marked liking for each other's company.

I seldom witnessed quarrels or heard bad language among married people. If a woman is a shrew (*uriweri*) and the husband not sufficiently dominated to bear the fact meekly, or *vice versa*, marriage is so easily dissolved that there is hardly ever an unsuccessful match which survives the first outbreak long.

Jealousy, with or without adequate reason, and adultery are the two factors in tribal life which put most strain on the marriage tie.

In law, custom and public opinion, sexual appropriation is exclusive. There is no lending of wives, no exchange, no waiving of marital rights in favour of another man. Any such breach of marital fidelity is as severely condemned in the Trobriands as it is in Christian principle and European law; indeed the most puritanical public opinion among ourselves is not more strict. Needless to say, however, the rules are as often and as easily broken, circumvented, and condoned as in our own society.

In the Trobriands the norms are strict, and though deviations from them are frequent, they are neither open nor, if discovered, unatoned; they are certainly never taken as a matter of course.

A tragic story is told in Omarakana about a man called Taytapola, belonging to a generation now passed away. He caught his wife Bulukwau'ukwa in the very act of adultery with Molukwayawa, a man of the same village. The adulterer succeeded in making his escape. The husband pursued him spear in hand, but failing to overtake him, came back to his hut and blew the conch shell. His maternal kinsmen (*veyola*) rallied round him; and they all repaired to the adversary's end of the village, where they accused the culprit and insulted him in front of his sub-clan. A village fight ensued, the two principals facing each other, each supported by his kinsmen. The offender was speared and died. In such a case, the attack was probably concentrated on him personally, and the defence of the wrongdoer lacked the impetus of conviction.

Kouta'uya, a chief of the compound village of Sinaketa, went on a Kula expedition to Gumasila. One of his wives, Bogonela, had a lover, by name Kaukweda Guya'u. The eldest wife of the absent chief, Pitaviyaka, was suspicious of her fairer companion and watched her. Hearing a noise one night, she went to Bogonela's hut and found the two lovers together. A great scandal broke out in the village. The guilty wife was publicly harangued and insulted by the female relatives of her husband: 'You like carnal pleasures too much; you are too fond of male charms.' Bogonela did as the custom and ideal of personal honour dictated. In her best attire and adorned with all her valuable ornaments, she climbed a tall coconut palm on the central place of the village. Her little daughter, Kaniyaviyaka, stood under the tree and cried. Many people were assembled. She commended her child to the care of the eldest wife and jumped from the tree. She was killed on the spot.

5 The harvest tribute: *urigubu*

When, after their 'honeymoon' in the boy's parental house, the couple set up for themselves, they have to erect a yam-store as well as a dwelling-hut, and the former, as we know, will stand in the inner ring facing the latter. The yam-house has a ceremonial compartment, contained between the beams of a square well, and into this the annual contribution of the wife's family is regularly stowed at harvest. At the same time the master of the new household is himself delivering a large quantity of yams to his own sister or female relatives. He keeps for himself only the inferior tubers, stowed under the thatch in the top compartment and in the inferior yam-houses, *sokwaypa*. He also produces his own seed yams and all other vegetables.

Thus everyone keeps back a fraction of his garden-yield for himself. The rest goes to his female relatives and their husbands. When a boy is young, his duty is to provide for his nearest female relative, his mother. Later on, he has to maintain his sister when she marries; or perhaps a maternal aunt, or a maternal aunt's daughter, if these have no nearer male kinsmen to provide for them.

There are several types of garden, each of a different nature and with a different name. There are the early gardens, *kaymugwa*, planted with mixed crops, which begin to yield new food after the last year's harvest has been exhausted. This keeps the household going until the new, main harvest has begun. And there is the taro garden, *tapopu*. Both of these every family makes for its own use. Then there is the main garden, *kaymata*, the yield of which is chiefly devoted to the supply of the female relatives. All that the man produces for his own use is called by the generic term *taytum-wala*; what he grows for his women-folk and their husbands is called *urigubu*.

The harvest of the main gardens inaugurates a long and elaborate series of activities, associated with the offering of annual gifts. The members of each household – for digging is always done *en famille* – repair to their own garden-plot within the large, communal enclosure. The yams of the small variety, called *taytu*, which are by far the most important of all native vegetables, are then dug up by means of pointed sticks and carried to a shady arbour (*kalimomyo*) made of poles and yam vine, where the family group sit down and carefully clean the dug-up tubers, shaking the earth from them and shaving off the hairs with sharpened shells. Then a selection is made. The best yams are placed in a large conical heap in the middle, and this is the *urigubu* yield. The rest are stowed away in the corners in less regular and much smaller heaps. The main heap is constructed with almost geometrical precision, with the best yams carefully distributed all over its surface, for it will remain in the little shed for some time, to be admired by people from the village and neighbouring communities. All this part of the work, which, as can easily be seen, has no utilitarian value, is done eagerly, with interest and *con amore*, under the stimulus of vanity and ambition. The chief pride of a Trobriander is to gain renown as a 'master-gardener' (*tokwaybagula*). And to achieve this, he will make great efforts and till many plots in order to produce a considerable number of heaps with a large quantity of yams in each. It must also be remembered that the marriage gift is the chief and most ostentatious product of the garden work.

In about a week or a fortnight, the *taytu* (small yams) are brought in from the gardens to the village. The owner then engages a number of helpers – men, women, and children – to carry the gift to his sister's husband, perhaps right at the other end of the district. These put on semi-festive dress, paint their faces, adorn themselves with flowers and set out in a merry crowd; this is a time for gaiety and rejoicing. The carrier parties walk about all over the gardens, inspect and admire or criticize the crops. Perhaps a man, through special luck or excess of zeal in labour, has an outstandingly good yield, and the renown (*butura*) of this has spread. Or there may be a famous master-gardener in the village, and his crops have to be viewed and compared with his previous achievements. Sometimes a village community, or several of them, agree to have a *kayasa* (competitive) harvest, and all strive to the utmost to do themselves and their community credit. The rivalry is so strong that in old days there was seldom a *kayasa* harvest without a war, or at least fights, to follow.

After they have rested and admired the gardens, the crowd of carriers engaged for the occasion repair to the owner's plot. There the yams are dealt out and measured with a standard basket. For each basketful, a small petal is torn off a cycas leaf. Each tenth petal is left standing, to mark the tithe. For a big plot, several cycas leaves may have to be used. The carriers then proceed to the recipient's village, men and women mixing together, with jokes and laughter. The owner supplies them with dainties on the road: coco-drinks to quench their thirst, betel-nut as a stimulant, succulent bananas to refresh them. The village is entered at high speed; the men run ahead, pandanus petals streaming from their armlets, and the women follow closely. As they come among the houses, a collective litany is shouted, the fore-runner repeating a series of meaningless traditional words very quickly at the top of his voice: '*Bomgoy, yakakoy, siyaloy . . .*' while the whole crowd thunder back in unison a loud and strident 'Yah'. Then in front of the recipient's yam-house, they build the yams into a circular heap, quite as fine as the one made before in the garden. It is only after a few days that the next ceremonial event takes place, when the vege-tables are removed to the inside of the yam-house.

Returning now to the sociological and economic importance of the annual marriage endowment, it not only has very considerable effect on the marriage institution itself, but on the whole economy and constitution of the tribe. Looked at from the point of view of the recipient, it is clear that every man has to guide his marital choice according to his needs, and to his prospective wife's endowment. For he will be dependent, not only on his own industry and capacity, but also on that of his relatives-in-law. A fortune-hunter will lay siege to a girl who is the only sister of several brothers – the very existence of whom would at once cool the ardour of a European with a similar end in view. Only a man who could face destitution with equanimity would court a girl who had several sisters and but a single brother. As a man's wife bears sons and they grow up, he acquires as it were home-made relatives-in-law – for in a matrilineal society children are naturally classed with relatives-in-law – and their first duty is to provide for the parental household. Ordinarily the husband receives the main part of his wife's endowment from one relative-in-law only; but in the case of a chief or a man of importance, though one man will nominally be responsible, many others will co-operate with him to provide a suitable gift. Even a commoner, however, receives, besides the *urigubu* from his chief donor, a number of smaller gifts named *kovisi* or *taytupeta* from his wife's other relatives. They are all presented at harvest time and consist of several baskets of yams and other vegetables.

A man also receives from his relatives-in-law various services,

given as occasion demands. They have to assist him when he builds
a house or canoe, arranges for a fishing expedition, or takes part in
one of the public festivals. In illness, they must keep watch over
him against sorcerers, or carry him to some other place where he
hopes to get better. In feuds or in other emergencies he may, given
certain circumstances, command their services. Finally, after his
death, the bulk of mortuary duties will fall upon them. Only from
time to time has the man to repay the annual services of his relatives-in-law by a gift of valuables – such occasional gifts being
called *youlo*.

6   The significance of *urigubu*

Let us focus our attention on the group consisting of mother and
children and the mother's brother. This group, as we know, forms
the real unit of kinship in native theory. The females continue the
line, the males represent it in each generation. The males inherit the
property, the females through the *urigubu* gift are made to benefit
from a large part of the males' stewardship. The males of several
generations work for the females; the females, under the guardian-
ship of their husbands or fathers, lead their sexual and reproductive
lives, continuing the lineage of the kindred.

It must be emphatically stated here that it is not the 'clan' which
acts as a unit in this complementary division of functions, but definitely the group consisting of brother, sister and her offspring.

The woman's brother then is her natural legal guardian. But he is
not enough. He cannot enter in any way into his sister's sexual life,
not even indirectly, not even from a great distance. He leases his
sister's procreative life as well as her offspring to her husband, as
his maternal uncle has leased his mother's reproductive life to his
father. Since he has to keep at a distance, physically as well as
morally, the marriage must be patrilocal. But with all this the
fundamental principles of matrilineal kinship oppose the development of any strong patrilocal or patrilineal family life. In the first
place, the matrilineal, that is to the Trobriander the real, kindred of
the husband, do not want him to bestow too much attention,
privileges and gifts on his children; for a man's possessions and
advantages should be kept within his own matrilineal kindred. On
the other hand the real, that is matrilineal, kindred of the children,
want them back in their community, want them as helpmates and

legal successors. The patrilocal household thus is usually broken up, the girls leave the paternal house to marry, the boys return to their maternal uncle. Husband and wife, both old, decrepit and dependent now, remain alone and are still maintained by the wife's family, including her sons.

The *urigubu* is the endowment by its real head of the matrilineal unit of filiation, and this real head is neither within the household, nor even, as a rule, in the same village. The patrilocal household, on the other hand, which benefits by this endowment has its real head within it. This head also contributes economically to it, but is regarded as a stranger in matters of kinship and his position is legal only in virtue of a series of reciprocities which bind him to his wife, to his wife's brother, and to her offspring.

The *urigubu* is, therefore, the expression of the real constitution of Trobriand kinship grouping. This grouping is not simple as with us, where it consists of one household, one family, and one unit of filiation. The kinship grouping in the Trobriands embraces on the one hand the unit of filiation – brother, sister and offspring; and on the other hand, the household – husband, wife and children, including sometimes old parents and more distant relatives. The core of the household is always the family; that is, to the sociologist, the reproductive unit, husband, wife and offspring; to the Trobriander, the matrimonial grouping, founded on the contract of marriage, which makes the husband the deputy guardian of his wife and her immature children. The *urigubu*, therefore, is the outcome and economic expression of a compromise or adjustment between the principles of the patrilocal household and matrilineal filiation. Into the composition of the *urigubu*, however, there also enters the brother–sister taboo, the principle of legitimacy which decrees that all children must have a father, and the customary rule that adult man and adult woman must enter into permanent and full sexual partnership.

We can now understand not merely the legal sanctions, but also the personal motives for the *urigubu*. If the *urigubu* is regarded as a gift from an outsider to a household which he is scarcely even permitted to visit, it appears absurd, unfair and cumbersome. But when the *urigubu* is understood as the endowment of his own kindred group by its head, it becomes natural, almost obvious. Exactly as in a patriarchal society the *paterfamilias* feeds his household and works for its firm economic foundation to endure after his death, so in the Trobriand matrilineal community the maternal uncle provides for his descendants freely, generously and with a will. In the process he also feeds his sister's husband, but the latter repays by reciprocal gifts that share of the *urigubu* which falls to him and furthermore himself contributes to the feeding of his wife and her children, that is of the filiational group, a group which is not his kindred. All in all, the economic arrangements of a household reflect very neatly the various sociological, legal, moral and personal inclinations, interests and reciprocal duties of the native.

We can also perceive now why it is that a man will not procure *taytu* locally at so much a basket for his sister's household and pay for it by some service rendered in his own community. According to native law, custom and morals, his real duty lies with his sister's household. It is consequently for this household that he has to raise and harvest the *taytuwala* (real *taytu*), the *taytumwaydona* (the full *taytu*). It is on the size and quality of this part of the result of his labours that his reputation as a gardener depends. Moreover, in the giving of it he satisfies both his vanity and his sentiment. For on the one hand he is giving to a stranger – a man who by definition belongs to another clan – his sister's husband, and of such a gift he is allowed to brag. But on the other hand he is providing for his sister, for his own descendants, for those who will in future work for him and for the glory of his lineage, and therefore his heart is in the work.

The whole ceremonial side of the transactions is not merely an expression of a strong individual inclination; it contains also an effective sanction. The display, the measurement in public, the taking and recording of tally, provide both a psychological spur to the giver and a handle to the community, whether it be for praise or blame. When his work has been successful as well as efficient, the generous gift is appreciated, the glory of the giver and his lineage extolled, and the moral approbation of the community bestowed, and this to a Trobriander is a great satisfaction and a real reward.

We can also understand why a man may be a good gardener as long as his object is to satisfy the fundamental obligations of the *urigubu*, but that it is dangerous to be a good gardener on his own behalf. To have large gardens and to use them for his own food runs obviously counter to one of the fundamental principles of Trobriand sociology, and the community, there as elsewhere, reacts with a sound conservatism and a deep hostility to anything which offends its established conceptions.

We can now quite briefly assess the functions of the *urigubu*, the influence, that is to say, which it exerts on Trobriand social life. From all that has been said above it can be seen that it is one of the main elements in the stability of marriage. It is closely connected with the position of the father and his relations to the offspring, as well as with the latter's relations to the maternal uncle. But one of the most important elements in the *urigubu* is that it is the channel through which every headman of a village community, every chief of subsidiary rank in his district, as well as the paramount chief of Omarakana, levies his tribute.

While the harvest gift received by a poor man is small and simple, in the case of a chief it is large and the sources of it are very complex on the sociological and economic side. Terminologically the ethnographer becomes easily confused, in that the word *urigubu* is often used to designate the chief's tribute as well as his harvest gifts. As a matter of fact most of the chief's tribute, though not all, is given as a glorified contribution from wife's brother to sister's husband, only, in the case of a woman married to a chief, her whole sub-clan would labour for her and not merely one of her male relatives. Hence a chief's wife brings her husband a much bigger quantity of food than she would have received had she been married to a commoner (about five times as much, I estimated), her gift consists of finer *Taytu* and is offered with greater display. Now the chief has the privilege of polygamy. Before the decline of their power, the chiefs profited by this to the extent of some fourscore wives, and To'uluwa had a couple of dozen at the beginning of his reign. Even in 1918, when he had only a dozen, his *urigubu* was, on a rough estimate, sixty times that received by a commoner and, at the beginning of his reign, when he had twice as many wives, it must have been at least double this. In fact, I think it was much more than that, since at that time the power of the chief was unquestionably greater. In the old days when a paramount chief had some sixty wives or more he must have received something like four hundred times as much as commoners. The brother of a chief's wife and the maternal kinsmen of this man would also have to render a much wider range of services than is normally due from brother to sister's husband.

Thus the chief's *urigubu* became a tribute levied on a number of

village communities, but always levied in virtue of his position as a
glorified brother-in-law of the whole community. Some of the
chief's *urigubu*, however, although it went by this name, was not
given by people related to him by marriage, but by vassals, who
paid it on account of their residence in his village, and still other of
the tribute he received could not be brought within the term
urigubu, but was named *pokala* and *tabubula*.

So far, by the word *chief* I have meant, primarily; the paramount
chief of Omarakana, but between his *urigubu* and the amount
received by an ordinary tribesman or by a poor commoner with
some fifty baskets a year, there was a whole range of gradations.
There were the sub-chiefs, *gumguya'u*, with about half-a-dozen
wives each; and of lower rank but even greater power was the
toliwaga of Kabwaku. Next came the lesser chiefs with a couple of
wives each, and after them the headmen of villages, who were
better endowed than the ordinary citizen, though as a rule
monogamous.

7 Divorce

Divorce, called by the natives *vaypaka* (*vay* = marriage; *paka*,
from *payki*, to refuse), is not infrequent. Whenever husband and
wife disagree too acutely, or whenever bitter quarrels or fierce
jealousy make them chafe too violently at the bond between them,
this can be dissolved – provided the emotional situation does not
lead instead to a more tragic issue. This solution, or rather dissolution, of the difficulty is a weapon used by the woman rather than
the man. A husband very seldom repudiates his wife, though in
principle he is entitled to do so. For adultery, he has the right to kill
her; but the usual punishment is a thrashing, or perhaps merely
remonstrance or a fit of the sulks. If he has any other serious
grievance against her, such as bad temper or laziness, the husband,
who is little hampered by marriage ties, easily finds consolation
outside his household, while he still benefits by the marriage tribute
from his wife's relatives.

There are, on the other hand, several instances on record of a
woman leaving her husband because of ill-treatment or infidelity
on his part, or else because she had become enamoured of someone
else.

Sometimes extraneous conditions, more especially quarrels

between the husband and the wife's family, lead to divorce. In a dispute between two communities, marriages are often dissolved for the same reason.

The formalities of divorce are as simple as those by which marriage is contracted. The woman leaves her husband's house with all her personal belongings, and moves to her mother's hut, or to that of her nearest maternal kinswoman. There she remains, awaiting the course of events, and in the meantime enjoying full sexual freedom. Her husband, as likely as not, will try to get her back. He will send certain friends with 'peace offerings' (*koluluvi*, or *lula*) for the wife and for those with whom she is staying. Sometimes the gifts are rejected at first, and then the ambassadors are sent again and again. If the woman accepts them, she has to return to her husband, divorce is ended and marriage resumed. If she means business, and is determined not to go back to her wedded life, the presents are never accepted; then the husband has to adjust himself as best he may, which means that he begins to look for another girl. The dissolution of marriage entails in no case the restitution of any of the inaugural marriage gifts exchanged, unless, as we shall see, the divorced woman should re-marry.

The girl, if she is still young enough, now resumes her prenuptial life and leads the free, untrammelled existence of a *nakubukwabuya* (unmarried girl), entering upon liaison after liaison, and living in bachelors' houses. One of the liaisons may lengthen out and develop into a new marriage. Then the new husband must present a valuable object (*vaygu'a*) to his predecessor, in recompense for the one given to the wife's family at the beginning of the first marriage. The new husband must also give another *vaygu'a* to his wife's relatives, and he then receives from them the first annual harvest gift – *vilakuria* – and the subsequent yearly tribute in yams. It seemed to me that a divorcée was much more independent of family interference in choosing her new husband than an ordinary unmarried girl. The initial gifts of food (*pepe'i*, etc.) are not given in the case of such a remarriage. There is, apparently, no social stigma on a girl or a man who has been married and divorced, although as a matter of *amour propre* no one wishes to own that he or she has been abandoned by the other.

It goes without saying that the children, in case of divorce, always follow their mother; and this is no doubt another reason why divorce is less popular with men than with women. During the interim, when their mother is living as a spinster, they remain in the household of her nearest married maternal relative.

8 Death and the bereaved

When a man dies, his wife is not set free by the event. It may be said without paradox that, in a way, the strictest and heaviest shackles of marriage are laid on her after the real tie has been dissolved by death. Custom compels her to play the burdensome rôle of chief mourner; to make an ostentatious, dramatic, and extremely onerous display of grief for her husband from the moment of his demise until months, at times years, afterwards. She has to fulfil her part under the vigilant eyes of the public, jealous of exact compliance with traditional morals, and under the more suspicious surveillance of the dead man's kindred, who regard it as a special and grievous offence to their family's honour if she flags for a single moment in her duty. The same applies in a smaller degree to a widower, but in his case the mourning is less elaborate and burdensome, and the vigilance not so relentless.

Let us take the death of a man of consequence in the fullness of age, leaving behind a widow, several children and brothers. From the moment of his death, the distinction between his real, that is matrilineal, kinsmen (*veyola*) on the one hand, and his children, relatives-in-law and friends on the other, takes on a sharp and even an outwardly visible form. The kinsmen of the deceased fall under a taboo; they must keep aloof from the corpse. They are not allowed either to wash or adorn or fondle or bury it; for if they were to touch or to come near it, pernicious influences from the body would attack them and cause their disease and death. These pernicious influences are conceived in the form of a material exhalation, issuing from the corpse and polluting the air. It is called *bwaulo*, a word which also designates the cloud of smoke which surrounds a village especially on steamy, calm days. The necrogenic *bwaulo*, invisible to common eyes, appears to a witch or sorcerer as a black cloud shrouding the village. It is innocuous to strangers, but dangerous to kinsmen.

The kindred must also not display any outward signs of mourning in costume and ornamentation, though they need not conceal their grief and may show it by weeping. Here the underlying idea is that the maternal kinsmen are hit in their own persons;

that each one suffers because the whole sub-clan to which they belong has been maimed by the loss of one of its members. 'As if a limb were cut off, or a branch lopped from a tree.' Thus, though they need not hide their grief, they must not parade it. This abstention from outward mourning extends, not only to all the members of the sub-clan beyond the real kinsmen, but to all the members of the clan to which the dead man belonged. On the other hand, the taboo against touching the corpse applies primarily to the members of the sub-clan and especially to the actual kinsmen, to whom, of course, the temptation to touch the corpse, as an expression of love, would be strongest.

Quite different, in the native idea, is the relation of the widow, and of the children and relatives-in-law, to the dead and to his corpse. They ought, according to the moral code, to suffer and to feel bereaved. But in feeling thus they are not suffering directly; they are not grieving for a loss which affects their own sub-clan (*dala*) and therefore their own persons. Their grief is not spontaneous like that of the *veyola* (maternal kinsmen), but a duty almost artificial, springing as it does from acquired obligations. Therefore they must ostentatiously express their grief, display it, and bear witness to it by outward signs. If they did not, they would offend the surviving members of the dead man's sub-clan. Thus an interesting situation develops, giving rise to a most strange spectacle: a few hours after the death of a notable, the village is thronged by people, with their heads shaven, the whole body thickly smeared with soot, and howling like demons in despair. And these are the non-kinsmen of the dead man, the people not actually bereaved. In contrast to these a number of others are to be seen in their usual attire, outwardly calm and behaving as if nothing had happened. These represent the sub-clan and clan of the deceased, and are the actually bereaved. Thus by a devious reasoning, tradition and custom produce the reverse of what would seem natural and obvious to us or any observer from almost any other culture.

Among those who display their grief, it is easy to distinguish several groups and grades. There is the rank and file of mourners, comprising all the people belonging to the remaining three clans; for, when a notable dies, everyone in the village community puts on mourning, except the members of his own clan. A small group is busy about the body and the grave; this consists of the male children and brothers-in-law of the deceased. Nearest to the corpse and plunged most deeply in the mimicry of grief are seated a few women, among whom one, the widow, is conspicuous, supported by her daughters and sisters. In this group, and it may be in that of the sons also, an observer well acquainted with these natives would be able to distinguish an interesting interplay of feigned and merely histrionic grief with real and heartfelt sorrow.

With this sociological scheme before us, we can now follow the sequence of event and ritual which begins automatically with a man's death. When death is seen to be approaching, the wife and children, kinsmen and relatives-in-law crowd round the bed, filling the small hut to overflowing. The consummation of death is marked by a frantic outburst of wailing. The widow, who generally stands at the head of the dying man, utters the first piercing shriek, to which immediately other women respond, till the village is filled with the strange harmonies of the melodious dirge. From this moment all the varied activities of the days, and even weeks, which follow will be carried on to the choral accompaniment of a long-drawn wail which never stops for one instant.

First the corpse is washed, anointed, and covered with ornaments, then the bodily apertures are filled with coconut husk fibre, the legs tied together, and the arms bound to the sides. Thus prepared, it is placed on the knees of a row of women who sit on the floor of the hut, with the widow or widower at one end holding the head. They fondle the corpse, stroke the skin with caressing hands, press valuable objects against chest and abdomen, move the limbs slightly and agitate the head. The body is thus made to move and twist with slow and ghastly gestures to the rhythm of the incessant wailing. The hut is full of mourners, all intoning the melodious lamentation. Tears flow from their eyes and mucus from their noses, and all the liquids of grief are carefully displayed and smeared over their bodies or otherwise conspicuously disposed. Outside, certain women, usually relatives-in-law of the dead man, perform a slow rhythmic dance (the *vaysali*) with relics in their hands.

The sons in the meantime dig the grave, which in olden days was always on the central place of the village, but which now, by the white man's decree, must be on the outskirts. A few hours after death the body is laid in it, wrapped in mats, and is covered with logs, which leave a shallow space above. On this layer of logs the widow lies down to keep vigil over the corpse. Her daughter may be beside her; round the brink of the grave are her sisters, kinswomen and friends, and the other relatives-in-law of the dead man. As night draws on, the central place fills with people; for even nowadays the white man's regulations against burial in the *baku* are circumvented by making a temporary grave there, or placing the corpse on the ground. Here the mourners, the kinsmen, all the villagers and many guests from far afield congregate to hold a most remarkable wake (*yawali*).

The chief mourners and kinsmen in appropriate groups keep the central position round the grave. Outside this inner ring, the villagers and guests are seated, each community in a separate body, their mood and behaviour becoming less tragic as they are farther removed from the corpse, until on the outskirts of the crowd, we find people in animated conversation, eating and chewing betel nut. The central group of mourners intones the deep wail of sorrow, the others sing songs, and, as the night goes on, people will stand up and recite fragments of magic in honour of the departed, chanting them over the heads of the crowd.

The body is not allowed to remain long in peace – if the weird, noisy, and discordant din of singing, wailing, and haranguing can be so described. On the following evening, the body is exhumed, and inspected for signs of sorcery. Such an inspection yields most important clues, as to who caused the death by witchcraft and for what motive this was done.

Before daybreak after the first exhumation, the body is taken out of the grave, and some of the bones are removed from it. This anatomical operation is done by the man's sons, who keep some of the bones as relics and distribute the others to certain of their relatives.

The excision of the bones and their subsequent use as relics is an act of piety; the process of detaching them from the putrefying corpse, a heavy, repugnant, and disgusting duty. The sons of the deceased are expected by custom to curb and conceal their disgust, and to suck some of the decaying matter when they are cleaning the bones. Speaking with virtuous pride they will say: 'I have sucked the radius bone of my father; I had to go away and vomit; I came back and went on.' After they have cleansed the bones, which is always done on the seashore, they return to the village, and the dead man's kinswomen ceremonially 'wash their mouths' by giving them food and purify their hands with coconut oil. The bones are converted to various purposes, serviceable and ornamental: the skull is made into a lime pot to be used by the widow; the jaw-bone is turned into a neck ornament to hang on her breast; the radius, ulna, tibia, and some other bones are carved into lime spatulae to be used with betel and areca nut.

A curious mixed sentiment underlies this complex of customs. On the one hand, it should be the wish of the widow and children to keep a part of the beloved dead. 'The relic (*kayvaluba*) brings the departed back to our mind and makes our inside tender.' On the other hand, the use of these relics is regarded as a harsh and unpleasant duty, as a sort of pious repayment for all the benefits received from the father. As it was explained to me: 'Our mind is grieved for the man who has fed us, who has given us dainties to eat; we suck his bones as lime spatulae.' Or again: 'It is right that a child should suck the father's ulna. For the father has held out his hand to its excrement and allowed it to make water on to his knee.' Thus the use of relics is at the same time a relief to the bereaved widow and children, and an act of filial piety which must be rigorously observed.

To the dead man's maternal kinsmen (*veyola*) the use of his bones is strictly tabooed. If they break this taboo they would fall ill, their bellies would swell and they might die. The contact is most dangerous when the bone is still wet with the dead man's bodily juices. When, after a few years, the bones are handed over to the kinsmen, they are presented carefully wrapped in dry leaves, and are then only gingerly handled by them. They are finally deposited on rocky shelves overlooking the sea. Thus the bones pass several times from hand to hand before they come to their final rest.

More distant relatives-in-law and friends of the dead man have his nails, teeth and hair, which they make into all sorts of mourning ornaments and wear as relics. The dead man's personal possessions are used in the same way, and nowadays, when the bodily relics have frequently to be concealed, this practice is very much in favour.

After the second exhumation the body is buried, the wake is over, and the people disperse; but the widow, who, during all this time, has not stirred from her husband's side, nor eaten nor drunk nor stopped in her wailing, is not yet released. Instead she moves into a small cage, built within her house, where she will remain for months together, observing the strictest taboos. She must not leave the place; she may only speak in whispers; she must not touch food or drink with her own hands, but wait till they are put into her mouth; she remains closed up in the dark, without fresh air or light; her body is thickly smeared over with soot and grease, which will not be washed off for a long time. She satisfies all the necessities of life indoors, and the excreta have to be carried out by her relatives. Thus she lives for months shut up in a low-roofed, stuffy, pitch-dark space, so small that with outstretched hands she can almost touch the walls on either side; it is often filled with people who assist or comfort her, and pervaded by an indescribable atmosphere of human exhalations, accumulated bodily filth, stale food, and smoke. Also she is under the more or less active control and surveillance of her husband's matrilineal relatives, who regard her mourning and its inherent privations as their due. When the term of her widowhood has almost run its course – its length depends upon the status of her husband and varies from about six months to two years – she is gradually released by the dead man's kinsmen. Food is put into her mouth according to a ritual which gives her permission to eat with her own hands. Then, ceremonially, she is allowed to speak; finally she is released from the taboo of confinement and, still with appropriate ritual, requested to walk forth. At the ceremony of her complete release by the female *veyola* of the dead man, the widow is washed and anointed, and dressed in a new gaudy grass skirt in three colours. This makes her marriageable again.

9 The ideology of mourning

Throughout the rigorous ritual of mourning, in which the widow, the orphans, and to a much lesser degree the other relatives-in-law of the deceased are caught and held as in a vice, we can observe the working of certain ideas belonging to the tribal tradition of the Trobrianders. One especially, the taboo on maternal kinsmen, which forces them to keep aloof since it is both dangerous to approach the corpse and superfluous to show grief, is strikingly visible throughout the whole course of burial, exhumation, and grave-tending. The corresponding idea, that it is the imperative duty of the widow and her relatives to show grief and perform all the mortuary services, emphasizes the strength and the permanence of marriage bonds as viewed by tradition. It is also a posthumous continuation of the remarkable system of services which have to be given to a married man by his wife's family, including the woman herself and her children.

In the mortuary phase of these services, however, the dead man's sub-clan have to render payment more strictly and more frequently than he had to do in his life-time. Immediately after the bones have been cut out and the remains buried, the dead man's sub-clan organise the first big distribution of food and valuables, in which the widow, children, and other relatives-in-law, as well as the unrelated mourners, are richly paid for the various services rendered in tending the corpse and digging the grave. Other distributions follow at stated intervals. There is one expressly for women mourners; one for the tenders of the grave; one for the rank and file of mourners; one, by far the largest, in which presents of valuables and enormous quantities of food are given to the widow and children, in so far as they, in grief and piety, have used the bones of the dead man for their lime-chewing or as ornaments. This intricate series of distributions stretches out into years, and it entails a veritable tangle of obligations and duties; for the members of the deceased's sub-clan must provide food and give it to the chief organiser, the headman of the sub-clan, who collects it and then distributes it to the proper beneficiaries. These, in their turn, partially at least, re-distribute it. And each gift in this enormous complex trails its own wake of counter-gifts and obligations to be fulfilled at a future date.

The ostentation with which the widow and children have to display their grief, the thickness – literally and metaphorically speaking – with which they put on their mourning are indeed striking; and the underlying complex psychology of these things must have become apparent in the above account. In the first place, it is a duty towards the dead and towards his sub-clan, a duty strongly enjoined by the code of morals and guarded by public opinion, as well as by the kinsmen. 'Our tears – they are for the kinsmen of our father to see', as one of the mourners simply and directly told me. In the second place, it demonstrates to the world at large that the wife and children were really good to the dead and that they took great care of him in his illness. Lastly, and this is very important, it allays any suspicion of their complicity in his murder by black magic. To understand the last queer motive, one has to realise the extreme fear, the ever-vigilant suspicion of sorcery, and the unusual lack of trust in anyone at all with reference to it. The Trobrianders regard every death without exception as an act of sorcery, unless it is caused by suicide or by a visible accident, such as poisoning or a spear thrust. It is characteristic of their idea of the bonds of marriage and fatherhood – which they regard as artificial and untrustworthy under any strain – that the principal suspicion of sorcery attaches always to the wife and children. The real interest in a man's welfare, the real affection, the natural innocence of any attempt against him are, by the traditional system of ideas, attributed to his maternal kinsmen. His wife and children are mere strangers, and custom persists in ignoring any real identity of interest between them.

6   Principles of land tenure

1   Introduction

There are a few fundamental principles which underlie all claims
and control all practices referring to land. These principles, or
doctrines, as I prefer to call them, can be briefly enumerated.

A. There is one main conviction, an *idée maîtresse*, which
dominates the whole attitude of man to soil in the Trobriands. A
man or woman have rights over a given territory in virtue of the
fact that their ancestress in matrilineal filiation emerged from the
soil at a definite sacred spot situated in that territory. The system of
matrilineal descent, therefore, combined with what we might call
the doctrine of first emergence, constitute the legal and mythological foundation of Trobriand land tenure.

B. The law of exogamous and patrilocal marriage compels a man
to take in wedlock a woman who is not of his sub-clan nor yet of his
clan. She joins him in his community and remains there till the end
of her life or the end of her marriage. Her children, though belonging to her sub-clan and community, have the right of residence
until they reach maturity. This law of exogamous and patrilocal
marriage is independent of the doctrine of first emergence. It
affects land tenure in a two-fold manner: (i) It separates the woman
from her own land, while her rights in the ancestral soil are recognised in the institution of *urigubu*. (ii) It constitutes her and her
offspring into non-citizen residents of her husband's community,
and through that it entitles them to join the gardening team, i.e.
the group of agricultural producers in the husband's community.

C. The doctrine of magical leadership establishes a united team
who cultivate one garden within one enclosure and in one organised
activity. This doctrine is perhaps not quite independent of the
previous ones. In so far as magic is also a product of local emergence, the doctrine is derivative of A. In so far as the membership

in the gardening team is the result of the right of citizenship and right of residence, this doctrine is derived from A and B at the same time. The organising influence of magic is moreover associated with the organising political power of the headman and of the chief. With all that, this doctrine plays an important part in native belief in the spiritual claims of the magician to be the real master of the soil in virtue of his magic, and this even when he is not the same person as the headman. This doctrine also affects land tenure in so far as it is the expression of the unity and solidarity of the gardening team.

D. The affirmation that rank outweighs the claim of local emergence. This doctrine might also be formulated – as it often is by the natives themselves – in the principle that the highest sub-clan, the Tabalu, are masters of all soil and can claim and use it wherever they like; while other sub-clans of high rank share in this prerogative according to their degree. This doctrine is expressed historically by the gradual shifting of sub-clans of higher rank from their original territory to more fertile districts, while the Tabalu, the highest sub-clan, gradually came to occupy all the centres of agriculture, political influence and economic exploitation.

These four doctrines are not, of course, codified in any explicit native tradition. We find them here and there formulated in myths, in historical traditions, in the legal principles of marriage, with all that these mean to the Trobriander. It would be possible to show, point by point, both that the doctrines work within the institutions and also to document them by means of genuine native statements. What the sociologist has to do is to place the facts and statements in relation to each other and to extract from them the really relevant principles. I think that the four doctrines contain the full legal theory of, and sum up the most important economic usages connected with, land tenure. Doctrine A is fundamental from the legal point of view. Doctrine B, in its two-fold influence, affects profoundly the actual organisation of gardening. Doctrine C represents rather the native emphasis on the importance of magic, and it does not add very much to what has already been contained in doctrines A and B. Doctrine D affects the past and therefore the present practice.

If we want briefly to summarise our results in a synoptic table, we could list in the first column the four doctrines, subdividing B according to its two sociological effects. We shall see then that we can roughly attribute a type of social grouping to each doctrine, the second one obviously having a two-fold social influence. In the third column we can list the main influences of each principle. As with all such representations, it is essential not to make a fetish of this diagram. It is merely a convenient summary of some of our results. The first column shows the four fundamental doctrines, legal and mythological. It shows also that in the systematic statement of Trobriand land tenure it will be best to proceed by the analysis of these doctrines. And since these doctrines are at the same time independent of and adjusted to each other, it will be necessary to examine how they combine.

The second column shows the social consequences of each doctrine, and the integration through that doctrine of people into a specific mode of grouping. The third column shows how a doctrine of land tenure defines the mode of settlement and the legal, economic and political relations of a community to the land.

Doctrine		Social grouping	Aspect
A First emergence		Sub-clan	Legal, mythological
B Law of marriage, matriliny and exogamy	*urigubu*	Matrilineal kindred: mother, brother, children	Legal and economic (consumption)
	Right of residence of wife and children	Family and village community as agglomeration of families	Legal and economic (production)
C Magical organisation		Garden team	
D Rank		Political units: Paramount chief's domain; districts; compound village communities	(Historical) political

2 The doctrine of first emergence

Every Trobriander, man or woman, believes that by birth and descent he or she is connected with a definite spot, and through this with a village community and with a territory. For everyone believes that his lineage, in the person of his first female ancestress in direct line, issued from a definite spot in the Trobriand territory. The myth of first emergence is definitely a matrilineal one. It always refers to a woman, at times accompanied by a man who is her brother not her husband. This belief, combined with the principles of matrilineal descent, furnishes the charter of citizenship and land tenure to every Trobriander. For by the act of first emergence all the descendants in direct female line of the original woman have acquired the right of citizenship in the territory surrounding the spot of her emergence. This belief is the foundation of almost all territorial rights and claims. The most famous of such holes of emergence, called Obukula, differs from all the others in that from it are supposed to have emerged the original animal ancestors of the four clans which were the first to come out upon the surface of the earth. From that hole also a great many of the aristocratic or ancient sub-clans trace their original emergence – and in this the hole of Obukula is also anomalous. The highest of the high, the Tabalu sub-clan of the Malasi clan, the Mwauri, Tudava and Mulobwayma sub-clans of the Lukuba clan, and the Kaylavasi sub-clan of the Lukulabuta clan – all these came out of the Obukula hole. The bearing of this myth on land tenure we shall have to consider later.

While speaking about myths of first emergence, I must make clear their dogmatic character. It is not, however, easy to draw a clear line between a simple assertion – the bald statement of an original occurrence – and such a statement developed and embellished by incidents. In the Trobriands only one myth of first emergence is expanded into a long and dramatised story, and that is the myth of the first emergence of the four ancestors of the four main clans. The other statements are usually very simple. They reduce themselves to a mere affirmation: 'From the hole of Bulimaulo there emerged first Kaluva'u and his sister, Bokaluva'u. They brought with them the magic of our soil and many other herbs.' But this assertion enters into any discussion about the pedigrees of the sub-clan, about the division of land, about the respective claims to territory of the various contiguous sub-clans. At times, when some special magic is discussed, such a myth becomes fuller. Thus in connexion with the magic of rain and drought, we have a story about the emergence from Bulimaulo of an ancestral woman, Bopadagu. We are told subsequently how she gave birth to various animals associated with rain magic, to rain itself and to one or two children, and we are told in a developed and dramatised story how she handled that important but dangerous fruit of her womb – rain. But where there is no question of special magic the myth of first emergence takes the extremely simple form of the mere mention of the spot, of the names of first ancestors, of the insignia of rank and dignity which they brought with them, and of the types of magic, sometimes reduced to gardening magic only, which they carried from underground.

Of particular interest for us is the fact that with such a hole of emergence there is always connected a village, or part of a village, and a territory, or what we might call an assortment of lands, both of which belong to the people who came out of the hole. As a rule this comprises some waste land, a tabooed grove or two, a portion of the *rayboag* and perhaps one or two fields in the *dumya* (swamps); in every case it includes a large portion of cultivable bush (*odila*), divided into a number of fields which are subdivided into plots. Those villages which are near the open sea own a part of the eastern seashore (*momola*) with a fishing and bathing beach and a few sheds for their canoes. On the lagoon the beach is called *kovalawa* and here canoes are kept. Thus a hole of emergence is always the centre of a contingent territory which encloses a village, or part of it, and affords the following economic opportunities to its members: access to fertile, cultivable soil, invariably; at times access to navigation and fishing areas; a certain district for recreation and, of course, a system of roads communicating with other villages.

Thus we see that the combined doctrines of first emergence and matrilineal descent sanction the direct and full economic and general use and enjoyment of a given territory, ownership of the cultivable lands included in it; and invest the sub-clan with a number of traditional, magical and religious claims. All members can claim this territory as their own, and every member has his share in this joint claim. It is only the members of the sub-clan who can use the title *toli* (owner of) with regard to village garden lands and mythological spots: *tolivalu* (owners of village); *tolipway-pwaya* (owners of soil); *toliboma* (owners of tabooed grove). The members of the sub-clan have the right of citizenship, that is, the absolute and unquestionable right of residence. They can also deny residence to any of the people who live in the village in virtue of one or the other of the derived rights of residence or the customary indulgences. The citizens also have the ultimate right to cultivate as many plots of the common soil as is necessary for any one of them. The right to cultivate the soil is inextricably bound up with the right to claim a village as theirs, to inhabit it and to perform magic.

The permanence of the sub-clan and the immutability in every individual of his sociological nature are expressed by what might be called a spiritual continuity which also has a territorial or local character. After death man migrates into the other world, which is situated somewhere under or on a real island, Tuma, to the north-west. There the spirits still keep together and to one locality; they till common gardens on communally owned land, much as in this world. When during the festival of *milamala* the spirits return to their own locality they are tended by their own kindred and given offerings of food grown on their own soil. The material remains of man also continue to be bound up with the soil which gave his lineage birth. A man or woman must be buried in his own village, and after the bones have been interred, dug up and have passed through several vicissitudes, they will finally come to rest in a communal cave belonging to his sub-clan and situated on its aboriginal primeval territory.

United by common mythological sentiment, united by a great many economic interests, united also in a political community of joint armed forces, not for the defence of the territory but for the enhancement of their renown, the citizens identify themselves with their territory and own it in virtue of this identification. The principle: one hole of emergence, one sub-clan, one territory – or a definite part of it – and one headman, runs through the whole social organisation of the Trobriands. The first principle gives every man a right of residence, a right to a portion of land in it, a real asylum and a place from which he can never forcibly be moved.

Doctrine A, in short, in so far as it contains the charter of the constitution of the sub-clan, makes this the legal unit of ownership in land. Through the brother and sister taboo and the correlated sub-clan exogamy, it makes the sub-clan into a group which though it owns land is prevented from using it either in production or in consumption. As it stands, Doctrine A contains therefore an inner contradiction and its results would be completely nihilistic for land tenure as an effective force in the economic exploitation of the soil.

Doctrine A, however, does not stand alone. It is supplemented by the law of marriage which we have listed as Doctrine B. This doctrine completely remoulds the constitution of the local group. The sub-clan remains as the core of the local group, but to this are added new members, that is, the wives and children of the citizens. These wives bring with them, in addition to their membership, an economic endowment in the form of the *urigubu*. Marriage, therefore, leads to the formation of a producing and consuming group – the household; while a number of households compound into the village community. This again, reorganised into the gardening team, becomes the effective unit of agricultural production. Also marriage, in conjunction with the doctrine of rank, introduces another disturbing influence into the workings of Doctrine A. We can see at first glance, therefore, that the final result of the working of these doctrines will give us a very different picture from the simple, legally clear, mythologically founded charter of land tenure.

3 The law of marriage

At this juncture marriage interests us in that it affects the residence of the wife and of her children. Since residence is the basis for effective economic co-operation, above all in agriculture, residence is deeply connected with land tenure.

It would be perhaps more correct to say that residence, as related to titles in land, is one of the main elements in Trobriand land tenure. From this point of view, the law of marriage has a two-fold consequence with regard to land tenure. In the first place, it establishes a new economically co-operative unit – the family; and since the village community consists of a number of families, the law of marriage also is at the basis of the constitution of the village community. In the second place, while the woman becomes a resident and effective co-operative member of the village community, she legally remains a member of her own sub-clan. This membership entitles her to a share in the produce of another community – her sub-clan's – that is to *urigubu*.

How far is the *urigubu* connected with land tenure? We have seen that the *urigubu* contributes greatly to the position of the woman in marriage. We have seen also that it is the endowment by the wife's brother of her household in virtue of the native principle of kinship which makes a man, his sister and her offspring into the real unit of filiation.

Let us look more closely at the woman's economic position throughout her life. As a girl in her parents' household she works on her father's soil and contributes towards the raising of the crops which will be in part consumed within the parental household. When she grows up she will share in her husband's gardens and benefit by part of the produce from them. But where is her own soil? Her mother's brother holds it, her own brother will later inherit it. The former is now annually furnishing the *urigubu* gift to her parental household. She, together with her mother and father and the other children, subsists partly on the produce of the soil which is her own. When in her turn she receives the *urigubu* for her own household, this also will be raised on her own soil. We can, therefore, from the point of view of land tenure, regard the *urigubu* as the annual return from the joint patrimony, the portion which is due to the woman from her brother; because the land which he husbands is partly his own, partly held in trust for the females of each generation. The *urigubu* gift, which must be raised on this land, is given by one who uses the land to a group of people who have a right to it, but who are, under the law of patrilocal marriage, 'absentee owners'.

Let us also remember that the *urigubu*, although formally offered by the wife's brother to her husband, is really a gift *ad personam*, the person being the recipient's wife. At her death it automatically stops; the children should return to their own community, but if they remain in their father's community, the maternal uncle need not, though I think in practice he very often does, continue to supply them with vegetable food.

It is necessary to emphasise that *urigubu* and land tenure follow from the same set of ideas concerning kinship and the territorial apportionment of land. The natives, in describing *urigubu*, would not naturally define it as the result of a woman's title to her land. But they are quite clear that it is due to her household, because she and her children are really part and parcel of her brother's kinship group. They are also fully aware that she and her children are real owners of the soil on which the *urigubu* is raised. Thus while the juridical generalisation has to be made by the observer, all its concrete presuppositions exist in native legal theory. In reality the *urigubu* makes a great difference in the married status of the woman, in her influence at home and in her position in the village community. The *urigubu* also allows women, especially if they have many brothers, to exercise a wide choice in husbands.

We could say that the claims to land are vested in men and women; but that the men can exploit their land directly, while the women, and their children before maturity, profit by it indirectly.

The bearing of the *urigubu* upon land tenure is now quite clear. If land tenure in the widest sense be defined as the effective use of titles in the utilisation of land, the *urigubu* is a principle which annually diverts part of the crops into the hands of those members of a sub-clan who, because of their female sex, cannot reside in the sub-clan's territory and yet have a claim to part of its produce. The law of marriage establishes households with divided kinship. These households, as we know, are financed from two sources, corresponding to this two-fold kinship. The family subsists partly on the soil on which they reside, but partly also on the soil to which the alien residents, the woman and her offspring, have the traditionally founded legal claims.

The family, however, is not merely a group where agricultural produce is consumed. It is also a productive unit. And here again the law of marriage affects land tenure profoundly. Land tenure vests the title to land in the father of the family. He is the citizen of the local group, the member of the sub-clan, and as such has the fundamental right to cultivate soil. The law of marriage joins his wife to him. By marriage she acquires the right to assist him in garden work – a right which is also a duty; and she acquires a claim to part of the joint produce. In a way the claims to land of a woman resident by marriage are as firm and unquestionable as those of her husband. They are less fundamental because they depend on the contract of marriage which, in the Trobriands, can be dissolved by divorce.

It might be incidentally remarked that normally a Trobriand woman never lives in that section of the village of which she is the real citizen. As a child she lives in her father's village; he is not of her mother's clan and his community cannot be hers. The only exception – for there are exceptions to every sociological rule – is when under cross-cousin marriage the arrangement is matrilocal and it is the girl who moves to her own community, which is also the community of her maternal uncle, that is, of her husband's father.

Throughout gardening, the family is in a way the most important joint exploiter of the soil. Once a portion of land is assigned to a man at the garden council, he, his wife and his children have an un-questionable right to use it productively during the whole gardening cycle. The right of the man is primary, that of his wife and children is derived. But in practice all these claims form one unified system, indeed one claim. This allows them to cultivate the land and then to appropriate as much of the produce as is necessary for the house-hold, the amount being limited only by the husband's pride and kinship sentiments which compel him to devote a substantial portion to the endowment of his own sister, sisters, or kinswomen.

4   The gardening team

Let us now pass to the organisation of the gardening team and to its rôle in land tenure. In the first place then, the garden team is either a village community as a whole or else one or more self-contained parts of a village. For – and this must be made quite clear – when a compound village such as Omarakana and Kasana'i split into two gardening teams, this split follows exactly the local subdivision of the village.

As to the inner organisation of the garden team we will only rapidly summarise the relevant points. The gardening team consists first of the headman and garden magician, who may be the same person. The magician is the actual leader in work as well as in magic. The headman, when he is distinct from the magician, may perform one or two ceremonial and legal acts. He opens the proceedings at the *kayaku* and directs the allotment of the plots. But after that he hands over the whole conduct of affairs to the garden magician. The rank and file of the gardening team are dif-ferentiated on several counts. First of all we have the adult males who appear at the *kayaku*, to whom plots are personally allotted, and who do the gardening in their own name. In the actual economic work this group is supplemented by their women folk, and to a smaller extent by the children. Within the first group, how-ever, we must make a further distinction. The gardening team consists of citizen residents who own land in their own right and alien residents who are allotted one or more plots by the secondary claim of residence.

The garden team then is a special unit of social organisation which comes into being by the integrating influence of agricultural work on land tenure. This latter, as we know, resolves itself largely into the workings of the two doctrines of first emergence and of marriage. In the organisation of the garden team one more effective force enters – that of magic, or perhaps we might better say: the economic leadership of the magician. In our analysis above we spoke of it as an independent doctrine of land tenure (Doctrine C). We can see now clearly, however, that it does not affect land tenure in any way comparable to the influence of the two previous doctrines.

Nevertheless, it is by no means negligible. The effective use of land, the exploitation of the sources of fertility in the soil, is definitely vested in the gardening team. This is the case both in economic reality and in native ideas. For over and above the efforts of each individual and the co-operation within the family, a considerable amount of concerted work is necessary in order to make Trobriand agriculture as productive as it is. Thus there are a number of tasks which the members of the gardening team must execute simultaneously and to a certain standard in order to protect the garden as a whole. The building of the joint fence is the most important of such activities, but the same applies to a smaller extent to most garden work. Although it is not necessary that every plot should be completely cut down, yet when too much bush is left standing, the burning is less effective on the plots already cut, since the flames do not sweep evenly and the fire cannot assume proper dimensions. One of the effects of team organisation and of the influence of the *towosi* is that people are not allowed to lag too far behind or in too great numbers. In weeding, also, when a woman is very slack and allows her plot to be overgrown with noxious herbs, these will naturally spread into other plots. Here also the natives both expect and practise a certain solidarity in garden work. At thinning, especially if there is any disease among the roots and the bad ones have to be taken out, neglect on the part of one gardener harms his neighbours. Thus the organisation of the gardening team affects the economic use of the territory – in other words, it affects the exploitation of titles to land, that is land tenure.

It is clear, therefore, that the magician's claim to be the master of the soil is not an idle one. We see also that the solidarity established by common work in the field – a solidarity which unites citizen members, their wives, and families, as well as non-citizen residents

– is an additional force in the effective use of land. The gardening team is a highly derived and complicated product of the working of Doctrines A, B, and C. Our analysis has shown us precisely how these doctrines work together in producing the most important group in Trobriand agricultural exploitation: the gardening team. The constitution of this group, however, as well as the working of Doctrine A, is affected by one more principle, to which we now turn.

5 The principle of rank

In Trobriand society there are obviously two forces or influences at work: the one personified by the father of the family, the other by the wife's brother. Since these two in the Trobriands as elsewhere are human beings, and not mere cyphers, they behave accordingly: each one tries to get as much as he can out of his legal claims and at the same time he tries to weaken the legal claims which work against his influence and power. The father of the family, on the one hand, is fully satisfied with the privileges which matriliny bestows on him: he gladly receives the full instalment of *urigubu* or even a surplus; he accepts the services of his wife's brother and other kinsmen; and he claims the services of his children, notably his sons, in the name of matriarchal law, by which his sons are classed with his relatives-in-law and thus are beholden to him. On the other hand, he asserts the principle of patriarchy and, more than that, he behaves as a loving father. Thus, for instance, he is not satisfied with legal prestations from his sons at a distance. He tries to keep them at home even after maturity, very largely because he is attached to them and craves their presence and company; thereby attempting to override the matrilineal principle of readjustment – the custom of split residence and of the return at maturity to the ancestral village. He attacks thus the authority of his sons' matrilineal uncle. Not only that: by keeping his sons at home he attacks the matrilineal principle in his own person, in so far as he is the head and representative of his own sub-clan. Because when the sons remain with him he always bestows on them various privileges and offices which belong by strict law to his sister's male offspring. This he can do; he is in fact aided and abetted by such customary arrangements as cross-cousin marriage, and usages of tolerance which allow a man to hand over to his sons certain personal goods,

traditional privileges, the exercise of magic, which by strict matrilineal law they should never possess or exercise.

We might describe the conditions in the Trobriands as a dynamic
adjustment between the patriarchal and matriarchal principle. It is
not a static balance but rather a perpetual conflict – a conflict
which enters into personal relations within the family, within the
village community, within the constitution of the tribe as a whole.
Yet it is obvious that there would be no room for conflict, for
readjustments or encroachments, if naturally and normally the
personal influence of the two men – the father and the mother's
brother – were even. There might be the inevitable variations
according to personality, but these could not produce any lasting or
profound effect. In the Trobriands, however, there is one element
of a sociological nature which enters here and tips the scale on one
side or the other. For, as we shall presently see, this principle does
not act invariably or even predominantly on the side of the
partiarchal influence. The principle obviously is that of rank, and it
acts in a two-fold manner.

Let us first briefly recapitulate how rank enhances the power of a
man within his household and community, that is, the power of a
man *qua* patriarch. A man of rank has the privilege of polygamy,
to which is superadded the advantage of a more substantial *urigubu*
for each wife. Thus, through the working of the matrilineal
principle associated with the essentially patriarchal personal status,
such a man diverts to himself a considerable amount of wealth.
Speaking in terms of production and land tenure, this means that
he obtains through rank, matriliny and patriarchy a system of
effective claims over a more or less extended territory.

But this action of rank does not bear directly on the readjustment
between the matrilineal and patriarchal principle. This readjustment is achieved in so far as a man of rank can easily overrule the
matrilineal influence with regard to his own sons. No matrilineal
uncle will contest any claims to his nephews, if the father of these
nephews is a man of rank higher than his own. It is a privilege for
the sons to remain in a village of high rank. Their matrilineal uncle
gains personal influence through it and very often does not want to
regain them; especially since, by being a chief's sons, they develop a
certain arrogance and a number of extravagant claims which would
make them undesirable as subordinate kinsmen. But even if a man
wanted to exercise his rights as matrilineal uncle he could not do so

against the wishes of his superior brother-in-law.

The position of a chief, whether paramount or not, within his own community is less untrammelled in the matter of favouring sons. To a certain extent a man of rank can overrule the claims of his own kinsmen in favour of his sons more readily than a man of low rank; for rank in the person of the eldest head of a sub-clan becomes effective political power. But the rank of the chief, say the paramount chief, is not higher than that of his brothers and matrilineal nephews.

In all this, we see that rank overrules the workings of Doctrines A and B as regards residence, and hence in the use of the territory; even more, it may override the right of the sub-clan to exercise garden magic and to control its lands. The fact that, in the very capital of the Trobriands, the most important magical instrument of power – the magic of rain and drought – is performed by an alien, that the economically most relevant magic, that of the *towosi*, has been repeatedly in the hands of aliens, shows how powerfully the influence of rank can overrule the workings of Doctrine A through the instrumentality of Doctrine B. For, let us remember, it is always rank acting through the relationship of father to son – a relationship based in the Trobriands essentially on their law of marriage.

Rank, however, as we have said already, acts both ways. It not only overrules matriliny by allowing a father of higher rank to set aside the fundamental principles of filiation and to introduce his own sons into the community. It may also tip the balance in favour of the matrilineal principle. This occurs when a wife of higher rank marries a man of lower rank and settles in his community. Her children, notably her sons, will be personally dear to their father. As father he wishes to retain them in his community quite as much as a father of high rank wants to retain lower-rank sons in his own village. And here rank helps him, though in a slightly different manner. He is backed up, not by his own rank, but by that of his wife and her offspring. Since such a woman would normally marry a headman of the community he would have some power of his own over his own kinsmen. This power, however, would not be sufficient to allow him to keep his sons with him permanently. But since they are of a higher rank, and backed up by their matrilineal uncle, they can have their way. If they consent, they can remain in their father's village, and no one would dare to oppose them. The greater the difference in rank, the more nobly born the wife, the less the force of any objections to their permanent residence in the village. Hence the noblest lineage, that of the Tabalu, was able to take root all over the district. The feeling of the members of the autochthonous sub-clan is complex. On the one hand they are proud of retaining a lineage of high rank in their village. It adds prestige to the whole community and it enhances the power and standing of every individual. At the same time, the autochthonous elders resent being put into a subordinate place. For whenever men of a high sub-clan settle in the village they gradually acquire an increasing power. For when a headman retains sons of a rank higher than his own, not merely a single individual becomes definitely associated with the village community, but a whole lineage. The high rank son of a headman or notable of lower rank obtains rights of lifelong residence, not in virtue of his father's rank, power and influence, but because of his own personal status. This status allows him to remain where he wishes and makes him automatically the most important person in the community. Since the new community becomes subject to him, it also becomes the home of his descendants in mother line. From his new home he will prepare the *urigubu* for his sisters, and the sons of these sisters will naturally come back to him and reside with him, and also succeed him in his offices. A sub-clan of high rank takes roots in its new community by degrees, acquiring the various offices and privileges one by one, the exercise of garden magic being usually the last to come.

It is clear now that although the adoption of a son by a chief in virtue of the latter's superior rank is on the whole more frequent and at times more dramatic, it is less important than the settlement of high-rank people in villages of low rank through the mechanism of a woman's marriage into an inferior sub-clan. The residence of a lower-rank son in a high-rank father's village is a phenomenon which never can outlast a generation. If the son has married his father's matrilineal niece, the offspring will automatically be full-titled citizens and the introduced lineage becomes eliminated. If he has remained in his father's village while marrying a woman of a sub-clan who has no right of citizenship, the offspring of that woman will belong to the mother's sub-clan and the influence of the father's father – who is the chief or headman of high rank – is never sufficient to keep his son's sons in the community.

To sum up then: rank operating through the father brings about the phenomenon of a constantly recurring but sporadic influx of alien residents. It is an important phenomenon but produces no lasting imprint on the constitution of the local community and the fundamental rights of land tenure. Operating from father to son, rank cannot override Doctrine A. Operating through the wife and allowing sons of high rank to settle in an inferior village, Doctrine D, as we have called it, that is the doctrine of rank, brings about the permanent shifting of authority and sovereignty to new territories. It also overrides and modifies powerfully Doctrine A.

One more point might here be added. We know that besides the myths of local emergence there is one important and explicit story of how the four clans came out of the soil in the sacred grove of Obukula near Laba'i. This story tells us how the rank of the four clans became graded. The Malasi finally became the most important – the ruling clan. But there is not the slightest doubt in the minds of the natives that this distinction belongs only to one sub-clan of the Malasi, that is, the Tabalu. There is no doubt that, in the minds of the natives, this general myth establishes the Tabalu as overlords of the whole district. Their rights to spread, to settle wherever they like, to assume the lordship over any community, is to a large extent based on this myth. Whenever there is a conflict between two influences – and such conflicts I have found in a marked degree in Vakuta and Tukwa'ukwa and in a slightly different form revived in Kavataria – the Tabalu would refer to the fact that all the soil of that district belongs to them in virtue of their first emergence.

We can thus say that the doctrine of first emergence has two aspects: one is represented by the numerous local myths of first emergence, the other by the general or national myth of the first emergence of the four clans. Thus completed and complemented, Doctrine A in a way embraces Doctrine D. And its validity is not so much overruled as complemented by the principle of rank. Whichever way we take it, however, and whether we prefer to think of Doctrines A and D as independent or as interrelated, we can see now how Doctrines A, B and D work in together.

We can also briefly summarise the specific contribution of the doctrine of rank as regards land tenure. (1) It organises village lands into the bigger units representing a district. Within such a district the exploitation of land is associated with the substantial tribute given to the chief in the form of the *urigubu*, of *pokala* and of other gifts. The chief, on the other hand, accumulates and stores this quota of the district's yield and uses it later in connection with tribal enterprise, warfare and public ceremonies. Besides Kiriwina, where this economy assumes the biggest dimensions, we have such districts as Tilataula, Kuboma, Kayleula, Luba. In Sinaketa this district economy is not very pronounced. (2) The influence of rank supplies the effective force in the shifting of sub-clans from one local community to another. Thereby it partly overrides the principle of first emergence. In reality, however, it combines with this and derives its ultimate force therefrom in so far as it becomes an effective charter of land tenure. (3) When a sub-clan of high rank settles, it does not oust its predecessors but acquires from them, through their consent, the effective claims over the land. (4) Rank also introduces the patriarchal anomaly within a matrilineal system, whereby adult members who have no legal claim to citizenship and to the lands are included in the garden team. The position of such individuals is the more remarkable in that they often play a leading part, not only in the community as such, but in the magic of gardening and the organisation of garden work.

Part three
The Kula

Editor's note to part three

Sources

Section 4 of chapter 7 is taken from Malinowski's first publication on the Kula (1920, pp. 101–5). With this exception, the three chapters which follow have been assembled from *Argonauts of the Western Pacific*, pp. 81–3, 86–8, 507–8, 91–6 and 98–9 (chapter 7); 118–20, 208–11, 275–81, 352–60, 362–4, 480–1, 468–75, 489–90 (chapter 8); 424, 229–30, 236, 238–47, 392–6, 400–1, 403–18, 306, 311–21, 327–30 and 510–13 (chapter 9).

Further reading

Critical comment upon and reappraisals of Malinowski's data on the Kula can be found in Brookfield and Hart (1971), Brunton (1975), Firth (1957b), Forge (1972) and Uberoi (1962). For additional information on the Kula in other Massim societies see Belshaw (1955), Fortune (1932) and Lauer (1970). Another large Melanesian maritime trading system is described by Harding (1967). Malinowski's analyses of Trobriand magic are discussed by Nadel (1957) and Tambiah (1968).

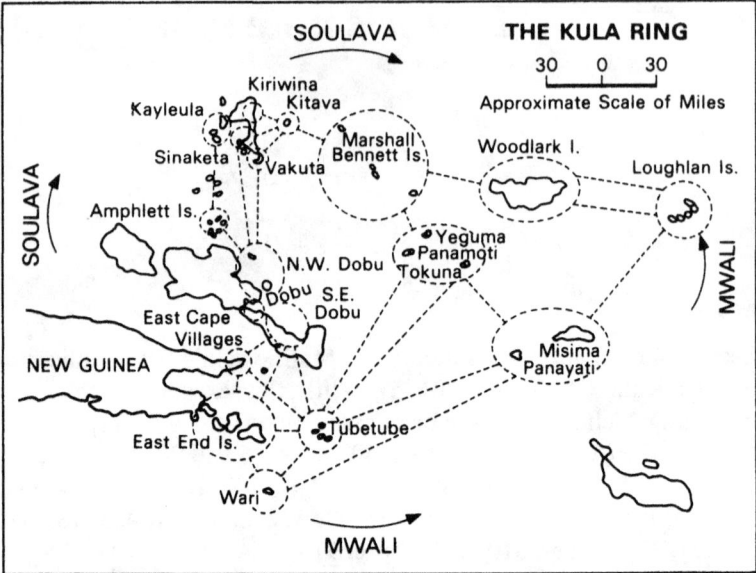

Figure 6 The Kula ring

7 Essentials of the Kula

1 A concise definition

The Kula is a form of exchange, of extensive, inter-tribal character; it is carried on by communities inhabiting a wide ring of islands, which form a closed circuit. This circuit can be seen on Fig. 6, where it is represented by the lines joining a number of islands to the north and east of the east end of New Guinea. Along this route, articles of two kinds, and these two kinds only, are constantly travelling in opposite directions. In the direction of the hands of a clock, moves constantly one of these kinds – long necklaces of red shell, called *soulava*. In the opposite direction moves the other kind – bracelets of white shell called *mwali*. Each of these articles, as it travels in its own direction on the closed circuit, meets on its way articles of the other class, and is constantly being exchanged for them. Every movement of the Kula articles, every detail of the transactions is fixed and regulated by a set of traditional rules and conventions, and some acts of the Kula are accompanied by an elaborate magical ritual and public ceremonies.

On every island and in every village, a more or less limited number of men take part in the Kula – that is to say, receive the goods, hold them for a short time, and then pass them on. Therefore every man who is in the Kula, periodically though not regularly, receives one or several *mwali* (arm-shells), or a *soulava* (necklace of red shell discs), and then has to hand it on to one of his partners, from whom he receives the opposite commodity in exchange. Thus no man ever keeps any of the articles for any length of time in his possession. One transaction does not finish the Kula relationship, the rule being 'once in the kula, always in the Kula', and a partnership between two men is a permanent and lifelong affair. Again, any given *mwali* or *soulava* may always be found travelling and changing hands, and there is no question of its ever settling down, so that the principle 'once in the Kula, always in the Kula' applies also to the valuables themselves.

The ceremonial exchange of the two articles is the main, the fundamental aspect of the Kula. But associated with it, and done under its cover, we find a great number of secondary activities and features. Thus, side by side with the ritual exchange of arm-shells and necklaces, the natives carry on ordinary trade, bartering from one island to another a great number of utilities, often unprocurable in the district to which they are imported, and indispensable there. Further, there are other activities, preliminary to the Kula, or associated with it, such as the building of sea-going canoes for the expeditions, certain big forms of mortuary ceremonies, and preparatory taboos.

The Kula is thus an extremely big and complex institution, both in its geographical extent, and in the manifoldness of its component pursuits. It welds together a considerable number of tribes, and it embraces a vast complex of activities, interconnected, and playing into one another, so as to form one organic whole.

The definition of the Kula must now be amplified, and we must describe one after the other its fundamental characteristics and main rules, so that it may be clearly grasped by what mechanism the mere exchange of two articles results in an institution so vast, complex, and deeply rooted.

2 Arm-shells and necklaces

First of all, a few words must be said about the two principal objects of exchange, the arm-shells (*mwali*) and the necklaces (*soulava*). The arm-shells are obtained by breaking off the top and the narrow end of a big, cone-shaped shell (*Conus millepunctatus*), and then polishing up the remaining ring. These bracelets are highly coveted by all the Papuo-Melanesians of New Guinea, and they spread even into the pure Papuan district of the Gulf.

The use of the small discs of red spondylus shell, out of which the *soulava* are made, is also of a very wide diffusion. There is a manufacturing centre of them in one of the villages in Port Moresby, and also in several places in Eastern New Guinea, notably in Rossel Island, and in the Trobriands. I have said '*use*' on purpose here, because these small beads, each of them a flat, round disc with a hole in the centre, coloured anything from muddy brown to carmine red, are employed in various ways for ornamentation. They are most generally used as part of earrings, made of rings of turtle shell, which are attached to the ear lobe, and from which hang a cluster of the shell discs. These earrings are very much worn, and, especially among the Massim, you see them on the ears of every second man or woman, while others are satisfied with turtle shell alone, unornamented with the shell discs. Another everyday ornament, frequently met with and worn, especially by young girls and boys, consists of a short necklace, just encircling the neck, made of the red spondylus discs, with one or more cowrie shell pendants. These shell discs can be, and often are, used in the make-up of the various classes of the more elaborate ornaments, worn on festive occasions only. Here, however, we are more especially concerned with the very long necklaces, measuring from 2 to 5 metres, made of spondylus discs, of which there are two main varieties, one, much the finer, with a big shell pendant, the other made of bigger discs, with a few cowrie shells or black banana seeds in the centre.

The arm-shells on the one hand, and the long spondylus shell strings on the other, the two main Kula articles, are primarily ornaments. As such, they are used with the most elaborate dancing dress only, and on very festive occasions such as big ceremonial dances, great feasts, and big gatherings, where several villages are represented. Never could they be used as everyday ornaments, nor on occasions of minor importance, such as a small dance in the village, a harvest gathering, a love-making expedition, when facial painting, floral decoration and smaller though not quite everyday ornaments are worn. But even though usable and sometimes used, this is not the main function of these articles. Thus, a chief may have several shell strings in his possession, and a few arm-shells. Supposing that a big dance is held in his or in a neighbouring village, he will not put on his ornaments himself if he goes to assist at it, unless he intends to dance and decorate himself, but any of his relatives, his children or his friends and even vassals, can have the use of them for the asking. If you go to a feast or a dance where there are a number of men wearing such ornaments, and ask anyone of them at random to whom it belongs, the chances are that more than half of them will answer that they themselves are not the owners, but that they had the articles lent to them. These objects are not owned in order to be used; the privilege of decorating oneself with them is not the real aim of possession.

Casting now a glance at the Kula ring we see that one class of Kula article, the *mwali* or arm-shells, are produced within the ring at two points, that is, in Woodlark Island and in western Boyowa. The other article, that is the *soulava* or *bagi* (necklaces) are poured into the ring at its southernmost point. One of these sources (Rossel Island) is still active, the other (Port Moresby) most probably furnished a good supply in olden days, but is now disconnected with the Kula ring. The necklaces produced in Sinaketa are not the real Kula article, and though they are sometimes exchanged they sooner or later disappear from the ring according to a sort of Gresham's Law, which operates here on an article which is not money, and therefore acts in the opposite sense! The third type of valuable which sometimes flows in the Kula stream but is not really of it, the large green-stone axe blades, finely polished all over, are, or more correctly were, quarried in Woodlark Island, and polished in the district of Kiriwina in the Trobriands. Another polishing centre is, or was, I believe, the island of Misima.

We see that the two sources of the *mwali* and *soulava* are at the northern and southern ends of the ring; the arm-shells being manu-factured in the extreme north, the necklaces entering at the southern end. It is noteworthy that on the eastern portion of the ring, on the section Woodlark-Boyowa-Dobu-Tubetube, the two articles travel in the natural direction, that is, each is exported from the districts of its origin towards one, where it is not made or pro-cured. On the other branch, Woodlark-Yeguma-Tubetube, the current of the Kula is inverse to a natural, commercial movement of the articles, for here, the Tubetube people import arm-shells into Murua, thus bringing coals to Newcastle, while the Muruans bring necklaces to Tubetube and Wari, that is, to the points at which the necklaces flow into the ring from the outside. These considerations are important for anyone who would like to reflect on the origins, or history of the Kula, since the natural movement of valuables was no doubt the original one, and the western half of the Kula from this point of view appears to be the older.

3 The rules of the Kula

The exchange of these two classes of *vaygu'a*, of the arm-shells and the necklaces, constitutes the main act of the Kula. This exchange is not done freely, right and left, as opportunity offers, and where the whim leads. It is subject indeed to strict limitations and regulations. One of these refers to the sociology of the exchange, and entails that Kula transactions can be done only between partners. A man who is in the Kula – for not everyone within its district is entitled to carry it on – has only a limited number of people with whom he deals. This partnership is entered upon in a definite manner, under fulfilment of certain formalities, and it constitutes a life-long relationship. The number of partners a man has varies with his rank and importance. A commoner in the Trobriands would have a few partners only, whereas a chief would number hundreds of them. There is no special social mechanism to limit the partnership of some people and extend that of the others, but a man would naturally know to what number of partners he was entitled by his rank and position. And there would be always the example of his immediate ancestors to guide him. In other tribes, where the distinction of rank is not so pronounced, an old man of standing, or a headman of a hamlet or village would also have hundreds of Kula associates, whereas a man of minor importance would have but few.

Two Kula partners have to kula with one another, and exchange other gifts incidentally; they behave as friends, and have a number of mutual duties and obligations, which vary with the distance between their villages and with their reciprocal status. An average man has a few partners near by, as a rule his relations-in-law or his friends, and with these partners, he is generally on very friendly terms. Again, the average man will have one or two chiefs in his or in the neighbouring districts with whom he kulas. In such a case, he would be bound to assist and serve them in various ways, and to offer them the pick of his *vaygu'a* when he gets a fresh supply. On the other hand he would expect them to be specially liberal to him.

The overseas partner is, on the other hand, a host, patron and ally in a land of danger and insecurity. Nowadays, though the feeling of danger still persists, and natives never feel safe and comfortable in a strange district, this danger is rather felt as a magical one, and it is more the fear of foreign sorcery that besets them. In olden days, more tangible dangers were apprehended, and the partner was the main guarantee of safety. He also provides with food, gives presents, and his house, though never used to sleep in, is the place in which to foregather while in the village. Thus the Kula partnership provides every man within its ring with a few friends near at hand, and with some friendly allies in the far-away, dangerous, foreign districts. These are the only people with whom he can kula, but, of course, amongst all his partners, he is free to choose to which one he will offer which object.

Let us now try to cast a broad glance at the cumulative effects of the rules of partnership. We see that all around the ring of Kula there is a network of relationships, and that naturally the whole forms one interwoven fabric. Men living at hundreds of miles' sailing distance from one another are bound together by direct or intermediate partnership, exchange with each other, know of each other, and on certain occasions meet in a large intertribal gathering. Objects given by one, in time reach some very distant indirect partner or other, and not only Kula objects, but various articles of domestic use and minor gifts. It is easy to see that in the long run, not only objects of material culture, but also customs, songs, art motives and general cultural influences travel along the Kula route. It is a vast, inter-tribal net of relationships, a big institution, consisting of thousands of men, all bound together by one common passion for Kula exchange, and secondarily, by many minor ties and interests.

Returning again to the personal aspect of the Kula, let us take a concrete example, that of *an average man* who lives, let us assume, in the village of Sinaketa, an important Kula centre in the southern Trobriands. He has a few partners, near and far, but they again fall into categories, those who give him arm-shells, and those who give him necklaces. For it is naturally an invariable rule of the Kula that arm-shells and necklaces are never received from the same man, since they must travel in different directions. If one partner gives the arm-shells, and I return to him a necklace, all future operations have to be of the same type. More than that, the nature of the operation between me, the man of Sinaketa, and my partner, is determined by our relative positions with regard to the points of the compass. Thus I, in Sinaketa, would receive from the north and east only arm-shells; from the south and west, necklaces are given to me. If I have a near partner next door to me, if his abode is north or east of mine, he will always be giving me arm-shells and receiving necklaces from me. If, at a later time he were to shift his residence within the village, the old relationship would obtain, but if he became a member of another village community on the other side of me the relationship would be reversed. The partners in villages to

the north of Sinaketa, in the district of Luba, Kulumata, or Kiriwina all supply me with arm-shells. These I hand over to my partners in the south, and receive from them necklaces. The south in
this case means the southern districts of Boyowa, as well as the
Amphletts and Dobu.

Thus every man has to obey definite rules as to the geographical
direction of his transactions. At any point in the Kula ring, if we
imagine him turned towards the centre of the circle, he receives the
arm-shells with his left hand, and the necklaces with his right, and
then hands them both on. In other words, he constantly passes the
arm-shells from left to right, and the necklaces from right to left.

Applying this rule of personal conduct to the whole Kula ring, we
can see at once what the aggregate result is. The sum total of
exchanges will not result in an aimless shifting of the two classes of
article, in a fortuitous come and go of the arm-shells and necklaces.
Two continuous streams will constantly flow on, the one of necklaces following the hands of a clock, and the other, composed of
the arm-shells, in the opposite direction. We see thus that it is quite
correct to speak of the *circular* exchange of the Kula, of a ring or
circuit of moving articles. On this ring, all the villages are placed in
a definitely fixed position with regard to one another, so that one is
always on either the arm-shell or on the necklace side of the other.

Now we pass to another rule of the Kula, of the greatest importance. It seems almost incredible at first, but it is the fact, nevertheless, that no one ever keeps any of the Kula valuables for any length
of time. Indeed, in the whole of the Trobriands there are perhaps
only one or two specially fine arm-shells and shell-necklaces permanently owned as heirlooms, and these are set apart as a special
class, and are once and for all out of the Kula. 'Ownership,' therefore, in Kula, is quite a special economic relation. A man who is in
the Kula never keeps any article for longer than, say, a year or two.
Even this exposes him to the reproach of being niggardly, and certain districts have the bad reputation of being 'slow' and 'hard' in
the Kula. On the other hand, each man has an enormous number of
articles passing through his hands during his life time, of which he
enjoys a temporary possession, and which he keeps in trust for a
time. This possession hardly ever makes him use the articles, and he
remains under the obligation soon again to hand them on to one of
his partners. But the temporary ownership allows him to draw a
great deal of renown, to exhibit his article, to tell how he obtained

it, and to plan to whom he is going to give it. And all this forms one of the favourite subjects of tribal conversation and gossip, in which the feats and the glory in Kula of chiefs or commoners are constantly discussed and re-discussed. Thus every article moves in one direction only, never comes back, never permanently stops, and takes as a rule some two to ten years to make the round.

All the rules so far enumerated – looking at them from the individual point of view – limit the social range and the direction of the transactions as well as the duration of ownership of the articles. Looking at them from the point of view of their integral effect, they shape the general outline of the Kula, give it the character of the double-closed circuit. Now a few words must be said about the nature of each individual transaction, in so far as its *commercial technicalities* are concerned. Here very definite rules also obtain.

The main principle underlying the regulations of actual exchange is that the Kula consists in the bestowing of a ceremonial gift, which has to be repaid by an equivalent counter-gift, after a lapse of time, be it a few hours or even minutes, though sometimes as much as a year or more may elapse between payments. (In order not to be guilty of inconsistency in using loosely the word 'ceremonial' I shall define it briefly. I shall call an action ceremonial, if it is (1) public; (2) carried on under observance of definite formalities; (3) if it has sociological, religious, or magical import, and carries with it obligations.) But it can never be exchanged from hand to hand, with the equivalence between the two objects discussed, bargained about and computed. The decorum of the Kula transaction is strictly kept, and highly valued. The natives sharply distinguish it from barter, which they practise extensively, of which they have a clear idea, and for which they have a settled term – in Kiriwinian: *gimwali*. Often, when criticising an incorrect, too hasty, or indecorous procedure of Kula, they will say: 'He conducts his Kula as if it were *gimwali*.'

The second very important principle is that the equivalence of the counter-gift is left to the giver, and it cannot be enforced by any kind of coercion. A partner who has received a Kula gift is expected to give back fair and full value, that is, to give as good an arm-shell as the necklace he receives, or *vice versa*. Again, a very fine article must be replaced by one of equivalent value, and not by several minor ones, though intermediate gifts may be given to mark time before the real repayment takes place.

The two main principles, namely, first that the Kula is a gift repaid after an interval of time by a counter-gift, and not a bartering; and second, that the equivalent rests with the giver, and cannot be enforced, nor can there be any haggling or going back on the exchange – these underlie all the transactions. A concrete outline of how they are carried on will give a sufficient preliminary idea.

Let us suppose that I, a Sinaketa man, am in possession of a pair of big arm-shells. An overseas expedition from Dobu in the d'Entrecasteaux Archipelago, arrives at my village. Blowing a conch shell, I take my arm-shell pair and I offer it to my overseas partner, with some such words as 'This is a *vaga* (opening gift) – in due time, thou returnest to me a big *soulava* (necklace) for it!' Next year, when I visit my partner's village, he either is in possession of an equivalent necklace, and this he gives to me as *yotile* (return gift), or he has not a necklace good enough to repay my last gift. In this case he will give me a small necklace – avowedly not equivalent to my gift – and he will give it to me as *basi* (intermediary gift). This means that the main gift has to be repaid on a future occasion, and the *basi* is given in token of good faith – but it, in turn, must be repaid by me in the meantime by a gift of small arm-shells. The final gift, which will be given to me to clinch the whole transaction, would then be called *kudu* (clinching gift) in contrast to *basi*.

Although haggling and bargaining are completely ruled out of the Kula, there are customary and regulated ways of bidding for a piece of *vaygu'a* known to be in the possession of one's partner. This is done by the offer of what we shall call solicitary gifts, of which there are several types. If I, an inhabitant of Sinaketa, happen to be in possession of a pair of arm-shells more than usually good, the fame of it spreads, for it must be remembered that each one of the first-class arm-shells and necklaces has a personal name and a history of its own, and as they circulate around the big ring of the Kula, they are all well known, and their appearance in a given district always creates a sensation. Now, all my partners – whether from overseas or from within the district – compete for the favour of receiving this particular article of mine, and those who are specially keen try to obtain it by giving me *pokala* (offerings) and *kaributu* (solicitary gifts). The former (*pokala*) consist as a rule of pigs, especially fine bananas, and yams or taro; the latter (*kaributu*) are of greater value: the valuable, large axe-blades (called *beku*), or lime spoons of whale-bone are given.

4 Outline of a Kula expedition

Glancing at Fig. 6 we see a number of circles, each of which represents a certain sociological unit which we shall call a Kula community. A Kula community consists of a village or a number of
villages, who go out together on big overseas expeditions and who
act as a body in the Kula transactions – perform their magic in common, have common leaders, and have the same outer and inner
social sphere, within which they exchange their valuables. The Kula
consists, therefore, first of the small, inner trade within a Kula
community or contiguous communities, and secondly of the big
overseas expeditions in which the annual exchange of articles takes
place between two communities, divided by sea. In the first, there is
a chronic, permanent trickling of articles from one village to
another, and even within the village. In the second a whole lot of
valuables, amounting to over a thousand articles at a time, are
exchanged in one enormous transaction, or, more correctly in ever
so many transactions taking place simultaneously.

I will describe the normal and typical course of such a big overseas expedition as it takes place between the Kula community of
Sinaketa with its surrounding villages and the Amphlett Group and
Dobu districts to the south. Such an expedition would take place
about once a year, but only every second or third year would it be
carried out on a really big scale. On such occasions big preparations
take place. First of all the large sea-going canoes must be made
ready. As a rule a few new ones have to be built to replace those
worn out and unseaworthy, and then those in good order have to be
overhauled and redecorated. The building of a canoe is a big tribal
affair. A series of magical rites have to be performed by a specialist
or specialists, who are versed in the art of constructing and carving
– the magic being considered indispensable to both arts. The
magical rites aim successively at the expulsion of a wood spirit
(*tokway*) from the tree to be felled: at the imparting of stability,
swiftness and good luck to the canoe, and at the counteracting of
evil influences cast on the canoe by direct sorcery or by the unwitting breaking of taboos. The rites – some performed in a simple
manner by a magician alone, some ceremonially with the attendance of the whole community – are carried out in a series, associated with the various activities, inaugurating some, accompanying others. The magic is always interwoven with the technical

operations and is to the native mind absolutely indispensable to the successful accomplishment of the task. Another important feature of canoe-building is the communal labour, which is always used at certain stages and for certain tasks, as for sail-making, the piecing together and lashing, caulking and painting of the canoe. The owner of the canoe has to pay for the work by gifts of *vaygu'a* (valuables) and distribution of food, and the expert magician-constructor directs the work.

The building and overhauling of canoes lasts for about six months, for it is done slowly in the intervals of other work. As the expeditions take place usually in February–April, the canoe work begins some time in August or September. When all the canoes are ready, there is a big gathering from the whole district, and the canoes are launched ceremonially, and races and general festivities take place. Some days later all the canoes start on a preliminary trip to the neighbouring districts, that is, in the case of Sinaketa, to the northern half of the island, to Kiriwina proper. There is a custom, called *kabigidoya*, of ceremonially presenting a canoe, and the owner receives gifts, which form part of the subsidiary trade, to be used on the big expedition. More subsidiary trade is obtained by barter (*gimwali*), especially from the manufacturing districts on the north shore of the lagoon. Wooden combs, fibre armlets, baskets, mussel shells and other articles, abundant here and rare in the Amphletts and in Dobu, are thus acquired in great quantities. On this preliminary trip the Sinaketans also obtain a number of arm-shells from Kiriwina by inland Kula, and with their wealth thus replenished return to Sinaketa.

A period of taboos and initial magic now obtains as the imme-diate preliminary to main departure. The owner of each canoe is subject to the most stringent restrictions – mainly referring to sexual relations – and he also performs all the magic. On an evening he goes into a garden and uttering a spell he plucks a spray of aro-matic mint, which he brings home. Then he prepares some coconut oil, anoints the mint with it, and, putting some oil and the mint into a vessel, he medicates it all with another spell. The vessel – in olden days a contrivance of roasted and thus toughened banana leaves, now a small glass bottle – is then attached to the prow of the canoe. This magic aims at the softening of the Dobuan's mind, so that he may be unable to resist any appeal made to his generosity. This aim is explicitly stated by all natives, and an analysis of the magical

spells reveals it also as their leading idea. But the magic is full of
mythological allusions, of side ideas and of references to animals
and birds, and it contains interesting metaphorical circumlocutions
of the aims to be attained.

Other spells, all expressing more or less the same ideas, are used
in the magical rite performed over a special bundle of valuables and
goods, called *lilava*, which is placed in the centre of the canoe and
must not be opened before the arrival in Dobu: also in the rite over
the coconut leaves lining the canoe. Again, in the rite over the provisions of food taken on the journey, the main aim is to make it last
long.

After the rites are finished and the expedition is ready, many
people from the neighbouring villages assemble, the departing
chiefs enjoin chastity to their wives and warn all the neighbouring
male villagers to keep off Sinaketa, and prognosticate a speedy
arrival with much *vaygu'a* (valuables). They are assured that they
can depart in safety as no one will visit their village surreptitiously.
Indeed, during their absence, the village should be kept tabooed,
and if a man is found loitering about the place, especially at night,
he is likely to be punished (by sorcery, as a rule) on the chief's
return.

The fleet now sails south; but the first stage of the journey is
short, as the natives halt on a sandbank some ten miles off
Sinaketa, where they have a ceremonial distribution of food, which
imposes an obligation on the *usagelu* (members of the crews)
towards the *toliwaga* (owners of canoes) to carry out the expedition
even in the face of contrary winds and bad weather. Next morning
several rites are performed over the canoes to undo all evil magic
and to make them swift and steady.

The open sea now lies before the fleet with the high, distant
peaks of the d'Entrecasteaux mountains floating above the haze. In
very clear weather the nearer Amphletts can be seen – small steep
rocks, scattered over the horizon, misty, but more material against
the faint blue of the distant land. These far-off views must have
inspired generation after generation of Kiriwinian sailors with zest
for adventure, wonder and desire to see the much-praised marvels
of foreign lands, with awe and with superstitious fear. Mixed with
it all – associated in the native mind with the allurement of the
distant *koya* (mountains) – there was the ambition to return with
plenty of *vaygu'a*. In myths, in traditional legends, in real stories

and in songs, Kula expeditions were and are described and praised and there is a definite complex of Kula tradition and mythology, governed perhaps by two dominating emotions: the desire to obtain the *vaygu'a* and the dread of the dangers to be encountered.

These latter are real enough, as the wind in the N.W. season, when the expeditions take place, is changeable, and violent squalls obtain, and the sea is full of reefs and sandbanks. But the natives have added to that from their store of myth-making imagination, and have surrounded the real dangers with a fabric of imaginary perils and modes of escape. There exist for them big, live stones, lying in wait for a canoe – they jump up when they see one, and smash it to pieces and destroy the sailors. There is a giant octopus, which will take hold of a canoe and never let it go, unless a sacrifice is made of a small boy, adorned and anointed, who is thrown over-board to the *kwita* (octopus). There may come a big rain, which smashes and submerges the canoe. But the greatest danger comes from flying witches, who, whenever they hear that a canoe is drowning – and they possess the capacity of hearing it at enormous distances – assemble and wait till the men are in the water, and then fall on them. There is a deep belief that shipwreck in itself would not be fatal – the men would float ashore, carried by the *débris* of the canoe – unless the flying witches were to attack them. A whole cycle of beliefs centres round this main idea, and there is a system of rites which are always practised in shipwreck, and which, if carried out properly, would ensure safety to those shipwrecked.

One part of this magic is directed towards the flying witches; it blinds and bewilders them and they cannot attack the men in the waves. Another part is chanted by the *toliwaga* (master of the canoe) whilst he and his companions are drifting, suspended on the float of the outrigger, and it attracts a giant fish (*iraveaka*). This beneficent animal arrives and pulls the float and the men ashore. This is not the end; the shipwrecked party have to go through a series of ceremonies intended to make them immune from the flying witches, and only after that may they return to their village.

The normal expedition, however, sails in one day with good following wind, or in several days if the wind is weak or shifting, and arrives at its first stage, in the Amphletts. Some exchange is done here, as well as on the further two intermediate halts in Tewara and Sanaroa and the concomitant magic has to be per-formed here. There are also several mythologically famed spots in

these islands: some rocks from which magic originated – how, the
myths do not relate distinctly – and other rocks, formerly human
beings, who travelled to their present sites from very far, and to
whom the natives offer *pokala* (offerings in order to have a propitious Kula). The island of Gumasila in the Amphletts, that of
Tewara, and places on Fergusson Island, are important mythological centres.

But the main aim of the expedition is the district of Dobu, more
especially the north-east corner of Fergusson Island, where on the
flat and fertile foreshore, among groves of coconut, betel-palms,
mangoes and bread-fruit trees, there stretch for miles the populous
settlements of Tautauna, Bwayowa, Deidei and Begasi.

Before approaching them, the whole fleet stops on a beach called
Sarubwoyna, not far away from the two rocks, *Atu'a'ine* and
Aturamo'a, which are the most important, perhaps, of the rocks to
whom *pokala* offering is given. Here the final magic is performed.
All the *usagelu* (members of the crew) go ashore and collect leaves
for magic. Spells are pronounced over them by the members of
each canoe and everyone washes with sea-water and dries his skin
with the medicated leaves. Then spells are uttered over coconut oil,
red paint and aromatic herbs – and the natives anoint and adorn
themselves, the magic making them beautiful and irresistible. A
spell is uttered into the mouth of a conch-shell and the canoes get
under way. The last distance, a few miles only, is traversed by
paddling; and powerful spells are uttered by several men in each
canoe, who recite them simultaneously, and the medicated conch-
shell is blown. These spells have to 'shake the mountain' – that is,
to produce a deep agitation in the minds of the Dobuans, and
impress them with the arrival of the newcomers. One more important rite is uttered to prevent the Dobuans from becoming fierce
and angry and to suppress any attempt at attacking the visitors.

Finally the party arrive, and it is the custom for the Dobuans to
meet them with *soulava* (shell-disc necklaces) in their hands. The
conch-shells are blown and the necklaces are ceremonially offered
by the Dobuans to the newcomers. Then the party go ashore, every
man going to the house of his main partner. There the visitors
receive gifts of food, and they again give some of their minor trade
as *pari* (visitors' gifts) to the Dobuans. Then, during a several days'
stay, many more *soulava* are given to the visitors. Often it is necessary for a Kiriwinian to woo his partner by gifts, solicitations and

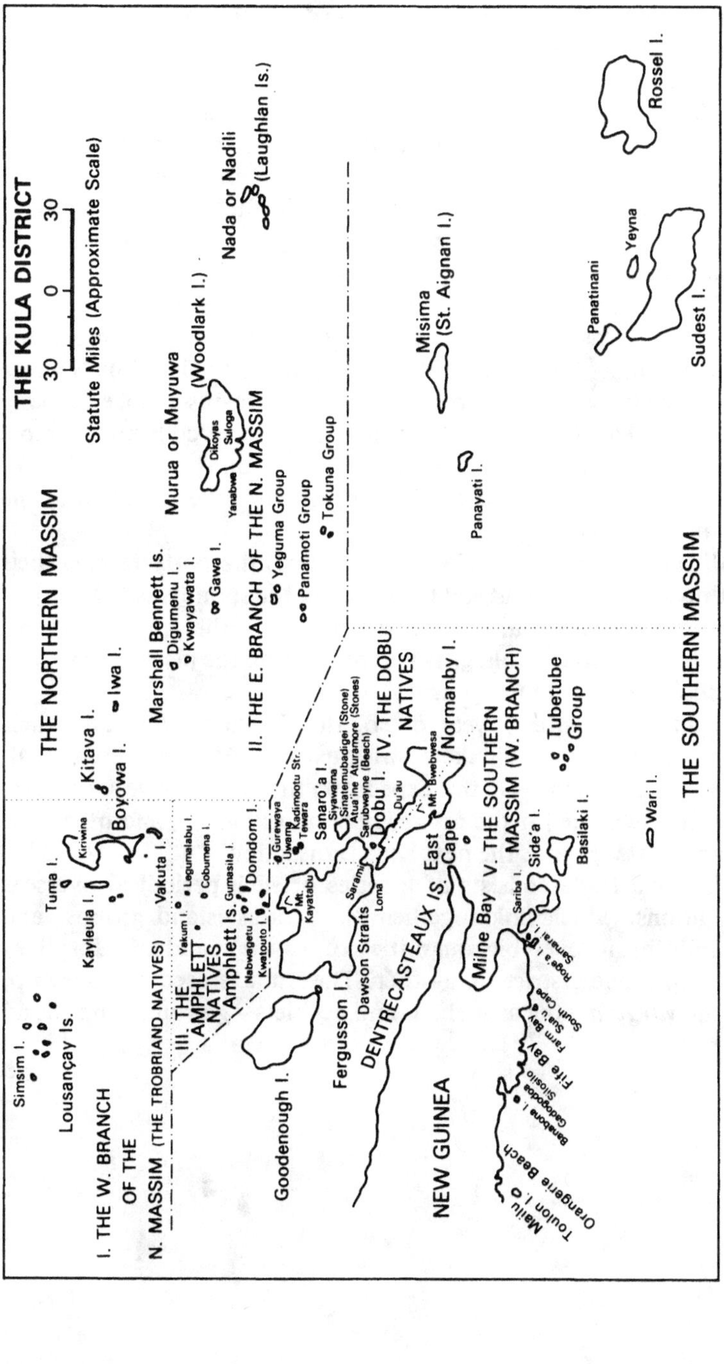

THE KULA DISTRICT

Statute Miles (Approximate Scale)

30   0   30

THE NORTHERN MASSIM

I. THE W. BRANCH OF THE N. MASSIM (THE TROBRIAND NATIVES)

Simsim I.
Lousançay Is.
Kayleula I.
Kitava I.
Tuma I.
Kiriwina
Boyowa I.
Vakuta I.
Iwa I.

Marshall Bennett Is.
Digumenu I.
Kwayawata I.
Gawa I.

Murua or Muyuwa (Woodlark I.)
Dikoyas
Suloga
Yanabwa

II. THE E. BRANCH OF THE N. MASSIM

Nada or Nadiii (Laughlan Is.)

Yeguma Group
Panamoti Group
Tokuna Group

III. THE AMPHLETT NATIVES

Yeum I.
Nabwageta I.
Kwetouto I.
Mt. Kayatabu
Gumasila I.
Cobumena I.
Legumalabu I.
Amphlett Is.
Domdom I.
Gureweya
Uwama
Tewara
Kadimootu Str.

Sanaro'a I.
Sivawawna
Sinatemubadigee (Stone)
Atua'ine Aturamore (Stones)
Sarubwoyna (Beach)
Loma
Suram

IV. THE DOBU NATIVES

DOBU I.
Du'au
Mt. Bwebwesa
Normanby I.

Fergusson I.
Goodenough I.
Dawson Straits
DENTRECASTEAUX IS.
East Cape

V. THE SOUTHERN MASSIM (W. BRANCH)

Milne Bay
Seriba I.
Side'a I.
Basilaki I.
Tubetube Group

Wari I.

Rawa I.
Rope I.
Samarai I.
South Cape
Siau I.
Farm Bay
Fife Bay
Silosilo
Gadogadoa I.
Banahona I.
Orangerie Beach
Maiiu I.
Touion I.

NEW GUINEA

Misima (St. Aignan I.)
Panayati I.
Panatinani
Yeyna
Sudest I.

Rossel I.

THE SOUTHERN MASSIM

Figure 7   The Kula district, showing the sub-divisions of the Massim and places of importance in the Kula

magical rites, transparently performed, if the latter possesses a specially good and desirable article. All the transactions are carried out according to the rules set forth above.

Side by side with the Kula, the subsidiary trade goes on, the visitors acquiring a great number of articles of minor value, but of great utility, some of them unprocurable in Kiriwina, as, for instance, rattan, fibre belts, cassowary feathers, certain kinds of spear wood, obsidian, red ochre and many other articles. This subsidiary trade is carried on by means of gifts and counter-gifts with one's own partners; by means of barter (*gimwali*) with other people; whereas certain articles are procured directly. Among the latter, the most important is the spondylus shell, fished by Sinaketans in the lagoon of Sanaroa, again under the observance of many taboos, and with the aid of magic, private and collective, simple and ceremonial. The shell called *kaloma* is, on their return home, worked out into the red shell-discs, which serve for making the *soulava* necklaces.

All the transactions in Dobu concluded, the party receive their parting gifts (*talo'i*) and sail back, doing the spondylus fishing just mentioned in Sanaroa, trading for pots with the Amphletts, and receiving additional Kula gifts and *talo'i* in all the places where they go ashore on their return journey.

In due time, after a year or so, the Dobuans will make their return expedition to Sinaketa, with exactly the same ceremonial, magic and sociology. On this expedition they will receive some arm-shells in exchange for the necklets previously given, and others, as advance gifts towards the next Kula transaction.

The Kula trade consists of a series of such periodical overseas expeditions, which link together the various island groups, and annually bring over big quantities of *vaygu'a* and of subsidiary trade from one district to another. The trade is used and used up, but the *vaygu'a* – the arm-shells and necklets – go round and round the ring.

8   Technicalities of the Kula

1   Canoe ownership: the *toliwaga*

The natives, to whom the Kula and the sailing expeditions are so important, will associate the name of a canoe with that of its *toli* (owner); they will identify his magical powers and its good luck in sailing and in the Kula; they will often speak of so-and-so's sailing here and there, of his being very fast in sailing, etc., using in this the man's name for that of the canoe.

The title of *toliwaga*, besides the general social distinction which it confers, implies further a definite series of social functions with regard to its individual bearer.

(1) There are first the formal and ceremonial privileges. Thus, the *toliwaga* has the privilege of acting as spokesman of his community in all matters of sailing or construction. He assembles the council, informal or formal as the case may be, and opens the question of when the sailing will take place. This right of initiative is a purely nominal one, because both in construction and sailing, the date of enterprise is determined by outward causes, such as reciprocity to overseas tribes, seasons, customs, etc. Nevertheless, the formal privilege is strictly confined to the *toliwaga*, and highly valued. The position of master and leader of ceremonies, of general spokesman, lasts right through the successive stages of the building of the canoe, and its subsequent use, and we meet with it in all the ceremonial phases of the Kula.

(2) The economic uses and advantages derived from a canoe are not limited to the *toliwaga*. He, however, gets the lion's share. He has, of course, in all circumstances, the privilege of absolute priority in being included in the party. He also receives always by far the greatest proportion of Kula valuables, and other articles on every occasion. This, however, is in virtue of his general position as chief or headman, and should perhaps not be included under this

179

heading. But a very definite and strictly individual advantage is that
of being able to dispose of the canoe for hire, and of receiving the
payment for it. The canoe can be, and often is, hired out from a
headman, who at a given season has no intention of sailing, by
another one, as a rule from a different district, who embarks on an
expedition. The reason of this is, that the chief or headman who
borrows, may at that time not be able to have his own canoe
repaired, or construct another new one. The payment for hire is
called *toguna*, and it consists of a *vaygu'a*. Besides this, the best
vaygu'a obtained on the expedition would be kulaed to the man
from whom the canoe was hired.

(3) The *toliwaga* has definite social privileges, and exercises definite functions, in the running of a canoe. Thus, he selects his
companions who will sail in his canoe, and has the nominal right to
choose or reject those who may go on the expedition with him.
Here again the privilege is much shorn of its value by many restrictions imposed on the chief by the nature of things. Thus, on the one
hand, his *veyola* (maternal kinsmen) have, according to all native
ideas of right and law, a strong claim on the canoe. Again, a man
of rank in a community could be excluded from an expedition only
with difficulty, if he wished to go and there were no special
grievance against him. But if there were such a cause, if the man
had offended the chief and were on bad terms with him, he himself
would not even try to embark. Another class of people having a *de
facto* right to sail are the sailing experts. In the coastal villages like
Sinaketa there are many of these; in inland ones, like Omarakana,
there are few. So in one of these inland places, there are men who
always go in a canoe, whenever it is used; who have even a good
deal to say in all matters connected with sailing, yet who would
never dare to use the title of *toliwaga*, and would even definitely
disclaim it if it were given to them. To sum up: the chief's privilege
of choice is limited by two conditions, the rank and the seamanship
of those he may select.

(4) A special feature, implied in the title of *toliwaga*, is the performance of magical duties. Magic during the process of construction is done by the expert, but magic done in connection with
sailing and Kula is done by the *toliwaga*. The latter must, by definition, know canoe magic.

2 Competitive expeditions: the *uvalaku*

The *uvalaku* is a Kula expedition on an exceptionally big scale, carried on with a definite social organisation under scrupulous observance of all ceremonial and magical rites, and distinguished from the smaller expeditions by its size, by a competitive element, and by one or two additional features. On an *uvalaku*, all the canoes in the district will sail, and they will sail fully manned. Everybody will be very eager to take part in it. Side by side with this natural desire, however, there exists the idea that all the members of the crews are under an obligation to go on the expedition. This duty they owe to the chief, or master of the *uvalaku*. The *toli'uvalaku*, as he is called, is always one of the sectional chiefs or headmen. He plays the part of a master of ceremonies, on leaving the beach of Sinaketa, at the distributions of food, on arrival in the overseas villages, and on the ceremonial return home. A streamer of dried and bleached pandanus leaf, attached to the prows of his canoe on a stick, is the ostensible sign of the dignity. The headman, who is *toli'uvalaku* on an expedition, will as a rule receive more Kula gifts than the others. On him also will devolve the glory of this particular expedition. Thus the title of *toli*, in this case, is one of honorary and nominal ownership, resulting mainly in renown (*butura*) for its bearer, and as such highly valued by the natives.

From the economic and legal point of view, however, the obligation binding the members of the expedition to him is the most important sociological feature. He gives the distribution of food, in which the others participate, and this imposes on them the duty of carrying out the expedition, however hard this might be, however often they would have to stop or even return owing to bad weather, contrary winds, or, in olden days, interference by hostile natives. As the natives say,

> We cannot return on *uvalaku*, for we have eaten of the pig, and we have chewed of the betel-nut given by the *toli'uvalaku*.

Only after the most distant community with whom the Sinaketans kula has been reached, and after due time has been allowed for the collection of any *vaygu'a* within reach, will the party start on the return journey. Concrete cases are quoted in which expeditions had to start several times from Sinaketa, always returning within a few days after all the provisions had been eaten

on Muwa, from where a contrary wind would not allow the canoes
to move south. Or again, a memorable expedition, some few
decades ago, started once or twice, was becalmed in Vakuta, had to
give a heavy payment to a wind magician in the village of Okinai to
provide them with a propitious northerly wind, and then, sailing
south at last, met with a *vineylida*, one of the dreadful perils of the
sea, a live stone which jumps from the bottom of the sea at a canoe.
But in spite of all this, they persevered, reached Dobu in safety, and
made a successful return.

Thus we see that, from a sociological point of view, the *uvalaku*
is an enterprise partially financed by the *toli'uvalaku*, and therefore
redounding to his credit, and bringing him honour; while the
obligation imposed on others by the food distributed to them, is to
carry on the expedition to a successful end.

I have said that an *uvalaku* expedition is distinguished from an
ordinary one, in so far also as the full ceremonial of the Kula has to
be observed. Thus all the canoes must be either new or relashed,
and without exception they must be also repainted and redecorated.
The full ceremonial launching, *tasasoria*, and the presentation,
kabigidoya, are carried out with every detail only when the Kula
takes the form of an *uvalaku*. The pig or pigs killed in the village
before departure are also a special feature of the competitive Kula.
So is the *kayguya'u* ceremonial distribution held on Muwa, just at
the point of the proceedings at which we have now arrived. The
tanarere, a big display of *vaygu'a* and comparison of the individual
acquisitions at the end of an expedition, is another ceremonial
feature of the *uvalaku* and supplies some of the competitive
element. There is also competition as to the speed, qualities and
beauties of the canoes at the beginning of such an expedition. Some
of the communities who present their *vaygu'a* to an *uvalaku*
expedition vie with one another, as to who will give most, and in
fact the element of emulation or competition runs right through the
proceedings.

Finally, a very important distinctive feature is the rule, that no
vaygu'a can be carried on the outbound sailing of an *uvalaku*. It
must not be forgotten that a Kula overseas expedition sails, in order
mainly to receive gifts and not to give them, and on an *uvalaku* this
rule is carried to its extreme, so that no Kula valuables whatever
may be given by the visiting party. The natives sailing from
Sinaketa to Dobu on ordinary Kula may carry a few arm-shells with

them, but when they sail on a ceremonial competitive *uvalaku*, no arm-shell is ever taken. For it must be remembered that Kula exchanges never take place simultaneously. It is always a gift followed after a lapse of time by a counter-gift. Now on a *uvalaku* the natives would receive in Dobu a certain amount of gifts, which, within a year or so, would be returned to the Dobuans, when these pay a visit to Sinaketa. But there is always a considerable amount of valuables which the Dobuans owe to the Sinaketans, so that when now the Sinaketans go to Dobu, they will claim also these gifts due to them from previous occasions.

3 Participation in the Kula

Not everyone who lives within the cultural sphere of the Kula does participate in it. More especially in the Trobriand Islands, there are whole districts which do not practise the Kula. Thus a series of villages in the north of the main island, the villages on the Island of Tuma, as well as the industrial villages of Kuboma and the agricultural ones of Tilataula do not practise Kula. In villages like Sinaketa, Vakuta, Gumasila and Nabwageta, every man carries on the Kula. The same applies to the small islands which link up the big gaps of the Kula chain, the islands of Kitava, Iwa, Gawa and Kwayawata, strewn on the seas between the Trobriands and Woodlark Island, to Tubetube and Wari, etc., etc. In the Dobuan-speaking district, on the other hand, I think that certain village complexes either do not practise Kula at all, or else practise it on a small scale, that is, their headmen have only a few partners in the neighbouring villages.

In some of the big chiefs' villages in Kiriwina there are certain people who never practice Kula. Thus in a village where the headman has the rank of *guya'u* (chief) or *gumguya'u* (minor chief) the commoners of the lowest rank and unrelated to the headman are not supposed to carry on the Kula. In olden days this rule would be very strictly observed, and nowadays even, though somewhat relaxed, not many commoners of this description practice the Kula. Limitations as to entry into the Kula, therefore, exist only in big Kula districts such as that of Dobu and of the Trobriands, and they are partly local, excluding whole villages, and partly social, excluding certain people of low rank.

The relation of partnership

The name for an overseas partner is in the Trobriand language *karayta'u*; 'my partner' is styled *ulo karayta'u*, *ulo* being the possessive pronoun of remote relation. The inland partners are known in Kiriwinian by the term denoting a friend, '*lubaygu*', the suffixed possessive pronoun *gu* being that of nearest possession.

Only after this relationship has been established between two men, can the two make Kula with one another. An overseas visitor would as a rule go to his partner's house and offer him a small present as *pari*. This again would be returned by the local man by means of a *talo'i* present. There would not be any great intimacy between two overseas partners. But, in sharp contrast to the essential hostility between two strange tribesmen, such a relationship of friendship would stand out as the most remarkable deviation from the general rule. In inland relations between two partners of neighbouring villages, the closeness and intimacy would be relatively small as compared to other ties. This relation was defined to me in these words:

> My partner same as my clansman (*kakaveyogu*) – he might fight me. My real kinsman (*veyogu*), same navel-string, would always side with us.

The best way of obtaining detailed information, and of eliminating any errors which might have crept into ethnographic generalisations, is to collect concrete data. I have drawn up a complete list of the partners of Kouta'uya, who is one of the biggest Kula men in the whole Ring; another list of a smaller Sinaketa headman, Toybayoba; and of course I know several complements of partners of smaller men, who, as a rule, have about four to six partners each.

The full list of Kouta'uya includes fifty-five men in the northern half of Boyowa, that is, in Luba, Kulumata and Kiriwina. From these the chief receives arm-shells. To the south, his partners in the southern districts of Boyowa and Vakuta are twenty-three by number; in the Amphletts eleven, and twenty-seven in Dobu. Thus we see that the numbers to the south and north almost balance, the southern exceeding the northern by six. These numbers include his partners in Sinaketa, where he makes Kula with all his fellow chiefs, and with all the headmen of the divisional villages, and in his own little village he kulas with his sons. But even there, everyone of his partners is either south or north to him, that is, either gives him the necklaces or arm-shells.

All the clans are represented in the list. Often when asked with regard to the name of some man, why he is in partnership with him, the answer would be – 'Because he is my kinsman', which means, in this case, clansman of equal rank. Men of other clans are included, as 'friends', or relatives-in-law, or for some other reason more or less imaginary.

The list of Toybayoba's partners includes twelve men to the north, four in southern Boyowa, three in the Amphletts and eleven in Dobu, the balance here also being on the southern side. As said above, minor men might have anything between four to ten partners all told, whereas there are men in northern Boyowa who have only two partners, one on each side of the ring, so to speak, with whom they make Kula.

In drawing up these lists, another striking feature comes to light: on both sides, there is a definite geographical limit beyond which a man cannot have any partners. For all men in the village of Sinaketa, for instance, this limit, as regards the arm-shells, coincides with the furthest boundary of Kiriwina; that is, no man from Sinaketa has any partners in Kitava, which is the next Kula district beyond Kiriwina. South, in the direction from which the *soulava* are received, the villages at the south-east end of Fergusson Island are the last places where partners of Sinaketan men are still to be found. The small island of Dobu itself lies just beyond this boundary, and no man in this island or in any of the villages on Normanby Island makes Kula with the Sinaketans (compare the circles, indicating Kula communities on Fig. 6).

Beyond these districts, the men still know the names of what could be called their partners-once-removed, that is, the partners of their partners. In the case of a man who has only a couple of partners on each side, who, again being modest men, have also only one or two, this relationship is not devoid of importance. If I, in Sinaketa, have one partner, say in Kiriwina, who again has one partner in Kitava, it is no small matter for me to learn that this Kitava man just obtained a splendid pair of arm-shells. For this means that there is about a quarter of a chance of my receiving these arm-shells, on the supposition that the Kitavan and Kiriwinian have two partners each between whom they can choose in bestowing them. In the case of a big chief like Kouta'uya, however, the number of once-removed partners becomes so great that they lose any personal significance for him. Kouta'uya has some twenty-five partners in Kiriwina; among them To'uluwa, the big chief, makes Kula with more than half of all the men in Kitava. Some other of Kouta'uya's partners in Kiriwina, of lesser rank, yet quite important, also make Kula with a great number, so that probably practically everybody in Kitava is Kouta'uya's partner-once-removed.

If we were to imagine that on the Kula Ring there are many people who have only one partner on each side, then the Ring would consist of a large number of closed circuits, on each of which the same articles would constantly pass. Thus if A in Kiriwina always kulas with B in Sinaketa who kulas with C in Tubetube, who kulas with D in Murua, who kulas with E in Kitava, who kulas with A in Kiriwina, then A B C D E A would form one such strand in the big Kula circuit. If an arm-shell got into the hands of one of them, it could never leave this strand. But the Kula Ring is nothing approaching this, because every small Kula partner has, as a rule, on one side or the other, a big one, that is a chief. And every chief plays the part of a shunting-station for Kula objects. Having so many partners on each side, he constantly transfers an object from one strand to another. Thus, any article which on its rounds has travelled through the hands of certain men, may on its second round come through an entirely different channel. This, of course, supplies a large part of the zest and excitement of the Kula exchange.

Entering the Kula relationship

In order to become a practising member of the Kula, a man must have passed the stage of adolescence; he must have the status and rank required, that is in such villages where this condition is demanded; he must know the magic of the Kula; and last, not least, he must be in possession of a piece of *vaygu'a*. The membership, with all its concomitant implications, may be received from the father, who teaches his son the magic, gives him a piece of *vaygu'a*, and provides him with a partner, very often in his own person.

Supposing one of the sons of Kouta'uya has reached the stage where a lad may begin to kula. The chief will have been teaching him the spells for some time already. Moreover the lad, who from childhood has taken part in overseas expeditions, has many a time seen the rites performed and heard the spells uttered. When the time is ripe, Kouta'uya, having the conch-shell blown, and with all due formalities, presents a *soulava* to his son. This latter, soon afterwards, goes somewhere north. Perhaps he goes only to one of the neighbouring villages within Sinaketa, perhaps he accompanies his father on a visit as far north as Omarakana, and in any case he makes Kula, either with one of his father's friends and partners, or with a special friend of his own. Thus, at one stroke, the lad is equipped with magic, *vaygu'a*, and two partners, one of whom is his father. His northern partner will give him in due course an arm-shell, and this he will probably offer to his father. The transactions once started continue. His father soon gives him another *vaygu'a*, which he may kula with the same northern partner, or he may try to establish another partnership. The next *mwali* (arm-shells) he receives from the north, he will probably give to another partner in the south, and thus establish a new relationship. A chief's son, who is always a commoner himself (since the chief cannot marry within his own sub-clan and the son has the status of his mother), would not multiply his partners beyond the limit numerically given by the above mentioned partners of Toybayoba.

Not everyone, however, is as fortunate as to be the son of a chief, which in the Trobriands is, on the whole, one of the most enviable positions, since it confers many privileges, and entails no special responsibilities. A young chief himself would have to pay substantially for establishing his position in the Kula, for a chief is always the son of a woman of high rank, and the nephew of a chief, though his father may be a commoner of small influence only. In any case, his maternal uncle will expect from him some *pokala* (offerings by instalment), in payment for magic, *vaygu'a*, and finally for a leading position in the Kula. The young chief would marry, and thus acquire wealth within limits, and with this he would have to give presents to his maternal uncle, who in turn would introduce him into the Kula, exactly as a chief does his son, only not disinterestedly.

A commoner enters into the Kula like a chief, with the only exception that everything is on a smaller scale, the amount of the *pokala* which he gives to his maternal uncle, the *vaygu'a* which he receives, and the number of partners with whom he kulas. When a man gives to another a piece of *vaygu'a*, of the Kula kind, but not

as a Kula exchange but as a gift, let us say as *youlo* (gift in repayment for the harvest supply offerings), this *vaygu'a* does not leave
the Kula Ring. The receiver, if he had not been in the Kula yet,
enters into it by acquiring the *vaygu'a*, and can then choose his
partner, and go on with the exchange.

Participation of women in the Kula

The Kula is essentially a man's type of activity. Women do not sail
on the big expeditions. From Kiriwina young unmarried girls would
sail east to Kitava, Iwa, and Gawa, and from these islands even old,
married women, indeed whole families, come to Kiriwina. But they
do not carry on overseas Kula exchange, neither among themselves,
nor with men.

In Kiriwina, some women, notably the chief's wives, are
admitted to the honour and privilege of exchanging *vaygu'a*,
though in such cases the transactions are done *en famille*. To take a
concrete case, in October or November, 1915, To'uluwa, the chief
of Omarakana, brought a fine haul of *mwali* from Kitava. The best
pair of these he presented to his veteran wife, Bokuyoba, a wife
whom he had inherited from his elder brother Numakala.
Bokuyoba in turn gave the pair, without much delay, to Kadamwasila, the favourite wife of the chief, the mother of five sons and
one daughter. She again gave it to her son, Namwana Guyau, who
kulad it on to some of his southern partners. Next time he receives a
soulava necklace, he will give it, not to his father directly, but to his
mother, who will hand it over to her senior colleague, and this
venerable lady will give it to To'uluwa. The whole transaction is
evidently a complimentary interpolation of the two *giyovila* (chief's
wives) in between the simple transaction of the chief giving the
vaygu'a to his son. This interpolation gives the women much
pleasure, and is highly valued by them.

In southern Boyowa, that is in Sinaketa and Vakuta, the rôle of
women is similar, but they play besides another part. A man would
sometimes send his wife with a Kula gift to his partner in the neighbouring village. On some occasions, when he needs *vaygu'a* very
badly, as for instance when he is expecting some *uvalaku* visitors,
his wife may help him to obtain the *vaygu'a* from that partner. For,
though this latter might refuse to give it to his Sinaketan partner, he
would not do so to his wife. It must be added that no sexual

motives are associated with it, and that it is only a sort of customary compliment paid to the fair sex.

In Dobu, the wife or the sister of a man is always credited with a great influence over his Kula decisions. Therefore, there is a special form of magic, used by the Sinaketans, in order to act on the minds of the Dobuan women. Although, in matters of sex, a Trobriander would have absolutely to keep aloof from Dobuan women, married or unmarried, he would approach them with nice speeches and gifts in matters of Kula. He would reproach an unmarried girl with her brother's conduct towards him. She would then ask for a piece of betel nut. This would be given with some magic spoken over it, and the girl, it is believed, would then influence her brother to kula with his partner.

4 Gifts and modes of transaction

The main principle of the Kula exchange has been laid down in the previous chapter; the Kula exchange has always to be a *gift*, followed by a *counter-gift*; it can never be a barter, a direct exchange with assessment of equivalents and with haggling. There must be always in the Kula two transactions, distinct in name, in nature and in time. The exchange is opened by an initial or opening gift called *vaga*, and closed by a final or return present called *yotile*. They are both ceremonial gifts, they have to be accompanied by the blow of a conch-shell, and the present is given ostentatiously and in public. The native term 'to throw' a valuable describes well the nature of the act. For, though the valuable has to be handed over by the giver, the receiver hardly takes any notice of it, and seldom receives it actually into his hands. The etiquette of the transaction requires that the gift should be given in an off-hand, abrupt, almost angry manner, and received with equivalent nonchalance and disdain. A slight modification in this is introduced when, as it happens sometimes, in the Trobriands, and in the Trobriands only, the *vaygu'a* is given by a chief to a commoner, in which case the commoner would take it into his hand, and show some appreciation of it. In all other cases, the valuable would be placed within the reach of the receiver, and an insignificant member of his following would pick it up.

It is not very easy to unravel the various motives which combine to make up this customary behaviour on receiving and giving a gift. The part played by the receiver is perhaps not so difficult to interpret. Right through their ceremonial and commercial give and take, there runs the crude and fundamental human dissatisfaction with the value received. A native will always, when speaking about a transaction, insist on the magnitude and value of the gift he gave, and minimise those of the equivalent accepted. Side by side with this, there is the essential native reluctance to appear in want of anything, a reluctance which is most pronounced in the case of food. Both these motives combine to produce the, after all, very human and understandable attitude of disdain at the reception of a gift. In the case of the donor, the histrionic anger with which he gives an object might be, in the first place, a direct expression of the natural human dislike of parting with a possession. Added to this, there is the attempt to enhance the apparent value of the gift by showing what a wrench it is to give it away.

The two gifts of the Kula are also distinct in time. It is quite obvious this must be so in the case of an overseas expedition of an *uvalaku* type, on which no valuables whatever are taken with them by the visiting party, and so any valuable received on such an occasion, whether as *vaga* or *yotile*, cannot therefore be exchanged at the same time. But even when the exchange takes place in the same village during an inland Kula, there must be an interval between the two gifts, of a few minutes at least.

There are also deep differences in the nature of the two gifts. The *vaga*, as the opening gift of the exchange, has to be given spontaneously, that is, there is no enforcement of any duty in giving it. There are means of soliciting it (*wawoyla*), but no pressure can be employed. The *yotile*, however, that is, the valuable which is given in return for the valuable previously received, is given under pressure of a certain obligation. If I have given a *vaga* (opening gift of valuable) to a partner of mine, let us say a year ago, and now, when on a visit, I find that he has an equivalent *vaygu'a*, I shall consider it his duty to give it to me. If he does not do so, I am angry with him, and justified in being so. Not only that, if I can by any chance lay my hand on his *vaygu'a* and carry it off by force (*lebu*), I am entitled by custom to do this, although my partner in that case may become very irate. The quarrel over that would again be half histrionic, half real.

Another difference between a *vaga* and a *yotile* occurs in overseas expeditions which are not *uvalaku*. On such expeditions, valuables sometimes are carried, but only such as are due already for a past *vaga*, and are to be given as *yotile*. Opening gifts, *vaga*, are never taken overseas.

As mentioned above, the *vaga* entails more wooing or soliciting than the *yotile*. This process, called by the natives *wawoyla*, consists, among others of a series of solicitary gifts. One type of such gifts is called *pokala*, and consists of food. As a rule, a considerable amount of food is taken on an expedition, and when a good valuable is known to be in the possession of a man, some of this food will be presented to him, with the words: 'I *pokala* your valuable; give it to me.' If the owner is not inclined to part with his valuable, he will not accept the *pokala*. If accepted, it is an intimation that the *vaygu'a* will sooner or later be given to the man who offers the *pokala*. The owner, however, may not be prepared to part with it at once, and may wish to receive more solicitary gifts.

Another type of such a gift is called *kaributu*, and consists of a valuable which, as a rule, is not one of those which are regularly kulaed. Thus, a small polished axe blade, or a valuable belt is given with the words: 'I *kaributu* your necklace (or arm-shells); I shall take it and carry it off.' This gift again may only be accepted if there is an intention to satisfy the giver with the desired *vaygu'a*. A very famous and great valuable will often be solicited by gift of *pokala* and of *kaributu*, one following the other. If, after one or two of such solicitary gifts, the big *vaygu'a* is finally given, the satisfied receiver will often give some more food to his partner, which gift is called *kwaypolu*.

The food gifts would be returned on a similar occasion if it arises. But there would be no strict equivalence in the matter of food. The *kaributu* gift of a valuable, however, would always have to be returned later on, in an equivalent form. It may be added that the *pokala* offerings of food would be most often given from a district, where food is more abundant than in the district to which it is carried. Thus, the Sinaketans would bring *pokala* to the Amphletts, but they would seldom or never *pokala* the Dobuans, who are very rich in food. Again, within the Trobriands, a *pokala* would be offered from the northern agricultural district of Kiriwina to men of Sinaketa, but not inversely.

It must be noted that all these expressions are given in the language of the Trobriands, and they refer to the gifts exchanged between the northern and southern Trobriands on the one hand, and these latter and the Amphletts on the other. In an overseas expedition from Sinaketa to Dobu, the solicitary gifts would be rather given wholesale, as the visitors' gifts of *pari*, and the subtle distinctions in name and in technicality would not be observed. That this must be so becomes clear, if we realise that, whereas, between the northern and southern Trobriands the news about an exceptionally good valuable spreads easily and quickly, this is not the case between Dobu and Boyowa. Going over to Dobu, therefore, a man has to make up his mind, whether he will give any solicitary presents to his partner, what and how much he will give him, without knowing whether he has any specially fine valuables to expect from him or not. If, however, there was any exceptionally valuable gift in the visitors' *pari*, it will have to be returned later on by the Dobuans.

Another important type of gift essential to the Kula is that of the intermediary gifts, called *basi*. Let us imagine that a Sinaketan man has given a very fine pair of arm-shells to his Dobuan partner at their last meeting in Sinaketa. Now, arriving in Dobu, he finds that his partner has not got any necklace equivalent in value to the arm-shells given. He none the less will expect his partner to give him meanwhile a necklace, even though it be of inferior value. Such a gift is a *basi*, that is, not a return of the highly valuable *vaga*, but a gift given to fill in the gap. This *basi* will have to be repaid by a small equivalent pair of arm-shells at a later date. And the Dobuan on his side has still to repay the big arm-shells he received, and for which he has as yet got no equivalent in his possession. As soon as this is obtained, it will be given, and will close the transaction as a clinching gift, or *kudu*. Both these names imply figures of speech. *Kudu* means 'tooth', and is a good name for a gift which clinches or bites. *Basi* means to pierce, or to stab.

The equivalence of the two gifts, *vaga* and *yotile*, is expressed by the word *kudu* (tooth) and *bigeda* (it will bite). Another figure of speech describing the equivalence is contained in the word *va'i*, to marry. When two of the opposite valuables meet in the Kula and are exchanged, it is said that these two have married. The arm-shells are conceived as a female principle, and the necklaces as the male.

The idea of equivalence in the Kula transaction is very strong and definite, and when the receiver is not satisfied with the *yotile* (return gift) he will violently complain that it is not a proper 'tooth' (*kuda*) for his opening gift, that it is not a real 'marriage', that it is not properly 'bitten'.

A few more words must be said on the subject of the valuables used in the Kula. I said in chapter 7, stating the case briefly, that in one direction travel the arm-shells, whilst in the opposite, following the hands of the clock, travel the necklaces. It must now be added that the *mwali* – arm-shells – are accompanied by another article, the *doga*, or circular boar's tusks. In olden days, the *doga* were almost as important as the *mwali* in the stream of the Kula. Nowadays, hardly any at all are to be met as Kula articles. It is not easy to explain the reason for this change. In an institution having the importance and traditional tenacity which we find in the Kula, there can be no question of the interference of fashion to bring about changes. The only reason which I can suggest is that nowadays, with immensely increased intertribal intercourse, there is a great drainage on all Kula valuables by other districts lying outside the Kula. Now, on the one hand the *doga* are extremely valued on the mainland of New Guinea, much more, I assume, than they are within the Kula district. The drainage therefore would affect the *doga* much more strongly than any other articles, one of which, the spondylus necklaces, are actually imported into the Kula region from without, and even manufactured by white men in considerable quantities for native consumption. The arm-shells are produced within the district in sufficient numbers to replace any leakage, but *doga* are extremely difficult to reproduce as they are connected with a rare freak of nature – a boar with a circular tusk.

There is one important exception in the respective movements of necklace and arm-shell. A certain type of spondylus shell strings, much bigger and coarser than the strings which are used in the Kula, are produced in Sinaketa. These strings, called *katudababile* in Kiriwinian, or *sama'upa* in Dobuan, are sometimes exported from Sinaketa to Dobu as Kula gifts, and function therefore as arm-shells. These *katudababile*, however, never complete the Kula ring, in the wrong direction, as they never return to the Trobriands from the east. Part of them are absorbed into the districts outside the Kula, part of them come back again to Sinaketa, and join the other necklaces in their circular movement.

Another class of articles, which often take a subsidiary part in the Kula exchange, consists of the large and thin polished axe blades, called in the Kiriwinian language *beku*. They are never used for any practical purposes, and fulfil only the function of tokens of wealth and objects of parade. In the Kula they would be given as *kaributu* (solicitary gifts), and would go both ways. As they are quarried in Woodlark Island and polished in Kiriwina, they would, however, move in the direction from the Trobriands to Dobu more frequently than in the opposite one.

Although, as we have seen, there is both a good deal of ceremony attached to the transaction and a good deal of decorum, one might even say commercial honour, implied in the technicalities of the exchange, there is much room left as well for quarrelling and friction. If a man obtains a very fine valuable, which he is not already under an obligation to offer as *yotile* (return payment), there will be a number of his partners, who will compete to receive it. As only one can be successful, all the others will be thwarted and more or less offended and full of malice. Still more room for bad blood is left in the matter of equivalence. As the valuables exchanged cannot be measured or even compared with one another by an exact standard; as there are no definite correspondence or indices of correlation between the various kinds of the valuables, it is not easy to satisfy a man who has given a *vaygu'a* of high value. On receiving a repayment (*yotile*), which he does not consider equivalent, he will not actually make a scene about it, or even show his displeasure openly in the act. But he will feel a deep resentment, which will express itself in frequent recriminations and abuse. These, though not made to his partner's face, will reach his ears sooner or later. Eventually, the universal method of settling differences may be resorted to – that of black magic, and a sorcerer will be paid to cast some evil spell over the offending party.

When speaking about some celebrated *vaygu'a*, a native will praise its value in the words: 'Many men died because of it' – which does not mean that they died in battle or fight, but were killed by black magic. Again, there is a system of signs by which one can recognise, on inspecting the corpse the day after death, for what reasons it has been bewitched. Among these signs there are one or two which mean that the man has been done away with, because of his success in Kula, or because he has offended somebody in connection with it. The mixture of punctilio and decorum, on the one hand, with passionate resentment and greed on the other, must be realised as underlying all the transactions, and giving the leading psychological tone to the natives' interest. The obligation of fairness and decency is based on the general rule, that it is highly improper and dishonourable to be mean. Thus, though a man will generally strive to belittle the thing received, it must not be forgotten that the man who gave it was genuinely eager to do his best. And after all, in some cases when a man receives a really fine valuable, he will boast of it and be frankly satisfied. Such a success is attributed of course not to his partner's generosity, but to his own magic.

A feature which is universally recognised as reprehensible and discreditable, is a tendency to retain a number of valuables and be slow in passing them on. A man who did this would be called 'hard in the Kula'. The following is a native description of this feature as exhibited by the natives of the Amphletts.

> The Gumasila, their Kula is very hard; they are mean, they are retentive. They would like to take hold of one *soulava*, of two, of three big ones, of four perhaps. A man would *pokola* them, he would *pokapokala*; if he is a kinsman he will get a *soulava*. The Kayleula only, and the Gumasila are mean. The Dobu, the Du'a'u, the Kitava are good. Coming to Muyuwa – they are like Gumasila.

This means that a man in Gumasila would let a number of necklaces accumulate in his possession; would require plenty of food as *pokala* – a characteristic reduplication describes the insistence and perseverance in *pokala* – and even then he would give a necklace to a kinsman only. When I inquired from the same informant whether such a mean man would also run a risk of being killed by sorcery, he answered:

> A man, who is very much ahead in the Kula – he will die – the mean man not; he will sit in peace.

5 Trade in the Kula

The trade takes place between the visitors and local natives, who are not their partners, but who must belong to the community with whom the Kula is made. Thus, Numanuma, Tu'utauna and Bwayowa are the three communities which form what we have called the 'Kula community' with whom the Sinaketans stand in the relation of partnership. And a Sinaketa man will *gimwali* (trade) only with a man from one of these villages who is not his personal partner.

When the visiting party from Sinaketa arrive, the natives from the neighbouring districts, that is, from the small island of Dobu proper, from the other side of Dawson Straits, from Deyde'i, the village to the south, will assemble in the three Kula villages. These natives from other districts bring with them a certain amount of goods. But they must not trade directly with the visitors from Boyowa. They must exchange their goods with the local natives, and these again will trade them with the Sinaketans. Thus the hosts from the Kula community act as intermediaries in any trading relations between the Sinaketans and the inhabitants of more remote districts.

To sum up the sociology of these transactions, we may say that the visitor enters into a three-fold relation with the Dobuan natives. First, there is his partner, with whom he exchanges general gifts on the basis of free give and take, a type of transaction, running side by side with the Kula proper. Then there is the local resident, not his personal Kula partner, with whom he carries on *gimwali*. Finally there is the stranger with whom an indirect exchange is carried on through the intermediation of the local men. With all this, it must not be imagined that the commercial aspect of the gathering is at all conspicuous. The concourse of the natives is great, mainly owing to their curiosity, to see the ceremonial reception of the *uvalaku* party. But if I say that every visitor from Boyowa, brings and carries away about half-a-dozen articles, I do not under-state the case. Some of these articles the Sinaketan has acquired in the industrial districts of Boyowa during his preliminary trading expedition. On these he scores a definite gain. A few samples of the prices paid in Boyowa and those received in Dobu will indicate the amount of this gain. This table shows in its second column the prices paid by the Sinaketans to the industrial villages of Kuboma, a district in the northern Trobriands. In the third column what they receive in Dobu is recorded. The table has been obtained from a Sinaketan informant, and it probably is far from accurate, and the transactions are sure to vary greatly in the gain which they afford. There is no doubt, however, that for each article, the Sinaketan would ask the price which he paid for them as well as some extra article.

Kuboma to Sinaketa			Dobu to Sinaketa
1 *tanepopo* basket	= 12 coconuts	= 12	coconuts + sago + 1 belt
1 comb	= 4 coconuts	= 4	coconuts + 1 bunch of betel
1 armlet	= 8 coconuts	= 8	coconuts + 2 bundles of betel
1 lime pot	= 12 coconuts	= 12	coconuts + 2 pieces of sago

Thus we see that there is in this transaction a definite gain obtained by the middlemen. The natives of Sinaketa act as intermediaries between the industrial centres of the Trobriands and Dobu, whereas their hosts play the same rôle between the Sinaketans and the men from the outlying districts.

It will be best to say here at once all that is necessary about the trade between Kiriwina and Kitava. As these two districts are geologically and in other respects much more similar to one another than Sinaketa and Dobu are, the trade is not of such vital importance, with one notable exception, as we shall see. The articles of subsidiary trade, which a Kiriwinian expedition would carry with them to Kitava, are the following: wooden combs; various classes of lime pots; armlets, plaited of fern fibre; turtle-shell earrings; mussel shell; coils of lashing creeper (*wayugo*); plaited fern belts, made originally in the d'Entrecasteaux. Of these articles, the most important are probably the mussel shells, used for scraping and as knives, the various kinds of lime pots, which are a speciality of Kuboma, and last, but not least, the *wayugo*. I am not quite certain as to whether this creeper is not to be found in Kitava, but as it grows only on marshy soil, it is hardly probable that it would thrive on a high, raised, coral island. In that case, the creeper is certainly the most indispensable of all the trade articles imported into Kitava from the Trobriands.

The Trobrianders import from the smaller islands a class of grass skirt made of coconut leaves; exceptionally well finished urn-shaped baskets; small hand-baskets; specially bleached pandanus mats; ornaments made of fragments of conus shell; certain classes of cowrie shell, used for ornamenting belts; ebony lime spatulae; ebony walking staves; sword-clubs carved in ebony; and an aromatic black paint, made of charred sandalwood. None of these articles is of vital importance, as all of them, though perhaps in slightly different or even inferior quality, are manufactured or found in the Trobriands.

There was one article, however, which, in the olden days, was of surpassing utility to the Trobriand natives, and which they could obtain only from Kitava, though it came originally from further east, from Murua (Woodlark Island). These were the *kukumali*, or roughly shaped pieces of green-stone, which were then polished in the Trobriands, and in this state used as stone implements, while the biggest of them, very large and thin and well polished all over, became a specially important class of *vaygu'a* (articles of high value). Although the practical use of stone implements has naturally been done away with by the introduction of steel and iron, the *beku* (valuable axe blades) have still an undiminished, indeed, an increased value, as the white traders have to use them for purchasing pearls from the natives. It is important to note that although all the raw material for these stone implements and valuables had to be imported from Kitava, the finished valuables were and are re-exported again, as Kiriwina is still the main polishing district.

6 Inland Kula

Omarakana is still the centre of the Trobriand inland Kula, and, in certain respects, still one of the most important places on the ring. It is probably the only locality where the Kula is or ever was to some extent concentrated in the hands of one man, and it is also the capital of the important district of Kiriwina, which dominates all the inland Kula of the northern Trobriands, and links up the island of Kitava with the western islands of Kayleula and Kuyawa.

Previously, in the definition of the fundamentals of the Kula, we saw that the population of the Ring can be divided into what we called *Kula communities*. These divisions, as we remember, were distinguished by the fact that each one makes overseas expeditions of its own. For example, the Sinaketans, as we saw, make their trips to Dobu in a body, and although the Vakutans may go with them at the same time, the two fleets sail and act as independent units. Again, the whole district of Kiriwina sails to the east, to Kitava, as one fleet. But no Sinaketan canoe could ever form part of it. Another distinguishing characteristic of a Kula community is that the furthest limits of partnership are the same for all its members. There are again certain differences between the manner of conducting transactions within a Kula community on the one hand, and between members of two communities on the other.

Kiriwina is one of such Kula communities, and Sinaketa is another. Yet the two are not divided by sea, and the style of exchange, when this is carried on between two Kula communities which lie in the same district, differs also from that of overseas Kula. Our first task here will be therefore to mark out clearly the lines of distinction between:

1. The transactions of Kula carried on overseas, from one district to another.
2. Kula between two distinct but contiguous 'Kula communities'.
3. Transactions within a 'Kula community'.

The facts belonging to the first heading have been described at length, and it will be enough to point out in what the second type differs from the first. Obviously, when two districts on the same island, such as Kiriwina and Sinaketa, make the exchange there is no overseas sailing, no preparation of canoes, no launching, no *kabigidoya*. Sometimes big joint expeditions are made by the one community to the other and a great haul of *vaygu'a* is carried home. As an example of that, we may mention the visit made by the Sinaketans to Kiriwina in the last days of March, 1918, when a great number of *mwali* were brought, in readiness for the Dobuan *uvalaku* visit. When such an important visit is made from one Trobriand district to another, some of the Kula magic will be performed, but obviously not all, for there is no *lilava* bundle to be medicated, since no trade is carried; no dangerous cannibals have to be tamed by the *ka'ubana'i* rite, for the hosts are, and always have been, friendly neighbours. But some of the beauty magic, and the enticing formula over betel-nut would be recited to obtain as many valuables as possible. Of course there is no associated trade on such expeditions, for there is very little to exchange between Sinaketa and Kiriwina, and what there is, is done independently, in a regular manner all the year round. Partnership between people of two such Kula communities is very much the same as within one of them. It obtains between people speaking the same language, having the same customs and institutions, many of whom are united by bonds of actual kinship or relationship-in-law.

Let us pass now to the relation between categories 2 and 3, that is between Kula of two contiguous 'Kula communities', and the Kula within one of them. First of all, in the inland Kula within the same community, there never take place big, wholesale transactions. The circulation of *vaygu'a* consists of individual exchanges, sometimes

more frequent, that is, whenever an overseas expedition has come
home laden with many valuables, sometimes done at long intervals.
No magic is performed in this type of Kula, and though there is a
certain amount of ceremony accompanying each gift, there are no
big, public gatherings. A concrete description of an actual case may
serve best to illustrate these general statements.

During the eight months I stayed in Omarakana in 1915–16, I
had the opportunity of watching many cases of inland Kula, as
there was a constant come and go between Kiriwina and Kitava,
and subsequent to each influx of arm-shells from the east, a series
of exchanges took place. In the month of November, To'uluwa
went with his canoe on a small expedition across the sea to Kitava,
and brought back a good haul of *mwali* (arm-shells). He arrived on
an evening on the beach of Kaulukuba, and word was sent over to
the village that next day he would come up with his trophies. In the
morning, blowings of conch-shell, heard from the distance,
announced the approach of the returning party, and soon,
preceded by one of his small sons carrying the conch-shell,
To'uluwa made his appearance, followed by his companions. Each
man carried a few pairs which he had obtained, whilst the chief's
share was brought in on a stick, hanging down in a chaplet.

Next day, several *soulava* (spondylus shell necklaces) were
brought to Omarakana by the various men from neighbouring
villages to the west, and ceremonially offered to To'uluwa. This
was, in each case, a *vaga* (opening gift), for which the giver expected
to receive his *yotile* (clinching gift) at once from the store of *mwali*.
In this case we see the influence of chieftainship in the relation
between Kula partners. In the inland Kula of Kiriwina, all gifts
would be brought to To'uluwa, and he would never have to fetch or
carry his presents. Moreover, he would always be given and never
give the opening gift (*vaga*), while his gift would invariably be a
yotile. So that the chief sometimes owes a Kula gift to a commoner,
but a commoner never owes a gift to a chief. The difference
between the rules of procedure here and those of an *uvalaku* overseas expedition is clear: in a competitive overseas expedition,
valuables for exchange are never carried by the visiting party, who
only receive gifts and bring them back home; in the inland Kula,
the determining factor is the relative social position of the two
partners. Gifts are brought to the man of superior by the man of
inferior rank, and the latter has also to initiate the exchange.

The following entry is quoted literally from my notes, made in Omarakana, on November the 13th, 1915. 'This morning, the headman of Wagaluma brought a *bagido'u* (fine necklace). At the entrance to the village (it is Omarakana), they (the party) halted, blew the conch-shell, put themselves in order. Then, the conch-shell blower went ahead, the men of highest rank took the stick with the *bagido'u*, a boy carrying the heavy wooden bell pendant on a *kaboma* (wooden dish). The headman approached To'uluwa and said: "*Agukuleya, ikanawo*; *lagayla lamaye*; *yoku kayne gala mwali.*" This he said in thrusting the stick into the thatch of the chief's house.' The words literally mean: 'My *kuleya* (food left over), take it; I brought it today; have you perhaps no arm-shells?' The expression 'food left over,' applied to the gift was a depreciating term, meaning something which is an overflow or unwanted scrap. Thus he was ironically depreciating his gift, and at the same time implying that much wealth still remained in his possession. By this, in an oblique manner, he bragged about his own riches, and with the last phrase, expressing doubt as to whether To'uluwa had any arm-shells, he threw a taunt at the chief. This time the gift was returned immediately by a fine pair of arm-shells.

Many more transactions took place in those two days or so; sounds of conch-shells were heard on all sides as they were blown first in the village from which the men started, then on the way, then at the entrance to Omarakana, and finally at the moment of giving. Again, after some time another blast announced the return gift by To'uluwa, and the receding sounds of the conch marked the stages of the going home of the party. To'uluwa himself never receives a gift with his own hands; it is always hung up in his house or platform, and then somebody of his household takes charge of it; but the commoner receives the arm-shell himself from the hands of the chief.

Not all the arm-shells brought from Kitava were thus at once given away. Some of them were kept for the purposes of more distant Kula; or to be given on some future, special occasion when a present had to be handed over in association with some ceremony. In the inland Kula, there is always an outbreak of transactions whenever a big quantity of valuables is imported into the district. And afterwards, sporadic transactions happen now and then. For the minor partners who had received arm-shells from To'uluwa would not all of them keep them for any length of time,

but part of them would be sooner or later passed on in inland transactions. But, however these valuables might spread over the
district, they would be always available when an expedition from
another Kula community would come and claim them. When the
party from Sinaketa came in March, 1918, to Omarakana, all those
who owned arm-shells would either come to the capital or else be
visited in their villages by their Sinaketan partners. Of the 154 or so
arm-shells obtained in Kiriwina on that occasion, only thirty came
from To'uluwa himself, and fifty from Omarakana altogether,
while the rest were given from other villages.

Thus the inner Kula does not affect the flow of the main stream,
and however the valuables might change hands within the 'Kula
community', it matters little for the outside flow.

7   The Kula in Kitava

It has been mentioned before, in fact it is obvious from the account
of the *uvalaku* custom that the Kula does not run with an even
flow, but in violent gushes. Thus the *uvalaku* expedition from
Dobu in 1918 carried about 800 pairs of arm-shells from Boyowa.
Such sudden rushes of the Kula articles are associated with an
important institution, which is not known in the Trobriands or in
Dobu, but which we find in Kitava and further along the Ring, as
far as Tubetube. When a man dies, custom imposes a taboo upon
the inhabitants of that village. This means that no one on a visit is
received in the village, and no Kula articles are given away from
there. The community lying under the taboo, however, expect to
receive as many Kula gifts as possible, and busy themselves in that
matter. After a certain time, a big ceremony and distribution of
goods, called *so'i*, is held, and invitations are sent out to all the
Kula partners, and, in the case of a big affair, even to people from
districts beyond the boundary of partnership. A big distribution of
food takes place in which all the guests receive their share, and then
the Kula valuables are given in great quantities to the partners of
that community.

The importance of such economic taboos at times of mourning is
due to another widespread association, namely that which obtains
between mourning and feasts, or, more correctly, distributions of
food, which are made at intervals during a more or less prolonged
period after a person's death. An especially big feast, or rather

distribution, is made at the end of the period, and on this occasion the accumulated goods, usually coconut, betel-nut and pigs, are distributed. Death among all the coastal natives of eastern New Guinea causes a great and permanent disturbance in the equilibrium of tribal life. On the one hand, there is the stemming of the normal flow of economic consumption. On the other hand, an innumerable series of rites, ceremonies and festive distributions, which one and all create all sorts of reciprocal obligations, take up the best part of the energy, attention and time of the natives for a period of a few months, or a couple of years according to the importance of the dead. The immense social and economic upheaval which occurs after each death is one of the most salient features of the culture of these natives, and one also which on its surface strikes us as enigmatic and which entices into all sorts of speculations and reflections. What makes the problem still more obscure and complex is the fact that all these taboos, feasts, and rites have nothing whatever to do, in the belief of the natives, with the spirit of the deceased. This latter has gone at once and settled definitely in another world, entirely oblivious of what happens in the villages and especially of what is done in memory of his former existence.

9   Perils, magic and myths

1 Taboos

In native terminology, the realm of the magical is called by the word *megwa*, which describes the 'magical performance', the 'spell', the 'force' or 'virtue' of magic, and can be used as adjective to describe in general everything which presents a magical character. Used as a verb, the words *megwa*, *miga-megwa*, *miga*, all of which are variations of the same root, mean: 'to perform magic', 'to utter a spell', 'to carry out a rite'. If the natives want to express that certain actions are done in connection with magic, and not with work, and that certain effects are due to magical forces, and not to other efforts, they used the word *megwa* as a substantive or adjective. It is never used to describe any virtue residing in a man or a thing, nor for any action which is independent of a spell.

The associated concept of taboo is covered by the Kiriwinian word *bomala* (with suffixed possessive pronouns). It means a 'prohibition', something which a man is not allowed to do under any circumstances. It is used for magical taboos, for prohibitions associated with rank, for restrictions in regard to food generally considered as unclean, as, for example, the flesh of lizards, snakes, dogs and man. There is hardly any trace of the meaning of 'sacred' attached to the word *bomala*. If anywhere, it can be found in the use of the word *boma*, for a tabooed grove where men usually are not allowed to enter, and where traditional spots, often original holes where men came out and whence magic issued, are to be found. The expression *toboma* (*to-*, prefix denoting personal noun) means a man of high rank, but hardly a sacred man.

The canoe on a Kula expedition is surrounded by taboos, and many observances have to be strictly kept, else this or that might go wrong. Thus it is not allowed to 'point to objects with the hand' (*yosala yamada*), or those who do it will become sick. A new canoe has many prohibitions connected with it which are called *bomala wayugo* (the taboos of the lashing creeper). Eating and drinking are not allowed in a new canoe except after sunset. The breaking of this taboo would make the canoe very slow. On a very quick *waga* this rule might perhaps be disregarded, especially if one of the young boys were hungry or thirsty. The *toliwaga* would then bale in some sea-water, pour it over one of the lashings of the creeper with the words:

I sprinkle thy eye, O *kudayuri* creeper, so that our crew might eat.

After that, he would give the boy something to eat and drink. Besides this eating and drinking taboo, on a new *waga* the other physiological needs must not be satisfied. In case of urgent necessity, a man jumps into the water, holding to one of the cross sticks of the outrigger, or if it were a small boy, he is lowered into the water by one of the elders. This taboo, if broken, would also make the canoe slow. These two taboos, however, as was said, are kept only on a new *waga*, that is on such a one which either sails for the first time, or else has been relashed and repainted before this trip. The taboos are in all cases not operative on the return journey. Women are not allowed to enter a new *waga* before it sails. Certain types of yams may not be carried on a canoe which has been lashed with the rites of one of the *wayugo* magical systems. There are several systems of this magic, and each has got its specific taboos. These last taboos are to be kept right through the sailing. On account of the magic of safety, as it might be called, a canoe has to be kept free from contact with earth, sand and stones. Hence the natives of Sinaketa do not beach their canoes if they can possibly avoid it.

Among the specific taboos of the Kula, called *bomala lilava* (taboos of the magical bundle), there is a strict rule referring to the entering of a canoe. This must not be entered from any other point but on the *vitovaria*, that is, the front side of the platform, facing the mast. A native has to scale the platform at this place, then, crouching low, pass to the back or front, and there descend into the body of the canoe, or sit down where he is. The compartment facing the *lilava* (magical bundle) is filled out with other trade goods. In front of it sits the chief, behind it the man who handles the sheets. The natives have special expressions which denote the various manners of illicitly entering a canoe, and, in some of the canoe exorcisms, these expressions are used to undo the evil effects of the breaking of these taboos. Other prohibitions, which the natives call the taboo of the *mwasila*, though not associated with the *lilava*, are those which do not allow of using flower wreaths, red ornaments or red flowers in decorating the canoe or the bodies of the crew. The red colour of such ornaments is, according to native belief, magically incompatible with the aim of the expedition – the acquisition of the red spondylus necklaces. Also, yams may not be roasted on the outward journey, while later on, in Dobu, no local food may be eaten, and the natives have to subsist on their own provisions, until the first Kula gifts have been received.

There are, besides, definite rules referring to the behaviour of one canoe towards another, but these vary considerably with the different villages. In Sinaketa, such rules are very few; no fixed sequence is observed in the sailing order of the canoes, any one of them can start first, and if one of them is swifter it may pass any of the others, even that of a chief. This, however, has to be done so that the slower canoe is not passed on the outrigger side. Should this happen, the transgressing canoe has to give the other one a peace offering (*lula*), because it has broken a *bomala lilava*, it has offended the magical bundle.

2   Flying witches

Of all the dangerous and frightful beings met with on a sailing expedition, the most unpleasant, the best known and most dreaded are the flying witches, the *yoyova* or *mulukwausi*. The former name means a woman endowed with such powers, whereas *mulukwausi* describes the second self of the woman, as it flies disembodied through the air. Thus, for instance, they would say that such and such a woman in Wawela is a *yoyova*. But sailing at night, one would have to be on the look-out for *mulukwausi*, among whom might possibly be the double of that woman in Wawela. Very often, especially at moments when the speaker would be under the influence of fear of these beings, the deprecating euphemism – '*vivila*' (women) would be used. And probably our Boyowan mariners would speak of them thus in their talk round the campfire, for fear of attracting them by sounding their real name. Dangerous as they always are, at sea they become infinitely more dreaded. For the belief is deep that in case of shipwreck or mishap at sea, no real evil can befall the crews except by the agency of the dreaded women.

The orthodox belief is that a woman who is a *yoyova* can send forth a double which is invisible at will, but may appear in the form of a flying fox or of a night bird or a firefly. There is also a belief that a *yoyova* develops within her a something, shaped like an egg, or like a young, unripe coconut. This something is called as a matter of fact *kapuwana*, which is the word for a small coconut. This idea remains in the native's mind in a vague, indefinite, undifferentiated form, and any attempt to elicit a more detailed definition by asking him such questions, as to whether the *kapuwana* is a material object or not, would be to smuggle our own categories into his belief, where they do not exist. The *kapuwana* is anyhow believed to be the something which in the nightly flights leaves the body of the *yoyova* and assumes the various forms in which the *mulukwausi* appears. Another variant of the belief about the *yoyova* is that those who know their magic especially well can fly themselves, bodily transporting themselves through the air.

The flying witches are a nefarious agency, second in importance to the *bwaga'u* (male sorcerer), but in efficiency far more deadly even than he himself. In contrast to the *bwaga'u*, who is simply a man in possession of a special form of magic, the *yoyova* have to be gradually initiated into their status. Only a small child, whose mother is a witch, can become a witch herself. When a witch gives birth to a female child, she medicates a piece of obsidian, and cuts off the navel string. The navel string is then buried, with the recital of a magical formula, in the house, and not, as is done in all ordinary cases, in the garden. Soon after, the witch will carry her daughter to the sea beach, utter a spell over some brine in a coconut cup, and give the child to drink. After that, the child is submerged in water and washed, a kind of witch's baptism! Then she brings back the baby into the house, utters a spell over a mat, and folds her up in it. At night, she carries the baby through the air, and goes to a trysting place of other *yoyova*, where she presents her child ritually to them. In contrast to the usual custom of young mothers of sleeping over a small fire, a sorceress lies with her baby in the cold. As the child grows up, the mother will take it into her arms and carry it through the air on her nightly rounds. Entering girlhood at the age when the first grass skirt is put on a maiden, the little prospective witch will begin to fly herself.

Another system of training, running side by side with flying, consists in accustoming the child to participation in human flesh. Even before the growing witch will begin to fly on her own account, the mother will take her to the ghoulish repasts, where she and other witches sit over a corpse, eating its eyes, tongue, lungs and entrails. There the little girl receives her first share of corpse flesh, and trains her taste to like this diet.

There are other forms of training ascribed to mothers solicitous that their daughters should grow up into efficient *yoyova* and *mulukwausi*. At night the mother will stand on one side of the hut, with the child in her hands, and throw the little one over the roof. Then quickly, with the speed only possible to a *yoyova*, she will move round, and catch the child on the other side. This happens before the child begins to fly, and is meant to accustom it to passing rapidly through the air. Or again, the child will be held by her feet, head down, and remain in this position while the mother utters a spell. Thus gradually, by all these means, the child acquires the powers and tastes of a *yoyova*.

This does not mean that the character of a *yoyova* is publicly donned. Indeed, though a man often owns up to the fact that he is a *bwaga'u*, and treats his speciality quite openly in conversation, a woman will never directly confess to being a *yoyova*, not even to her own husband. But she will certainly be marked by everyone as such a one, and she will often play up to the rôle, for it is always an advantage to be supposed to be endowed with supernatural powers. And, moreover, being a sorceress is also a good source of income. A woman will often receive presents with the understanding that such and such a person has to be injured. She will openly take gifts, avowedly in payment for healing someone who has been hurt by another witch. Thus the character of a *yoyova* is, in a way, a public one and the most important and powerful witches will be enumerated by name. But no woman will ever openly speak about being one. Of course to have such a character would in no way spoil matrimonial chances, or do anything but enhance the social status of a woman.

So deep is the belief in the efficacy of magic, and in magic being the only means of acquiring extraordinary faculties, that all powers of a *yoyova* are attributed to magic. As we saw in the training of a young *yoyova*, magic has to be spoken at every stage in order to impart to her the character of a witch. A full-blown *yoyova* has to utter special magic each time she wishes to be invisible, or when she wants to fly, or acquire higher speed, or penetrate darkness and distance in order to find out whether an accident is happening there. But like everything referring to this form of witchcraft, these formulae never come to light. Although I was able to acquire a whole body of spells of the *bwaga'u* sorcery, I could not even lift the fringe of the impenetrable veil surrounding the magic of the *yoyova*. As a matter of fact, there is not the slightest doubt for me that not one single rite, not one single word of this magic, ever existed.

Once a *mulukwausi* is fully trained in her craft, she will often go at night to feed on corpses or to destroy shipwrecked mariners, for these are her two main pursuits. By a special sense, acquired through magic, she can 'hear', as the natives say, that a man has died at such and such a place, or that a canoe is in danger. Even a young apprenticed *yoyova* will have her hearing so sharpened that she will tell her mother: 'Mother, I hear, they cry!' Which means that a man is dead or dying at some place. Or she will say: 'Mother, a *waga* is sinking!' And then they both will fly to the spot.

When she goes out on such an errand, the *yoyova* leaves her body behind. Then she climbs a tree, and reciting some magic, she ties a creeper to it. Then, she flies off, along this creeper, which snaps behind her. This is the moment when we see the fire flying through the sky. Whenever the natives see a falling star, they know it is a *mulukwausi* on her flight. Another version is that, when a *mulukwausi* recites a certain spell, a tree which stands somewhere near her destination bends down towards the other tree on which she is perched. She jumps from one top to the other, and it is then that we see the fire. According to some versions, the *mulukwausi*, that is, the witch in her flying state, moves about naked, leaving her skirt round the body, which remains asleep in the hut. Other versions depict her as tying her skirt tightly round her when flying, and beating her buttocks with a magical pandanus streamer.

Arrived at the place where lies the corpse, the *mulukwausi*, with others who have also flown to the spot, perches on some high object, the top of a tree or the gable of a hut. There they all wait till they can feast on the corpse, and such is their greed and appetite that they are also very dangerous to living men. People who collect round the dead body to mourn and wake over it often have a special spell against the *mulukwausi* recited over them, by the one who knows it. They are careful not to stray away from the others, and, during burial of the dead and afterwards, they believe the air to be infested with these dangerous witches, who spread the smell of carrion around them.

The *mulukwausi* will eat out the eyes, the tongue and the 'insides' (*lopoula*) of the corpse; when they attack a living man they may simply hit him or kick him, and then he becomes more or less sick. But sometimes they get hold of an individual and treat him like a corpse and eat some of his organs, and then the man dies. It is possible to diagnose this, for such a person would quickly fail, losing his speech, his vision, sometimes suddenly being bereft of all power of movement. It is a less dangerous method to the living man when the *mulukwausi*, instead of eating his 'insides' on the spot, simply remove them. They hide them in a place only known to themselves, in order to have provision for a future feast. In that case there is some hope for the victim. Another *yoyova*, summoned quickly by the relations of the dying and well paid by them, will, in the form of a *mulukwausi*, go forth, search for the missing organs, and, if she is fortunate enough to find and restore them, save the life of the victim.

What interests us most about *mulukwausi* is their association with the sea and shipwreck. Very often they will roam over the sea, and meet at a trysting place on a reef. There they will partake of a special kind of coral, broken off from a reef, a kind called by the natives *nada*. This whets their appetite for human flesh, exactly as the drinking of salt water does with the *bwaga'u*. They have also some indirect power over the elements in the sea. Although the natives do not quite agree on the point, there is no doubt that a definite connection exists between the *mulukwausi* and all the other dangers which may be met in the sea, such as sharks, the 'gaping depth' (*ikapwagega wiwitu*), many of the small sea animals, crabs, some of the shells and the other things to be mentioned presently, all of which are considered to be the cause of death of drowning men. Thus the belief is quite definite that, in being cast into the water by the shipwreck, men do not meet any real danger except by being eaten by the *mulukwausi*, the sharks and the other animals. If by the proper magic these influences can be obviated, the drowning men will escape unscathed. The belief in the omnipotence of man, or rather, woman in this case, and of the equal power in antidoting by magic, governs all the ideas of these natives about shipwreck. The supreme remedy and insurance against any dangers lies in the magic of mist, called *kayga'u*, which, side by side with Kula magic, and the magic of the canoes, is the third of the indispensable magical equipments of a sailor.

As in all other magic, also here, there are various systems of *kayga'u*, that is, there are various formulae, slightly differing in their expressions, though usually similar in their fundamental wordings and in certain 'key' expressions. In each system, there are two main types of spells, the *giyotanawa*, or the *kayga'u* of the Underneath, and the *giyorokaywa*, or the *kayga'u* of the Above. The first one usually consists of a short formula or formulae spoken over some stones and some lime in a lime pot and over some ginger root. This *giyotanawa*, as its name indicates, is magic directed against the evil agencies, awaiting the drowning men from below. Its spells close up 'the gaping depth' and they screen off the shipwrecked men from the eyes of the sharks. They also protect them from the other evil things which cause the death of a man in drowning. The several little sea worms found on the beach, the crabs, the poisonous fish, *soka*, and the spiky fish, *baiba'i*, as well as the jumping stones, whether *vineylida* or *nu'akekepaki*, are all warded off and blinded by the *giyotanawa*. Perhaps the most extraordinary belief in this connection is that the *tokwalu*, the carved human figures on the prow boards, the *guwaya*, the semi-human effigy on the mast top, as well as the canoe ribs, would 'eat' the drowning men if not magically 'treated'.

The *kayga'u* of the 'Above', the *giyorokaywa*, consists of long spells, recited over some ginger root on several occasions before sailing, and during bad weather or shipwreck. They are directed exclusively against the *mulukwausi*, and form therefore the more important class of the two. These spells must never be recited at night, as then the *mulukwausi* could see and hear the man, and make his magic inefficient. Again, the spell of the Above, when recited at sea, must be spoken so that the magician is not covered with spray, for if his mouth were wet with sea water, the smell would attrack rather than disperse the flying witches. The man who knows the *kayga'u* must also be very careful at meal times. Children may not speak, play about, or make any noise while he eats, nor should anyone go round him behind his back while he is thus engaged; nor may they point out anything with the finger. Should the man be thus disturbed during his food, he would have to stop eating at once, and not resume it till the next meal time.

Now the leading idea of *kayga'u* is that it produces some sort of mist. The *mulukwausi* who follow the canoe, the sharks and live stones which lie in wait for it, the depth with all its horror, and the *débris* of the canoe ready to harm the owner, all these are blinded by the mist that arises in obedience to these spells. Thus the paralysing effect of these two main forms of magic and the specialised sphere of influence of each of them, are definite and clear dogmas of native belief.

3   The uses of magic

All the data which have been so far mustered disclose the extreme importance of magic in the Kula. But if it were a question of treating of any other aspect of the tribal life of these natives, it would also be found that, whenever they approach any concern of vital importance, they summon magic to their aid. It can be said without exaggeration that magic, according to their ideas, governs human destinies; that it supplies man with the power of mastering the forces of nature; and that it is his weapon and armour against the many dangers which crowd in upon him on every side. Thus, in what is most essential to man, that is in his health and bodily welfare, he is but a plaything of the powers of sorcery, of evil spirits and of certain beings, controlled by black magic. Death in almost all its forms is the result of one of these agencies. Permanent ill-health and all kinds of acute sickness, in fact everything except such easily explainable ailments as physical overstrain or slight colds, are attributed to magic. The *tauva'u*, who bring epidemics, and the *tokway*, who inflict shooting pains and minor ailments, are the only examples of non-human beings' exerting any direct influence on human destinies, and even the members of this restricted pantheon of demonology only occasionally descend among the mortals to put into action their potential powers. By far the deepest dread and most constant concern of the natives are with the *bwaga'u*, the entirely human sorcerers, who carry out their work exclusively by means of magic. Second to them in the quantity of magical output, and in the frequency of their exploits, are the *mulukwausi*, the flying witches. They are a good example of how every belief in a superior power is at the bottom a belief in magic. Magic gives to these beings the capacity to destroy human life and to command other agents of destruction. Magic also gives man the power and the means to defend himself, and if properly applied, to frustrate all the nefarious attempts of the *mulukwausi*. Comparing the two agencies, it may be said that in everyday life, the sorcerer is by far the most feared and is most frequently believed to be at work; while the *mulukwausi* enter upon the scene at certain dramatic moments, such as the presence of death, a catastrophe on land, and more especially at sea; but then, they enter with even deadlier weapons than the *bwaga'u*. Health, the normal state of human beings, can, if once lost, be regained by magic and by magic only. There is no such thing as natural recovery, return to health being always due to the removal of the evil magic by means of magical counter-action.

All those crises of life, which are associated with fear of danger, with the awakening of passions or of strong emotions, have also their magical accompaniment. The birth of a child is always ushered in by magic, in order to make the child prosper, and to neutralise the dangers and evil influences. There is no rite or magic at puberty; but then, with this people, puberty does not present any very definite crisis in the life of the individual, as their sexual life starts long before puberty arrives, and gradually shapes and develops as the organism matures. The passion of love, however, has a very elaborate magical counterpart, embodied in many rites and formulae, to which a great importance is attached, and all success in sexual life is ascribed to it. The evil results of illicit love can also be counteracted by a special type of magic.

The main social interests, ambition in gardening, ambition in successful Kula, vanity and display of personal charms in dancing – all find their expression in magic. There is a form of beauty magic, performed ceremonially over the dancers, and there is also a kind of safety magic at dances, whose object is to prevent the evil magic of envious sorcerers. Particular garden magic, performed by an individual over his crops and seeds, as well as the evil magic which he casts on the gardens of his rivals, express the private ambitions in gardening, as contrasted with the interests of the whole village, which are catered for by communal garden magic.

Natural forces of great importance to man, such as rain and sunshine, the appropriate alternative operation of which makes his

crops thrive; or wind, which must be controlled for purposes of
sailing and fishing, are also governed by magic. The magic of rain
and sunshine can be used for good, as well as for nefarious purposes, and in this they have a special interest in the Trobriands,
because the most powerful system of this magic is in the hands of
the paramount chiefs of Kiriwina. By bringing about a prolonged
drought, the chiefs of Omarakana have always been able to express
their general displeasure with their subjects, and thus enhance their
wholesale power, independently of any other mechanism, which
they might have used for forcing their will on private individuals or
on whole communities.

The passions of hatred, envy and jealousy, besides finding their
expression in the all-powerful sorcery of the *bwaga'u* and *mulukwausi*, are also responsible for many forms of witchery, known by
the generic term of *bulubwalata*. The classical forms of this magic
have as their object the estrangement of the affections of a wife or a
sweetheart, or the destruction of the domestic attachment of a pig.
The pig is sent away into the bush, having been made to take a
dislike to its master and to its domestic habits; the wife, though the
spells used to estrange her are slightly different, can be made also to
take a dislike to her domestic life, abandon her husband and return
to her parents. There is a *bulubwalata* of gardens, of canoes, of
Kula, in fact of everything, and a good deal of beneficial magic is
taken up with exorcising the results of *bulubwalata*.

The list of magic is not quite exhausted yet. There is the magic of
conditional curses, performed in order to guard property from possible harm inflicted by others; there is war-magic; there is magic
associated with taboos put on coconuts and betel-nuts, in order to
make them grow and multiply; there is magic to avert thunder and
resuscitate people who are struck by lightning; there is the magic of
tooth-ache, and a magic to make food last a long time.

All this shows the wide diffusion of magic, its extreme importance and also the fact that it is always strongest there, where vital
interests are concerned; where violent passions or emotions are
awakened; when mysterious forces are opposed to man's
endeavours; and when he has to recognise that there is something
which eludes his most careful calculations, his most conscientious
preparations and efforts.

At the same time, magic is conceived as something essentially
human. It is not a force of nature, captured by man through some

means and put to his service; it is essentially the assertion of man's intrinsic power over nature. In saying that, I, of course translate native belief into abstract terms, which they would not use themselves for its expression. None the less it is embodied in all their items of folk-lore and ways of using magic and thinking about it. In all the traditions, we find that magic is always in possession of man, or at least of anthropomorphic beings. It is carried out from underground by man. It is not conceived as having been there somewhere outside his knowledge and then captured.

The close sociological association of magic with a given sub-clan emphasises this anthropocentric conception of magic. In the majority of cases, indeed, magic refers to human activities or to the response of nature to human activities, rather than to natural forces alone. Thus, in gardening and in fishing, it is the behaviour of plants and animals tended or pursued by man; in the canoe magic, in the carver's magic, the object is a human-made thing; in the Kula, in love magic, in many forms of food magic, it is human nature on to which the force is directed. Disease is not conceived as an extraneous force, coming from outside and settling on the man, it is directly a man-made, sorcerer-made something. We may, therefore, amplify the above given definition, and say that magic is a traditionally handed on power of man over his own creations, over things once brought forth by man, or over responses of nature to his activities.

4   The three aspects of magic

I have spoken so far about 'magic' in a wholesale manner, as if it were all of one piece. As a matter of fact, magic all the world over, however rudimentary or developed it might be, presents three essential aspects. In its performance there enter always some words spoken or chanted, some actions carried out, and there are always the minister or ministers of the ceremony. In analysing the concrete details of magical performances, therefore, we have to distinguish the *formula, the rite,* and *the condition of the performer.*

These three factors stand out quite clearly and definitely in the Trobriand magic, whether we examine the facts themselves or the natives' way of looking at them. It may be said at once that in this society the relative importance of the three factors is not quite the same. The spell is by far the most important constituent of magic.

In their linguistic use, although these natives have a special word, *yopa*, they very often use the word magic, *megwa*, to describe a spell. The spell is the part of the magic which is kept secret and known only to the esoteric circle of practitioners. When a magic is handed over, whether by purchase, gift, or inheritance, only the spell has to be taught to the new recipient, and as already once said before, it is usually taught in instalments, while the payment is received in that manner. When one speaks about magical knowledge, or in inquiries whether an individual knows some magic, this invariably refers to the formula, for the nature of the rite is always quite public property. To direct questions on the subject, the natives always reply that the spell is the more important part. The question: 'where is the real strength of magic?' would receive the reply: 'in the spell.' The condition of the magician is, like the rite, essential to the performance of the magic, but it also is considered by the natives as subservient to the spell.

All this must be made clearer by the examination of actual facts. First of all, let us examine the relation between spell and rite; and to this purpose it will be best to group the various magical performances into several classes according to the complexity of the concomitant rite. We shall begin with the simplest rites.

Spells uttered directly without concomitant rite

The natives have a special expression for such acts; they say that the formula is recited 'by the mouth only', '*o wadola wala*'. This form of magic with such a rudimentary rite is, however, relatively uncommon. Although one could say that there is no rite at all in such cases, for the magician does not manipulate anything or perform any action beyond speaking, yet from another point of view, the whole performance is ritual in so far as he has always to cast his voice towards the element, or being, which he addresses. Indeed here, as in all other cases, the voice of the reciter has to be somehow or other conveyed to the object which he wishes to becharm. We see, moreover, that in all these instances, the nature of this object is such that it can be directly reached by the voice, whilst on the other hand, there would be some difficulty in applying any substance or performing any action over, let us say, wind, or a shell growing on a distant reef or the *koya* (mountain).

Spells accompanied by simple rites of impregnation

In all these performances an object is put well within reach of the voice, and in an appropriate position. Often, the object is placed within a receptacle or covering so that the voice enters an enclosed space and is concentrated upon the substance to be charmed. Thus, when the *lilava* is chanted over, the voice is cast into the mats, which are afterwards carefully wrapped up. The aromatic mint is charmed, lying at the bottom of a bag made of baked and thus toughened banana leaf, which afterwards is carefully folded together and bound with string.

In the magic of the conch-shell, immediately after the charm has been spoken, both holes of the instrument are carefully stuffed up. In all cases where an object is going to be used immediately, not so many precautions are taken, but always, without any exception, the mouth is put quite close to the object medicated and wherever possible, this latter is placed in some sort of cavity, such as a folded piece of leaf, or even the two palms of the hand put together. All this shows that it is essential to a correct performance of magic, that the voice should be conveyed directly to the substance, if possible enclosed and condensed round it, and then, imprisoned permanently there by means of some wrapping. Thus, in this type of rite, the action serves mainly to convey carefully and to retain the spell round the object.

It may be noted that in almost all cases described, the substance charmed in the rite is not the final aim of the magic, but forms only a constituent part of the object in view or is an accessory of it, or an instrument used in its making. Thus the *wayugo* creeper, the *kaybasi* (caulking), the paint, the prow boards, all these are constituent parts of the canoe, and the magic performed over them does not aim at giving them any qualities, but aims at imparting swiftness and lightness to the canoe of which they are parts only. Again, the herbs and the colours of the coconut ointment medicated in the Kula are accessories of the final end of this magic, that is, of the personal beauty and attractiveness of the performer. The adze, the breaking stone in *kaloma* magic are implements used in obtaining the object, towards which the magic is directed. There are only a few instances in which the simple rite of impregnation is directly performed on the object in view. If we compare this type of rite with the one of the previous category, we see that the difference lies

mainly in the size of the object. If you want to cast a charm over a
mountain, over a reef, or over the wind, you cannot put your
object into a little bag made of banana leaf. Nor can you put there
the human mind. And, as a rule, the final objects of magical rites
are not small things which could be easily handled.

Spells accompanied by a rite of transference

When we compare the rite of medicating the adze blade with the
rite of medicating some dried grass with which the canoe is afterwards beaten, we see that, in the second case, the magic is uttered
over a something, which has no intrinsic connection with the final
object of the magic, that is, with the canoe. It is neither to become a
part of it, nor to be used as an implement in its manufacture. We
have here the introduction for purposes of the rite, of a special
medium used to absorb the magical force, and to transfer it to the
final object. We can therefore call rites where such mediums are
used *rites of transference*. When a stick is charmed to be used afterwards for the magical knocking out of a canoe; or a mussel-shell,
with which the canoe will be scraped; or a piece of coconut husk,
which will be thrown into the water to remove the heaviness of the
canoe; or a pandanus streamer which will give it swiftness, there is
introduced into every one of these rites a substance which has to
play a magical rôle only. The rite, therefore, is not the simple
charming of a part or of a constructive implement, which will enter
into the composition or be used in the making of an object. The rite
here is more autonomous, possesses more of its own significance.
The beating of a canoe with two bunches of grass, one after the
other, in order first to extract its heaviness and then impart to it
lightness, has a meaning parallel to the spell but independent of it.
So has also the throwing down of the coconut husk. The flutter of
the pandanus streamers has direct association with speed, as the
natives explicitly state. As the *bisila* streamers flutter in the wind,
so should the canoe and the sail shake with the swiftness of their
going. In the case of the ginger, which is spat over the Dobuans
feigning hostility, the inherent quality of the substance, which our
pharmacopaeas describe as a *stimulant*, makes the meaning of the
rite plain.

Spells accompanied by offerings and invocations

There are a number of rites, accompanied by offerings given to ancestral spirits, whose participation in the offering is solicited. Such rites are performed in garden magic, in fishing magic and in weather magic. It must, however, be said at once that there is no worship and no sacrificial offering involved in these rites, that is, not of the usual description, because the spirits are not imagined to serve as agents of the magician, in carrying out the bidding of his magic.

This survey shows clearly that the virtue, the force, the effective principle of magic lies in the spell. We saw that in many cases, the spell is quite sufficient, if directly breathed upon the object. Again, in what may be called the prevalent type of ritual, the action which accompanies the utterance of the formula serves only to direct and condense the spell upon the object. In all such cases the rite lacks all independent significance, all autonomous function. In some cases, the rite introduces a substance which is used for magical purposes only. As a rule, the substance then intensifies, through a parallel action, the meaning of the spell. On the whole, it may be said that the main creative power of magic resides in the formula; that the rite serves to convey, or transfer it to the object, in certain cases emphasising the meaning of the spell through the nature of the transferring medium, as well as through the manner in which it is finally applied. It is hardly necessary to state that in the Trobriand magic there are no rites performed without the spell.

It is also evident in studying the manner in which the force of the spell is conveyed to the object, that the voice of the reciter transfers the virtue. Indeed, the magical words are, so to speak, rubbed in by constant repetition to the substance. To understand this better we must inquire into the natives' conceptions of psycho-physiology. The mind, *nanola*, by which term intelligence, power of discrimination, capacity for learning magical formulae, and all forms of non-manual skill are described, as well as moral qualities, resides somewhere in the larynx. The natives will always point to the organs of speech, where the *nanola* resides. The man who cannot speak through any defect of his organs, is identified in name (*tonagowa*) and in treatment with all those mentally deficient. The memory, however, the store of formulae and traditions learned by heart, resides deeper, in the belly. A man will be said to have a good *nanola*, when he can acquire many formulae, but though they enter through the larynx, naturally, as he learns them, repeating word for word, he has to stow them away in a bigger and more commodious receptacle; they sink down right to the bottom of his abdomen.

There exist also certain ideas about stratification of magic, namely, that certain forms of magic have to be learnt first, so that they sink down, while others come on top. But these ideas are vague and contradictory, whereas the main idea, that magic rests in the belly, is clear and definite. This fact gives us a new insight into native ideas about magic. The force of magic, crystallised in the magical formulae, is carried by men of the present generation in their bodies. They are the depositories of this most valuable legacy of the past. The force of magic does not reside in the things; it resides within man and can escape only through his voice.

So far, we only spoke of the relation between spell and rite. The last point, however, brings us to the problem of the condition of the performer. His belly is a tabernacle of magical force. Such a privilege carries its dangers and obligations. It is clear that you cannot stuff foreign matter indiscriminately into a place, where extremely valuable possessions are kept. Food restrictions, therefore, become imperative. Many of them are directly determined by the contents of the spell. In other cases, the object which is the aim of the magic, cannot be partaken by the magician. This is the rule in the case of shark fishing, *kalala* fishing and other forms of fishing magic. The garden magician is also debarred from partaking of new crops, up to a certain period. There is hardly any clear doctrine as to why things mentioned in magical formulae, whether they are the aims of the magic or only co-operating factors, should not be eaten. There is just the general apprehension that the formula would be damaged by it. There are other taboos binding the magician, some of them permanent, some of them temporary, during the season of his magical performance. We saw some permanent ones, as in the case of the man who knows Kayga'u magic, and is not allowed to eat while children make noises. The temporary ones, such as the sexual abstinence during the first rites of the Kula, could be supplemented by numerous examples from other forms of magic. Thus, in order to bring about rain, the magician paints himself black and has to remain unwashed and unkempt for some time. The shark magician has to keep his house open, to remove his pubic leaf and to sit with his legs apart, while the fishing and the magic last, 'so that the shark's mouth might remain gaping'. But we cannot enter too much into enumeration of these taboos and observances, and have only to make it clear that the proper behaviour of the magician is one of the essentials of magic, and that in many cases this behaviour is dictated by the contents of the spell.

The taboos and observances are not the only conditions which a man must fulfil in order to carry out certain forms of magic. In many cases the most important condition is his membership in a social group, for many forms of magic are strictly local, and must be performed by one, who is the descendant of the mythical, original owner of the magic.

The traditional character of magic and the magical filiation of the performer find their expression in another important feature of the spells. In some of them, as we have seen, references to mythical events are made, or names of mythical ancestors are uttered. Even more often, we find a whole list of names, beginning with the mythical founder of the magic, and ending with the name of the immediate predecessor, that is, of the man from whom the magic was obtained by the actual performer. Such a list links up the present magician by a sort of magical pedigree with all those who had previously been using this formula. In other formulae again, the magician identifies himself with some mythical individual, and utters the latter's name in the first person. Both the actual genealogical descent of the magician from the mythical ancestors, and the magical filiation expressed in the formulae show again the paramount importance of tradition, in this case acting on the sociological determination of the performer. He is placed in a definite social group of those, who by birth, or what could be called 'magical adoption', have had the right of performing this magic. In the very act of uttering the spell, the magician bears testimony to his indebtedness to the past by the enumeration of magical names, and by references to myth and mythical events. Both the sociological restrictions, wherever they still exist, and the magical filiation confirm once more the dependence of magic on tradition. On the other hand, both show, as also do the taboos, that the obligations imposed on the magician and the conditions he has to fulfil are largely derived from the spell.

5   Systems of magic

Closely connected with the questions discussed in the preceding division is the subject of the *systems of magic* and the distinction between 'systematic' and 'independent' magical rites and formulae. The whole body of magic naturally falls into several big divisions, each of them corresponding to a department of nature, such as wind or weather; to some activity of man, such as gardening, fishing, hunting or warfare; or to some real or imaginary force, such as artistic inspiration, witchcraft, personal charm or prowess.

There is, however, an important distinction to be made within each such division of magic; some of the rites and spells are isolated and independent, they can be used by themselves, whenever the need arises. Such are almost all the incantations of wind magic; some spells of individual garden magic; formulae against tooth-ache, and minor ailments; some spells of hunting and food collect-ing; a few rites of love magic and of the magic of carving. When a man, for instance, paddles along the Lagoon in his canoe and an unfavourable wind sets in, he will utter a spell to make it abate and change. The same spell would be recited in the village, when there arises a wind so strong as to be dangerous. The incantation is a free, individual act, which may be performed and is performed in any of the circumstances which require it.

It is quite another matter with the spells belonging to what I have called here *systematic magic*. Such magic consists of a connected and consecutive body of incantations and concomitant rites, no one of which can be torn out of its sequence and performed by itself. They have to be carried out one after the other in a determined order, and the more important of them, at least, can never be omit-ted once the series has been started. Such a series is always closely connected with some activity such as the building of a canoe or an overseas Kula voyage, a fishing expedition or the making and harvesting of a garden. It can be easily seen how this intimate association between enterprise and magic imparts to systematic magic its specific character. The consecutive progress of work and of magic are inseparable, just because, according to native ideas, work needs magic, and magic has only meaning as an indispensable ingredient of work.

Both work and magic are directed towards the same aim; to con-struct a swift and a stable canoe; to obtain a good Kula yield; to ensure safety from drowning and so on. Thus we see that systematic magic consists in a body of rites and spells associated with one enterprise, directed towards one aim, and progressing in a consecutive series of performances which have to be carried out in their proper place. The point – the proper understanding of what is meant by systematic magic – is of the greatest theoretical importance because it reveals the nature of the relation between magical and practical activities, and shows how deeply the two are connected with one another. It is one of these points, also, which cannot be properly explained and grasped without the help of a chart. In the appended Table of Kula Magic and of the Corresponding Activities, I have prepared such a chart. The Table allows of a rapid survey of the consecutive activities of the Kula in their relation to magic, beginning with the first act of canoe-building and finishing with the return home. It shows the salient features of systematic magic in general, and of the *mwasila* and canoe magic in particular. It shows the relation between magical, ritual and practical activities, the correlated sequence of the two, their rolling off, stage after stage, and side by side, towards one central aim – a successful Kula. The Table thus serves to illustrate the meaning of the expression 'systematic magic', and it provides a firm outline of the essentials, magical, ceremonial and practical, of the Kula.

Table of Kula magic and of the corresponding activities

I First stage of canoe-building

Season and approximate duration	Place	Activity		Magic
Beginning: June–August	*Raybwag*	Felling of tree (done by the builder and helpers);	inaugurated by	the *vabusi tokway* (offering and spell) aiming at the expulsion of the wood sprite from the tree (performed by owner or builder)
Immediately afterwards	Same place	Trimming of the log-canoe (done by builder with helpers)		No magic.
A few days later	Road	Pulling the log (done by all villagers);	helped out by	double rite of lightness (*kaymomwa'u* and *kayagabile*).
On morning after arrival at village	Main place in the village	The log is left as it is;	until	the magical act (*kapitunena duku*) ceremonially inaugurating the work over the canoe
Evening of the same day	Main place in the village	Working out of the outside of the log		No magic accompanying it
Several days or weeks following	Main place	Scooping out of the inside of the canoe;	inaugurated by	*ligogu* spell over the *kavilali*, the adze with the movable handle
Towards the end of the foregoing period	In the village before builder's house	Other parts of canoe made ready by builder and helpers		No magic
After all work is over				Concluding rite: *kapitunena nanola waga*

All the magic of this stage is canoe magic. It is performed only when a new canoe is built and not when an old one is renovated. The spells are uttered by the builder and not by the owner, except the first one. Work at this stage is done by one man mainly, the builder and carver, with the help of a few men; except for the pulling of the log, in which many men assist.

II Second stage of canoe-building

Time	Place	Activity		Magic
First day of work	On the sea-front of a Lagoon village, or on a beach of one of the Eastern villages	Fixing the prow-boards;	inaugurated by	*katuliliva tabuyo* rite, performed over the ornamental prow-boards by the *toliwaga*. It belongs to the *mwasila* (Kula magic)
		The following activities are	inaugurated by	*vakakaya* rite. A magical, cere-monial cleansing of the canoe, performed by the owner or builder to remove all evil in-fluence and thus to make the canoe fast
(At times, the lashing can-not be done in one day and has to be continued into another session)		Lashing of the canoe;	associated with	the *wayugo* spell (lashing creeper) rite; the most important of the magical performances in the second stage. Done by builder or owner to make canoe swifter and stronger
Second sitting: during this the caulking is done and the three exorcisms per-formed afterwards	On the sea-front of a Lagoon village or on a beach of one of the Eastern villages	Caulking of the canoe;	associated with	*kaybasi* (caulking) magic; spell uttered over caulking by builder or owner to make canoe safe
				vakasulu, an exorcism; *vaguri*, an exorcism; *kaytapena waga*, an exorcism
		Painting of the canoe;	associated with	Magic of: *kaykoulo* (black paint); *malakava* (red paint); *pwaka* (white paint)

III   The ceremonial launching of a canoe

Activity	Magic
The launching and trial run	inaugurated by	*kaytalula wadola waga* rite, belonging to the *mwasila* cycle of magic

After this, there comes the interval, filled out by the *kabigidoya* (ceremonial visiting), by the preliminary trade and other preparations for the expedition overseas.

IV   The magic during, and preparations before, the departure

Time: some three to seven days before setting sail

Activity		Magic
Preparing the canoe for sailing (placing of the mats on the platform, and of the frames in the body);	inaugurated by	*yawarapu* rite over the coco-palm leaves, done by the *toliwaga* to ensure success in the Kula
		kayikuna sulumwoya rite over the aromatic mint
		kaymwaloyo rite over the mint boiled in coconut oil, performed by the *toliwaga*
Packing of the trade goods;	associated with	*gebobo* rite (called also *Kipwo'i sikwabu*) made over four coconuts by a friend or relative in law of the *toliwaga*, to make all the food last (the spell expresses only the desire for a good Kula)

All this magic belongs to the *mwasila*, and it has to be performed by the *toliwaga*, with the exception of the last spell.

V   Canoe magic, performed at the final start on overseas voyage

The series of rites starts at the moment when the canoes are ready to set sail on the long voyage on Pilolu. They are not associated with a progressive series of acts; they all refer to one aim: canoe speed and reliability. They are all performed by the *toliwaga*.

Activity: overseas sailing, inaugurated by a series of magical rites

	kadumiyala, ritual rubbing or cleansing of the canoe with leaves charmed over
Time: morning of the second day of the expedition	*bisila* magic; pandanus streamers, previously chanted over are tied to the mast and rigging
Place: the beach of Muwa	*kayikuna veva*; swaying the sheet rope uttering an incantation
Aim of magic: imparting of speed to canoe	*vabusi momwa'u*; 'expelling the heaviness' out of a canoe by means of a stale potato
Performer of the Rites: the *toliwaga*	*bisiboda patile*; a rite of evil magic to make other canoes slow and thus achieve relative speed

VI   The *mwasila*, performed on arrival at the final destination

(A) Beauty magic

Activity: washing, anointing and painting

kaykakaya – ritual washing and rubbing with charmed leaves

Place: the beach, on or near which the party rest before starting on the last stage (on the way to Dobu; Sarubwoyna beach. On the way to Sinaketa: Kaykuyawa)

luya (coconut) spell – over the scraped coconut used for anointing

sinata (comb) spell – over the comb

Performers: the spells are uttered usually by the *toliwaga*, sometimes by an elder member of the crew

sayyaku – aromatic black paint

bowa – ordinary charcoal blacking

talo – red paint of crushed areca-nut

(B) Magic of the final approach

Activity: the fleet are paddling (on the approach to Dobu) or punting (to Sinaketa) in a body

ta'uya – the ritual blowing of the conch-shell, which has been charmed over before

Performers: in each canoe, simultaneously, the *toliwaga* and two members of the crew

kayikuna-tabuyo – the swaying of the front prow-board while the spell is being uttered

kavalikuliku – the spell by the *toliwaga*

Aim: to 'shake the mountain', to produce an impression on the partners awaiting on the beach

kaytavilena mwoynawaga – the incantation uttered at the stern towards the *koya*

(C) Magic of safety

Activity	Magic
Entering the Dobuan village (this magic is performed only when Boyowans come to the *koya*)	*ka'ubana'i*, charm uttered over ginger, which is then ritually spat over the Dobuan village and the partners, and makes their hearts soft

(D) Magic of persuasion

Activity	Magic
The wooing in Kula (*wawoyla*) of the overseas partner by the visitor	*kwoygapani* – a spell uttered over a piece of areca-nut, given subsequently to the partner

VII   A canoe spell, uttered on the departure home

Activity	Magic
Loading of the canoe with the gifts received from overseas partners, with the trade gain, and with the provisions for the home journey	*kaylupa* – a spell to make the canoe lighter, to 'lift' it out of the water

6   The myth of the flying canoe

The myths of the Kula are scattered along a section of the present
Kula circuit. Beginning with a place in eastern Woodlark Island,
the village of Wamwara, the mythological centres are spread round
almost in a semi-circle, right down to the island of Tewara. A very
important myth, localised in Kitava, is the one which serves as
foundation for canoe magic. I have obtained three independent
versions of this myth, and they agree substantially. I shall adduce at
length the story as it was told to me by the best informant, and
written down in Kiriwinian, and after that, I shall show on what
points the other versions vary. I shall not omit from the full
account certain tedious repetitions and obviously inessential
details, for they are indispensable for imparting to the narrative the
characteristic flavour of native folk-lore.

   To understand the following account, it is necessary to realise
that Kitava is a raised coral island. Its inland part is elevated to a
height of about three hundred feet. Behind the flat beach, a steep
coral wall rises, and from its summit the land gently falls towards
the central declivity. It is in this central part that the villages are
situated, and it would be quite impossible to transport a canoe
from any village to the beach. Thus, in Kitava, unlike what
happens with some of the Lagoon villages of Boyowa, the canoes
have to be always dug out and lashed on the beach.

The myth of the flying canoe of Kudayuri

Mokatuboda of the Lukuba clan and his younger brother
Toweyre'i lived in the village of Kudayuri. With them lived
their three sisters Kayguremwo, Na'ukuwakula and
Murumweyri'a. They had all come out from underground in
the spot called Labikewo, in Kitava. These people were the
u'ula (foundation, basis, here: first possessors) of the *ligogu*
and *wayugo* magic.

   All the men of Kitava decided on a great Kula expedition to
the Koya. The men of Kumwageya, Kaybutu, Kabululo and
Lalela made their canoes. They scooped out the inside of the
waga, they carved the *tabuyo* and *lagim* (decorated prow
boards), they made the *budaka* (lateral gunwale planks). They
brought the component parts to the beach, in order to make

the *yowaga* (to put and lash them together).

The Kudayuri people made their canoe in the village. Mokatuboda, the head man of the Kudayuri village, ordered them to do so. They were angry: 'Very heavy canoe. Who will carry it to the beach?' He said: 'No, not so; it will be well. I shall just lash my *waga* in the village.' He refused to move the canoe; it remained in the village. The other people pieced their canoe on the beach; he pieced it together in the village. They lashed it with the *wayugo* creeper on the beach; he lashed his in the village. They caulked their canoes on the sea-shore; he caulked his in the village. They painted their canoes on the beach with black; he blackened his in the village. They made the *youlala* (painted red and white) on the beach; he made the *youlala* in the village. They sewed their sail on the beach; he did it in the village. They rigged up the mast and rigging on the beach; he in the village. After that, the men of Kitava made *tasasoria* (trial run) and *kabigidoya* (visit of ceremoni: presentation), but the Kudayuri canoe did not make either.

By and by, all the men of Kitava ordered their women to prepare the food. The women one day put all the food, the *gugu'a* (personal belongings), the *pari* (presents and trade goods) into the canoe. The people of Kudayuri had all these things put into their canoe in the village. The headman of the Kudayuri, Mokatuboda, asked all his younger brothers, all the members of his crew, to bring some of their *pari*, and he performed magic over it, and made a *lilava* (magical bundle) of it.

The people of other villages went to the beach; each canoe was manned by its *usagelu* (members of the crew). The man of Kudayuri ordered his crew to man his canoe in the village. They of the other villages stepped the mast on the shore; he stepped the mast in the village. They prepared the rigging on the shore; he prepared the rigging in the village. They hoisted the sail on the sea; he spoke 'May our sail be hoisted,' and his companions hoisted the sail. He spoke: 'Sit in your places, every man!' He went into the house, he took his *ligogu* (adze), he took some coconut oil, he took a staff. He spoke magic over the adze, over the coconut oil. He came out of the house, he approached the canoe. A small dog of his called Tokulubweydoga jumped into the canoe. He spoke to his

crew: 'Pull up the sail higher.' They pulled at the halyard. He
rubbed the staff with the coconut oil. He knocked the canoe's
skids with the staff. Then he struck with his *ligogu* the *u'ula*
of his canoe and the *dobwana* (that is, both ends of the
canoe). He jumped into the canoe, sat down, and the canoe
flew!

A rock stood before it. It pierced the rock in two, and flew
through it. He bent down, he looked; his companions (that is,
the other canoes of Kitava) sailed on the sea. He spoke to his
younger brothers (that is to his relatives in the canoe): 'Bail
out the water, pour it out!' Those who sailed on the earth
thought it was rain, this water which they poured out from
above.

They (the other canoes) sailed to Giribwa, they saw a canoe
anchored there. They said: 'Is that the canoe from Dobu?'
They thought so, they wanted to *lebu* (take by force, but not
necessarily as a hostile act) the *buna* (big cowrie) shells of the
Dobu people. Then they saw the dog walking on the beach.
They said: 'Wi-i-i! This is Tokulubweydoga, the dog of the
Lukuba! This canoe they lashed in the village, in the village of
Kudayuri. Which way did it come? It was anchored in the
jungle!' They approached the people of Kudayuri, they spoke:
'Which way did you come?' 'Oh, I came together with you
(the same way).' 'It rained. Did it rain over you?' 'Oh yes, it
has rained over me.'

Next day, they (the men of the other villages of Kitava),
sailed to Vakuta and went ashore. They made their Kula. The
next day they sailed, and he (Mokatuboda) remained in
Vakuta. When they disappeared on the sea, his canoe flew.
He flew from Vakuta. When they (the other crews) arrived in
Gumasila, he was there on the promontory of Lububuyama.
They said: 'This canoe is like the canoe of our companions,'
and the dog came out. 'This is the dog of the Lukuba clan of
Kudayuri.' They asked him again which way he came; he said
he came the same way as they. They made the Kula in
Gumasila. He said: 'You sail first, I shall sail later on.' They
were astonished. 'Which way does he sail?' They slept in
Gumasila.

Next day they sailed to Tewara, they arrived at the beach of
Kadimwatu. They saw his canoe anchored there, the dog came

out and ran along the beach. They spoke to the Kudayuri
men, 'How did you come here?' 'We came with you, the same
way we came.' They made Kula in Tewara. Next day, they
sailed to Bwayowa (village in Dobu district). He flew, and
anchored at the beach Sarubwoyna. They arrived there, they
saw: 'Oh, look at the canoe, are these fishermen from Dobu?'
The dog came out. They recognised the dog. They asked him
(Mokatuboda) which way he came: 'I came with you, I
anchored here.' They went to the village of Bwayowa, they
made Kula in the village, they loaded their canoes. They
received presents from the Dobu people at parting, and the
Kitava men sailed on the return journey. They sailed first, and
he flew through the air.'

On the return journey, at every stage, they see him first, they ask
him which way he went, and he gives them some sort of answer as
the above ones.

From Giribwa they sailed to Kitava; he remained in
Giribwa; he flew from Giribwa; he went to Kitava, to the
beach. His *gugu'a* (personal belongings) were being carried to
the village when his companions came paddling along, and
saw his canoe anchored and the dog running on the beach.
All the other men were very angry, because his canoe flew.
They remained in Kitava. Next year, they made their
gardens, all the men of Kitava. The sun was very strong, there
was no rain at all. The sun burned their gardens. This man
(the head man of Kudayuri, Mokatuboda) went into the
garden. He remained there, he made a *bulubwalata* (evil
magic) of the rain. A small cloud came and rained on his
garden only, and their gardens the sun burned. They (the
other men of Kitava) went and saw their gardens. They
arrived there, they saw all was dead, already the sun had
burned them. They went to his garden and it was all wet:
yams, *taitu*, taro, all was fine. They spoke: 'Let us kill him so
that he might die. We shall then speak magic over the clouds,
and it will rain over our gardens.'
The real, keen magic, the Kudayuri man (i.e. Mokatuboda)
did not give to them; he gave them not the magic of the
ligogu (adze); he gave them not the magic of *kunisalili* (rain
magic); he gave them not the magic of the *wayugo* (lashing

creeper), of the coconut oil and staff. Toweyre'i, his younger
brother, thought that he had already received the magic, but
he was mistaken. His elder brother gave him only part of the
magic, the real one he kept back.

They came (to Mokatuboda, the head man of Kudayuri), he
sat in his village. His brothers and maternal nephews
sharpened the spear, they hit him, he died.

Next year, they decided to make a big Kula expedition, to
Dobu. The old *waga*, cut and lashed by Mokatuboda, was no
more good, the lashings had perished. Then Toweyre'i, the
younger brother, cut a new one to replace the old. The people
of Kumwageya and Lalela (the other villages in Kitava) heard
that Toweyre'i cuts his *waga*, and they also cut theirs. They
pieced and lashed their canoes on the beach. Toweyre'i did it
in the village.

Here the native narrative enumerates every detail of canoe
making, drawing the contrast between the proceedings on the beach
of the other Kitavans, and of Toweyre'i building the canoe in the
village of Kudayuri. It is an exact repetition of what was said at the
beginning, when Mokatuboda was building his canoe, and I shall
not adduce it here. The narrative arrives at the critical moment
when all the members of the crew are seated in the canoe ready for
the flight.

Toweyre'i went into the house and made magic over the
adze and the coconut oil. He came out, smeared a staff with
the oil, knocked the skids of the canoe. He then did as his
elder brother did. He struck both ends of the canoe with the
adze. He jumped into the canoe and sat down; but the *waga*
did not fly. Toweyre'i went into the house and cried for his
elder brother, whom he had slain; he had killed him without
knowing his magic. The people of Kumwageya and Lalela
went to Dobu and made their Kula. The people of Kudayuri
remained in the village.

The three sisters were very angry with Toweyre'i, for he
killed the elder brother and did not learn his magic. They
themselves had learnt the *ligogu*, the *wayugo* magic; they had
it already in their *lopoula* (belly). They could fly through the
air, they were *yoyova*. In Kitava they lived on the top of
Botigale'a hill. They said: 'Let us leave Kitava and fly away.'

They flew through the air. One of them, Na'ukuwakula, flew to the West, pierced through the sea-passage Dikuwa'i (somewhere in the Western Trobriands); she arrived at Simsim (one of the Lousançay). There she turned into a stone, she stands in the sea.

The two others flew first (due West) to the beach of Yalumugwa (on the Eastern shore of Boyowa). There they tried to pierce the coral rock named Yakayba – it was too hard. They went (further South on the Eastern shore) through the sea-passage of Vilasasa and tried to pierce the rock Kuyaluya – they couldn't. They went (further South) and tried to pierce the rock of Kawakari – it was too hard. They went (further South). They tried to pierce the rocks at Giribwa. They succeeded. That is why there is now a sea passage at Giribwa (the straits dividing the main island of Boyowa from the island of Vakuta).

They flew (further South) towards Dobu. They came to the island of Tewara. They came to the beach of Kadimwatu and pierced it. This is where the straits of Kadimwatu are now between the islands of Tewara and Uwama. They went to Dobu; they travelled further South, to the promontory of Saramwa (near Dobu island). They spoke: 'Shall we go round the point or pierce right through?' They went round the point. They met another obstacle and pierced it through, making the Straits of Loma (at the Western end of Dawson Straits). They came back, they returned and settled near Tewara. They turned into stones; they stand in the sea. One of them cast her eyes on Dobu, this is Murumweyri'a; she eats men, and the Dobuans are cannibals. The other one, Kayguremwo, does not eat men, and her face is turned towards Boyowa. The people of Boyowa do not eat man.

In its enumeration of the various details of tribal life, this myth is truly a fount of ethnographic information. Its statements, when made complete and explicit by native comment, contain a good deal of what is to be known about the sociology, technology and organisation of canoe-making, sailing, and of the Kula. If followed up into detail, the incidents of this narrative make us acquainted for instance, with the division into clans; with the origin and local character of these latter; with ownership of magic and its association with the totemic group. In almost all mythological narratives of the Trobriands, the clan, the sub-clan and the locality of the heroes are stated. In the above version, we see that the heroes have emerged at a certain spot, and that they themselves came from underground; that is, that they are the first representatives of their totemic sub-clan on the surface of the earth.

Passing to the following part of the tale, we find in it a description of canoe-building, and this was given to me in the same detailed manner in all three versions. Here again, if we would substitute for the short sentences a fuller account of what happens, such as could be elicited from any intelligent native informant; if for each word describing the stages of canoe-building we insert a full description of the processes for which these words stand – we would have in this myth an almost complete, ethnographic account of canoe-building. We would see the canoe pieced together, lashed, caulked, painted, rigged out, provided with a sail till it lies ready to be launched. Besides the successive enumeration of technical stages, we have in this myth a clear picture of the rôle played by the headman, who is the nominal owner of the canoe, and who speaks of it as his canoe and at the same time directs its building; overrides the wishes of others, and is responsible for the magic. We have even the mention of the *tasasoria* and *kabigidoya*, and several allusions to the Kula expedition of which the canoe-building in this myth is represented as a preliminary stage. The frequent, tedious repetitions and enumerations of customary sequences of events, interesting as data of folk-lore, are not less valuable as ethnographic documents, and as illustrations of the natives' attitude towards custom.

The dramatic effect of the climax of the story, of the unexpected flight of the canoe, is clearly brought out in the narrative, and it was given to me in all its three versions. In all three, the members of the crew are made to pass through the numerous preparatory stages of sailing. And the parallel drawn between the reasonable proceedings of their fellows on the beach, and the absurd manner in which they are made to get ready in the middle of the village, some few hundred feet above the sea, makes the tension more palpable and the sudden *dénouement* more effective. In all accounts of this myth, the magic is also performed just before the flight, and its performance is explicitly mentioned and included as an important episode in the story.

The incident of bailing some water out of a canoe which never touched the sea seems to show some inconsistency. If we remember, however, that the water is poured into a canoe, while it is building, in order to prevent its drying and consequently its shrinking, cracking and warping, the inconsistency and flaw in the narrative disappear.

The episode of the dog is more significant and more important to the natives, and is mentioned in all three versions. The dog is the animal associated with the Lukuba clan; that is, the natives will say that the dog is a Lukuba, as the pig is a Malasi, and the iguana a Lukulabuta.

In the second part of the story, we find the hero endowed again with magical powers far superior to those of the present-day wizards. They can make rain, or stay the clouds, it is true, but he is able to create a small cloud which pours copious rain over his own gardens, and leaves the others to be shrivelled up by the sun. This part of the narrative does not touch the canoe problem, and it is of interest to us only in so far as it again shows what appears to the natives the real source of their hero's supernatural powers.

The motives which lead to the killing of Mokatuboda are not stated explicitly in the narrative. No myth as a rule enters very much into the subjective side of its events. But, from the lengthy, indeed wearisome, repetition of how the other Kitava men constantly find the Kudayuri canoe outrunning them, how they are astonished and angry, it is clear that his success must have made many enemies to Mokatuboda. What is not so easily explained is the fact that he is killed, not by the other Kitava men, but by his own kinsmen. One of the versions mentions his brothers and his sister's sons as the slayers. One of them states that the people of Kitava ask Toweyre'i, the younger brother, whether he has already acquired the flying magic and the rain magic, and only after an affirmative is received, is Mokatuboda killed by his younger brother, in connivance with the other people. An interesting variant is added to this version, according to which Toweyre'i kills his elder brother in the garden. He then comes back to the village and instructs and admonishes Mokatuboda's children to take the body, to give it the mortuary attentions, to prepare for the burial. Then he himself arranges the *sagali*, the big mortuary distribution of food. In this we find an interesting document of native custom and ideas. Toweyre'i, in spite of having killed his brother, is still the man who has to arrange the mortuary proceedings, act as master of ceremonies and pay for the functions performed in them by others. He personally may neither touch the corpse, nor do any act of mourning or burial; nevertheless he, as the nearest of kin of the dead man, is the bereaved one, is the one from whom a limb has been severed, so to speak. A man whose brother has died cannot mourn any more than he could mourn for himself. To return to the motives of killing, as this was done according to all accounts by Mokatuboda's own kinsmen with the approval of the other men, envy, ambition, the desire to succeed the headman in his dignity, must have been mixed with spite against him. In fact, we see that Toweyre'i proceeds confidently to perform the magic, and bursts out into wailing only after he has discovered he has been duped.

Now we come to one of the most remarkable incidents of the whole myth, that namely which brings into connection the *yoyova*, or the flying witches, with the flying canoe, and with such speed of a canoe, as is imparted to it by magic. In the spells of swiftness there are frequent allusions to the *yoyova* or *mulukwausi*.

The *kariyala* (magical portent) of the *wayugo* spell consists in shooting stars, that is, when a *wayugo* rite is performed at night over the creeper coils, there will be stars falling in the sky. And again, when a magician, knowing this system of magic, dies, shooting stars will be seen. Now, as we have seen, falling stars are *mulukwausi* in their flight.

In this story of the Kudayuri we see the mythological ground for this association. The same magic which allowed the canoe to sail through the air gives the three sisters of Kudayuri their power of being *mulukwausi*, and of flying. In this myth they are also endowed with the power of cleaving the rocks, a power which they share with the canoe, which cleft a rock immediately after leaving the village. The three sisters cleave rocks and pierce the land in several places. My native commentators assured me that when the canoe first visited Giribwa and Kadimwatu at the beginning of this myth, the land was still joined at these places and there was a beach at each of them. The *mulukwausi* tried to pierce Boyowa at several spots along the Eastern coast, but succeeded only at Giribwa. The myth thus has the archaic stamp of referring to deep changes in natural features. The two sisters who fly to the south return from the furthest point and settle near Tewara, in which there is some analogy to several other myths in which heroes from the Marshall

Bennett Islands settle down somewhere between the Amphletts and Dobu. One of them turns her eyes northwards towards the non-cannibal people of Boyowa and she is said to be averse to cannibalism. Probably this is a sort of mythological explanation of why the Boyowan people do not eat men and the Dobuans do.

7 The function of myth

A strict adherence to custom, to that which is done by everyone else, is the main rule of conduct among our natives in the Trobriands. An important corollary to this rule declares that the past is more important than the present. What has been done by the father – or, as the Trobriander would say, by the maternal uncle – is even more important as norm of behaviour than what is done by the brother. It is to the behaviour of the past generations that the Trobriander instinctively looks for his guidance. Thus the mythical events which relate what has been done, not by the immediate ancestors but by mythical, illustrious forbears, must evidently carry an enormous social weight. The stories of important past events are hallowed because they belong to the great mythical generations and because they are generally accepted as truth, for everybody knows and tells them. They bear the sanction of righteousness and propriety in virtue of these two qualities of preterity and universality.

Thus, through the operation of what might be called the elementary law of sociology, myth possesses the normative power of fixing custom, of sanctioning modes of behaviour, of giving dignity and importance to an institution. The Kula receives from these ancient stories its stamp of extreme importance and value. The rules of commercial honour, of generosity and punctiliousness in all its operations, acquire through this their binding force. This is what we could call the normative influence of myth on custom.

The Kula myth, however, exercises another kind of appeal. In the Kula, we have a type of enterprise where the vast possibilities of success are very much influenced by chance. A man, whether he be rich or poor in partners, may, according to his luck, return with a relatively big or small haul from an expedition. Thus the imagination of the adventurers, as in all forms of gambling, must be bent towards lucky hits and turns of extraordinarily good chance. The Kula myths feed this imagination on stories of extreme good luck,

and at the same time show that it lies in the hands of man to bring
this luck on himself, provided he acquires the necessary magical
lore.

But, distinct as it is, the mythical world is not separated by an
unbridgeable gulf from the present order of events. Indeed, though
an ideal must be always beyond what actually exists, yet it must
appear just within reach of realisation if it is to be effective at all.
Now, after we have become acquainted with their stories, we can
see clearly what was meant when it was said, that magic acts as a
link between the mythical and the actual realities. In the canoe
myth, for instance, the flying, the super-normal achievement of the
Kudayuri canoe, is conceived only as the highest degree of the
virtue of speed, which is still being imparted nowadays to canoes by
magic. The magical heritage of the Kudayuri clan is still there,
making the canoes sail fast. Had it been transmitted in its complete
form, any present canoe, like the mythical one, could be seen
flying. In the Kula myths also, magic is found to give super-normal
powers of beauty, strength and immunity from danger. The
mythological events demonstrate the truth of the claims of magic.
Their validity is established by a sort of retrospective, mythical
empiry. But magic, as it is practised nowadays, accomplishes the
same effects, only in a smaller degree. Natives believe deeply that
the formulae and rites of *mwasila* magic make those who carry
them out attractive, irresistible and safe from dangers.

Another feature which brings the mythical events into direct
connection with the present state of affairs is the sociology of
mythical personages. They all are associated with certain localities,
as are the present local groups. They belong to the same system of
totemic division into clans and sub-clans as obtains nowadays.
Thus, members of a sub-clan, or a local unit, can claim a mythical
hero as their direct ancestor, and members of a clan can boast of
him as of a clansman. Indeed, myths, like songs and fairy stories,
are 'owned' by certain sub-clans. This does not mean that other
people would abstain from telling them, but members of the sub-
clan are supposed to possess the most intimate knowledge of the
mythical events, and to be an authority in interpreting them. And
indeed, it is a rule that a myth will be best known in its own locality,
that is, known with all the details and free from any adulterations
or not quite genuine additions and fusions.

This better knowledge can be easily understood if we remember that myth is very often connected with magic in the Trobriands, and that this latter is a possession kept by some members of the local group. Now, to know the magic, and to understand it properly, it is necessary to be well acquainted with the myth. This is the reason why the myth must be better known in the local group with which it is connected. In some cases, the local group has not only to practise the magic associated with the myth, but it has to look after the observance of certain rites, ceremonies and taboos connected with it. In this case, the sociology of the mythical events is intimately bound up with the social divisions as they exist now. But even in such myths as those of the Kula, which have become the property of all clans and local groups within the district, the explicit statement of the hero's clan, sub-clan and of his village gives the whole myth a stamp of actuality and reality. Side by side with magic, the sociological continuity bridges over the gap between the mythical and the actual. And indeed the magical and the sociological bridges run side by side.

Here it must be noted also that the mythically changed features of the landscape bear testimony in the native's mind to the truth of the myth. The mythical word receives its substance in rock and hill, in the changes in land and sea. The pierced sea-passages, the cleft boulders, the petrified human beings, all these bring the mythological world close to the natives, make it tangible and permanent. On the other hand, the story thus powerfully illustrated reacts on the landscape, fills it with dramatic happenings, which, fixed there for ever, give it a definite meaning.

8 The meaning of the Kula

The Kula seems to be, to a certain extent, a novel type of ethnological fact. Its novelty lies partly in the size of its sociological and geographical extent. A big, inter-tribal relationship, uniting with definite social bonds a vast area and great numbers of people, binding them with definite ties of reciprocal obligations, making them follow minute rules and observations in a concerted manner – the Kula is a sociological mechanism of surpassing size and complexity, considering the level of culture on which we find it. Nor can this wide network of social co-relations and cultural influences be considered for a moment as ephemeral, new or precarious. For its highly developed mythology and its magical ritual show how deeply it has taken root in the tradition of these natives and of what ancient growth it must be.

Another unusual feature is the character of the transaction itself, which is the proper substance of the Kula. A half commercial, half ceremonial exchange, it is carried out for its own sake, in fulfilment of a deep desire to possess. But here again, it is not ordinary possession, but a special type, in which a man owns for a short time, and in an alternating manner, individual specimens of two classes of objects. Though the ownership is incomplete in point of permanency, it is in turn enhanced in point of numbers successively possessed, and may be called a cumulative possession.

Another aspect of great, perhaps the greatest, importance and which perhaps reveals best the unusual character of the Kula is the natives' mental attitude towards the tokens of wealth. These latter are neither used nor regarded as money or currency, and they resemble these economic instruments very little, if indeed there is any resemblance at all, except that both money and *vaygu'a* represent condensed wealth. *Vaygu'a* is never used as medium of exchange or as measure of value, which are the two most important functions of currency or money. Each piece of *vaygu'a* of the Kula type has one main object throughout its existence – to be possessed and exchanged; has one main function and serves one main purpose – to circulate round the Kula ring, to be owned and displayed in a certain manner, of which we shall speak presently. And the exchange which each piece of *vaygu'a* constantly undergoes is of a very special kind; limited in the geographical direction in which it can take place, narrowly circumscribed in the social circle of men between whom it may be done, it is subject to all sorts of strict rules and regulations; it can neither be described as barter, nor as simply giving and receiving of presents, nor in any sense is it a play at exchange. In fact it is Kula, an exchange of an entirely novel type. And it is just through this exchange, through their being constantly within reach and the object of competitive desire, through being the means of arousing envy and conferring social distinction and renown, that these objects attain their high value. Indeed, they form one of the leading interests in native life, and are one of the main items in the inventory of their culture. Thus, one of the most important and unusual features of the Kula is the existence of the Kula *vaygu'a*, the incessantly circulating and ever exchangeable valuables, owing their value to this very circulation and its character.

The acts of exchange of the valuables have to conform to a definite code. The main tenet of this declares that the transaction is not a bargain. The equivalence of the values exchanged is essential, but it must be the result of the repayer's own sense of what is due to custom and to his own dignity. The ceremonial attached to the act of giving, the manner of carrying and handling the *vaygu'a* shows distinctly that this is regarded as something else than mere merchandise. Indeed it is to the native something that confers dignity, that exalts him, and which he therefore treats with veneration and affection. Their behaviour at the transaction makes it clear that the *vaygu'a* is regarded not only as possessing high value, but that it is treated also in a ritual manner, and arouses emotional reaction. This recognition is confirmed and deepened by the consideration of some other uses of *vaygu'a*, in which uses other valuables such as *kaloma* belts and large stone blades also function, besides the Kula articles.

Thus, when a malignant spirit, *tauva'u*, is found in or near the village in the shape of a snake or a land crab, some *vaygu'a* is put before it ceremonially and this is not done so much in order to bribe the spirit sacrificially by a gift as rather to exercise a direct action on his mind, and to make it benevolent. In the annual festive and dancing period, the *milamala*, the spirits return to their villages. The Kula valuables at that time in the hands of the community, as well as the permanent *vaygu'a*, such as stone blades, *kaloma* belts and *doga* pendants, are exhibited sacrificially to the spirits on a platform, an arrangement and custom called *yolova*. Thus the *vaygu'a* represent the most effective offering to be given to the spirits, through which they can be put into a pleasant state of mind; 'to make their minds good', as the stereotyped phrase of the natives runs. In the *yolova* an offering is made to the spirits of what is most valued by the living. The shadowy visitors are supposed to take the spirit or shadow part of the *vaygu'a* home. In all this there is a clear expression of the mental attitude of the natives, who regard the *vaygu'a* as supremely good in themselves, and not as convertible wealth, or as potential ornaments, or even as instruments of power. To possess *vaygu'a* is exhilarating, comforting, soothing in itself. They will look at *vaygu'a* and handle it for hours; even a touch of it imparts under circumstances its virtue.

This is most clearly expressed by a custom observed at death. A dying man is surrounded and overlaid with valuables which all his relatives and relatives-in-law bring in loan for the occasion, to take it back when all is over, while the man's own *vaygu'a* are left on the corpse for some time after death. Various rationalised versions and justifications of this custom are given. Thus it is said to be a gift to Topileta, the keeper of the nether world; or, again, that it has to be taken in its spiritual form to procure a high social standing in Tuma, or simply, that it is laid to adorn and make happier the last moments of the dying. All these beliefs no doubt exist side by side, and they are all compatible with, and indeed express, the underlying emotional attitude; the comforting action of the valuables. It is applied to the dying as something full of good, as something exercising a pleasant action, soothing and fortifying at the same time. They put it on his forehead, they put it on his chest, they rub his belly and his ribs with it, they dangle some of the *vaygu'a* before his nose. I have often seen them do that, in fact, observed them do it for hours, and I believe there is a complex, emotional and intellectual attitude at the bottom of it; the desire to inspire with life; and at the same time to prepare for death; to hold him fast to this one, and to equip for the other world; but above all, the deep feeling that the *vaygu'a* are the supreme comfort, that to surround a man with them, even in his most evil moment, makes the moment less evil. The same mental attitude is probably at the bottom of the custom which prescribes that the widow's brothers should give a *vaygu'a* to the brothers of the dead man, the same *vaygu'a* being given back on the same day. But it is kept just long enough to be of comfort to those, who, according to native kinship ideas, are most directly hit by the death.

In all this we find the expression of the same mental attitude, the extreme value attached to condensed wealth, the serious, respectful way of treating it, the idea and the feeling that it is the reservoir of highest good. The *vaygu'a* are valued in quite a different manner from that in which we value our wealth. The Biblical symbol of the golden calf might even be better applied to their attitude than to ours, although it would be not quite correct to say that they 'worship' the *vaygu'a*, for they worship nothing. The *vaygu'a* might perhaps be called 'objects of cult' in the sense expressed by the facts of the Kula and the data just adduced; that is, in so far as they are handled ritually in some of the most important acts of native life.

Bibliography

AUSTIN, L. (1934-5), 'Procreation among the Trobriand Islanders', *Oceania*, vol. 5, pp. 102-13.

AUSTIN, L. (1938-9). 'The seasonal gardening calendar of Kiriwina, Trobriand Islands', *Oceania*, vol. 9, pp. 30-53.

AUSTIN, L. (1945-6), 'Cultural changes in Kiriwina', *Oceania*, vol. 16, pp. 15-60.

AUSTIN, L. (1949-50), 'A note on Dr. Leach's "Primitive calendars"', *Oceania*, vol. 20, pp. 333-5.

BALDWIN, B. (1944-5), 'Usituma! Song of heaven', *Oceania*, vol. 15, pp. 201-38.

BALDWIN, B. (1949-50), 'Kadaguwai: songs of the Trobriand sunset isles', *Oceania*, vol. 20, pp. 263-85.

BALDWIN, B. (n.d.), 'Traditional and cultural aspects of Trobriand Island chiefs', unpubl. MS., Anthropology Department, R.S.Pac.S., Australian National University.

BARNES, J. A. (1963), Introduction, *The Family among the Australian Aborigines*, B. Malinowski (rev. ed.), Schocken Books, New York.

BARNES, J. A. (1967), 'Some ethical problems in modern fieldwork', in *Anthropologists in the Field*, D. G. Jongmans and P. C. W. Gutkind, eds, Van Gorcum, Assen.

BEIER, U. (1975), 'Kabisawali: the impact of a self-help movement on cultural life in the Trobriand Islands', *Gigibori*, vol. 2, pp. 18-24, Institute of Papua New Guinea Studies, Port Moresby.

BELLAMY, R. L. (1908), 'Notes on the customs of the Trobriand Islanders', *Papua, Annual Report*, 1906-7, pp. 63-6.

BELSHAW, C. S. (1955), 'In search of wealth', *American Anthropologist* (Memoirs no. 80), vol. 57, pt 2.

BLACK, R. H. (1957), 'Dr. Bellamy of Papua', *Medical Journal of Australia*, 10-24 August 1957, pp. 1-24.

BRADFIELD, R. M. (1973), *A Natural History of Associations*, vol. I., Duckworth, London.

BROOKFIELD, H. C. and HART, D. (1971), *Melanesia: a Geographical Interpretation of an Island World*, Methuen, London.

BRUNTON, R. (1975), 'Why do the Trobriands have chiefs?', *Man* (n.s.), vol. 10, pp. 544-58.

CHOWNING, A. (1969), 'The fertility of Melanesian girls, laboratory mice and prostitutes: a comment on the "Bruce effect"', *American Anthropologist*, vol. 71, pp. 1122–5.

FIRTH, R. (1957a), ed., *Man and Culture: An Evaluation of the Work of Bronislaw Malinowski*, Routledge & Kegan Paul, London.

FIRTH, R. (1957b), 'The place of Malinowski in the history of economic anthropology', in *Man and Culture*, R. Firth, ed., Routledge & Kegan Paul, London.

FIRTH, R. (1967), Introduction, *A Diary in the Strict Sense of the Term*, B. Malinowski, Routledge & Kegan Paul, London.

FORGE, A. (1972), 'The golden fleece', *Man* (n.s.), vol. 7, pp. 527–40.

FORTES, M. (1957), 'Malinowski and the study of kinship', in *Man and Culture*, R. Firth, ed., Routledge & Kegan Paul, London.

FORTUNE, R. F. (1932), *Sorcerers of Dobu*, George Routledge, London.

GEERTZ, C. (1967), 'Under the mosquito net', *New York Review*, 14 September, 1967, pp. 12–13.

GROVES, M. (1956), 'Trobriand Island clans and chiefs', *Man*, vol. 56, p. 164.

HARDING, T. G. (1967), *Voyagers of the Vitiaz Strait*, University of Washington Press.

HARRIS, M. (1968), *The Rise of Anthropological Theory*, Routledge & Kegan Paul, London.

HATCH, E. (1973), *Theories of Man and Culture*, Columbia University Press.

HOGBIN, H. I. (1946), 'The Trobriand Islands, 1945: Letter to the editor', *Man*, vol. 46, p. 72.

JAMES, W. (1973), 'The anthropologist as reluctant imperialist', in *Anthropology and the Colonial Encounter*, T. Azad, ed., Ithaca Press, London.

JARVIE, I. C. (1964), *The Revolution in Anthropology*, Routledge & Kegan Paul, London.

KASAIPWALOVA, J. (1973), '"Modernizing" Melanesian society – why and for whom?', in *Priorities in Melanesian Development*, R. J. May, ed., Sixth Waigani Seminar, R.S.Pac.S., Australian National University and University of Papua New Guinea.

KASAIPWALOVA, J. (1975), 'Philosophy and historical reality of Kabisawali', *Gigibori*, vol. 2, pp. 16–17, Institute of Papua New Guinea Studies, Port Moresby.

KLUCKHOHN, C. (1943), 'Bronislaw Malinowski 1884–1942', *Journal of American Folklore*, vol. 56, pp. 208–19.

KUPER, A. (1973), *Anthropologists and Anthropology: The British School 1922–1972*, Allen Lane, London.

LAUER, P. (1970), 'Amphlett Islands' pottery trade and the Kula', *Mankind*, vol. 7, pp. 165–76.

LEACH, E. R. (1949–50), 'Primitive calendars', *Oceania*, vol. 20, pp. 245–62.

LEACH, E. R. (1957), 'The epistemological background to Malinowski's empiricism', in *Man and Culture*, R. Firth, ed., Routledge & Kegan Paul, London.

LEACH, E. R. (1958), 'Concerning Trobriand clans and the kinship category *tabu*', in

The Developmental Cycle in Domestic Groups, J. Goody, ed., Cambridge University Press.

LEACH, E. R. (1966a), 'On the "Founding fathers"', *Current Anthropology*, vol. 7, pp. 560–76.

LEACH, E. R. (1966b), Introduction, *Coral Gardens and their Magic*, B. Malinowski (vol. I) (2nd ed.), Allen & Unwin, London.

LEACH, E. R. (1967), 'Virgin birth', *Proceedings of the Royal Anthropological Institute*, 1966, pp. 39–50.

LEACH, J. W. (1973), 'Making the best of tourism: the Trobriand situation', in *Priorities in Melanesian Development*, R. J. May, ed., Sixth Waigani Seminar, R.S.Pac.S., Australian National University and University of Papua New Guinea.

LEWIS, I. M. (1968), Review of *A Diary in the Strict Sense of the Term* by B. Malinowski, *Man* (n.s.), vol. 3, pp. 348–9.

LOMBARD, J. (1972), *L'Anthropologie britannique contemporaine*, Presses Universitaires de France, Paris.

LOUNSBURY, F. G. (1965), 'Another view of Trobriand kinship categories', in *Formal Semantic Analysis*, E. A. Hammel, ed., *American Anthropologist* Special Publication, vol. 67, no. 5, pt. 2.

MALINOWSKI, B. (1915), 'The natives of Mailu: preliminary results of the Robert Mond research work in British New Guinea', *Transactions and Proceedings of the Royal Society of South Australia*, vol. 39, pp. 494–706.

MALINOWSKI, B. (1916), 'Baloma: spirits of the dead in the Trobriand Islands', *Journal of the Royal Anthropological Institute*, vol. 46, pp. 354–430.

MALINOWSKI, B. (1920), 'Kula: the circulating exchange of valuables in the archipelagoes of eastern New Guinea', *Man*, vol. 20, pp. 97–105.

MALINOWSKI, B. (1922), *Argonauts of the Western Pacific*, George Routledge, London.

MALINOWSKI, B. (1926), *Crime and Custom in Savage Society*, Kegan Paul, London.

MALINOWSKI, B. (1927), *Sex and Repression in Savage Society*, Kegan Paul, London.

MALINOWSKI, B. (1929), *The Sexual Life of Savages in North-Western Melanesia*, George Routledge, London.

MALINOWSKI, B. (1930), 'The rationalization of anthropology and administration', *Africa*, vol. 3, pp. 405–29.

MALINOWSKI, B. (1932a), *The Sexual Life of Savages*, 3rd ed., George Routledge, London.

MALINOWSKI, B. (1932b), Introduction, *Sorcerers of Dobu*, R. F. Fortune, George Routledge, London.

MALINOWSKI, B. (1932c), 'Pigs, Papuans and police court perspective', *Man*, vol. 32, pp. 33–8.

MALINOWSKI, B. (1935), *Coral Gardens and their Magic*, vol. I: *Soil-Tilling and Agricultural Rites in the Trobriand Islands*, Allen & Unwin, London.

MALINOWSKI, B. (1944), *A Scientific Theory of Culture and other Essays*, University of North Carolina Press (Oxford University Press, New York: 1960 paperback ed.).

MALINOWSKI, B. (1945), *The Dynamics of Culture Change*, P. M. Kaberry, ed., Yale University Press.

MALINOWSKI, B. (1947), *Freedom and Civilization*, Allen & Unwin, London.

MALINOWSKI, B. (1967), *A Diary in the Strict Sense of the Term*, Routledge & Kegan Paul, London.

MÉTRAUX, R. (1968), 'Bronislaw Malinowski', *International Encyclopedia of the Social Sciences*, vol. 9, pp. 541–9.

MONTAGUE, S. (1971), 'Trobriand kinship and the virgin birth controversy', *Man* (n.s.), vol. 6, pp. 353–68.

NADEL, S. F. (1957), 'Malinowski on magic and religion', in *Man and Culture*, R. Firth, ed., Routledge & Kegan Paul, London.

NISBETT, A. (1975), 'Kula custom: giving till it hurts', *Listener*, vol. 94, pp. 859–60.

PANOFF, M. (1972), *Bronislaw Malinowski*, Petite Bibliothèque Payot, Paris.

POWDERMAKER, H. (1966), *Stranger and Friend*, Secker & Warburg, London.

POWELL, H. A. (1960), 'Competitive leadership in Trobriand political organization', *Journal of the Royal Anthropological Institute*, vol. 90, pp. 118–45.

POWELL, H. A. (1969a), 'Genealogy, residence and kinship in Kiriwina', *Man* (n.s.), vol. 4, pp. 177–202.

POWELL, H. A. (1969b), 'Territory, hierarchy and kinship in Kiriwina', *Man* (n.s.), vol. 4, pp. 580–604.

POWELL, H. A. (1976), Review of the BBC film 'The Trobriand Experiment', *Royal Anthropological Institute News*, no. 13, March–April 1976, pp. 3–6.

REDFIELD, R. (1954), Introduction, *Magic, Science and Religion and other Essays*, B. Malinowski, Doubleday, New York.

RENTOUL, A. C. (1931), 'Physiological paternity and the Trobrianders', *Man*, vol. 31, pp. 152–4.

RENTOUL, A. C. (1932), 'Papuans, professors and platitudes', *Man*, vol. 33, pp. 274–6.

RICHARDS, A. I. (1957), 'The concept of culture in Malinowski's work', in *Man and Culture*, R. Firth, ed., Routledge & Kegan Paul, London.

RICHARDS, A. I. (1969), 'Malinowski', in *The Founding Fathers of Social Science*, Y. Raison, ed., Penguin Books, Harmondsworth.

ROBINSON, M. S. (1962), 'Complementary filiation and marriage in the Trobriand Islands', in *Marriage in Tribal Societies*, M. Fortes, ed., Cambridge University Press.

SAVILLE, W. J. V. (1926), *In Unknown New Guinea*, Seeley, Service, London.

SELIGMANN, C. G. (1910), *The Melanesians of British New Guinea*, Cambridge University Press.

SIDER, K. B. (1967), 'Affinity and the role of the father in the Trobriands', *Southwestern Journal of Anthropology*, vol. 23, pp. 90–109.

SLOAN, W. N. (1974), 'Vegetables and valuables: an alliance theory investigation of Trobriand society', *Journal of Symbolic Anthropology*, vol. 1, pp. 99–126.

SPIRO, M. E. (1968), 'Virgin birth, parthenogenesis and physiological paternity', *Man* (n.s.), vol. 3, pp. 242–61.

STOCKING, G. W. (1974), 'Empathy and antipathy in the heart of darkness', in *Readings in the History of Anthropology*, R. Darnell, ed., Harper & Row, London.

SYMMONS-SYMONOLEWICZ, K. (1958), 'Bronislaw Malinowski: an intellectual profile', *Polish Review*, vol. 3, pp. 55–76.

SYMMONS-SYMONOLEWICZ, K. (1959), 'Bronislaw Malinowski: formative influences and theoretical evolution', *Polish Review*, vol. 4, pp. 17–45.

SYMMONS-SYMONOLEWICZ, K. (1960), 'Bronislaw Malinowski: individuality as a theorist', *Polish Review*, vol. 5, pp. 53–65.

TAMBIAH, S. J. (1968), 'The magical power of words', *Man* (n.s.), vol. 3, pp. 175–208.

UBEROI, SINGH, J. P. (1962), *Politics of the Kula Ring*, Manchester University Press.

URRY, J. (1972), '*Notes and Queries on Anthropology* and the development of field methods in British Anthropology, 1870–1920', *Proceedings of the Royal Anthropological Institute for 1972*, pp. 45–57.

VOGET, F. W. (1975), *A History of Ethnology*, Holt, Rinehart & Winston, New York.

WAX, M. L. (1972), 'Tenting with Malinowski', *American Sociological Review*, vol. 37, pp. 1–13.

WEINER, A. (1976), *Women of Value: Men of Renown*, University of Texas Press.

YOUNG, M. W. (1971), *Fighting with Food*, Cambridge University Press.

Index

abortion, 107
adultery, 123–4, 132
agriculture, 25, 26, 27, 28, 29, 31, 33, 47, 48; *see also* food; gardening
Amphlett Islands, 62, 169, 172, 173, 174, 175, 184, 185, 191, 195, 237
ancestral spirits, 35, 57, 60, 219; reincarnation of, 99–102
Argonauts of the Western Pacific, 1, 6
arm-shells (bracelets: *mwali*), ritual exchange of, 32, 50, 163, 164–6, 168–71, 178, 182–3, 184, 185, 187, 192, 193, 199, 200, 201–2
arts and crafts, 26, 30, 33, 47
Austin, L., 23, 75

Baloma: the Spirits of the Dead in the Trobriand Islands, 1, 5
Baldwin, B., 14–16
bananas, 26, 35, 40, 41, 42, 172
Barnes, John, 4, 16
barter, 27, 47–50, 164, 171, 173, 178, 196–7
baskets, 30, 45–6
Ba'u village, 29, 30, 43, 44
beauty, *see* magic
Beier, U., 18, 19, 20
Bellamy, R. L., 12n
Belshaw, C. S., 161
betel-nuts, betel chewing, 30, 46, 52, 197
bird-snaring, 27
Black, R. H., 12n
Boyowa, 25, 166, 184, 185, 188, 192, 196, 202, 236; *see also* Kiriwina
bracelets, *see* arm-shells
Bradfield, R. M., 23
Brookfield, H. C., 161
brother-sister relationship/taboo, *see* luguta
Brunton, R., 23, 161

bulubwalata, *see* gardening; magic, evil
buritila'ulo (competitive exchange of harvest gifts), 69–72
bwaga'u (male sorcerers), 52, 207, 208, 209, 212, 213, 214
Bwoytalu village, 31, 33, 42, 44, 48, 80; woodworkers and carvers, 29–30

canoes, 40, 146; for Kula expeditions 164, 172–3, 174–6; for *uvalaku* expeditions, 181, 182; *see also* magic; mythology; taboos; *toliwaga*
carving, 30, 222
chiefs, chieftainship, 38, 68, 155, 156; distribution of wealth and, 51–2; Kula and, 167, 179–80, 181, 183, 184, 186–7, 188, 200; land tenure and, 157–8; marriage and, 112, 120–2; *urigubu* of, 131–2; *see also* clans; garden magicians; rank; sub-clans
children, 213; divorce and, 133–4; sex prohibitions and, 87–9; sociological paternity and, 109–11; spirit-, 99–102; *see also* illegitimacy; infant betrothal
Chowning, A., 75
clans, clanship, 77–80, 233, 234; choice of marriage partner and, 114; doctrine of first emergence and, 79, 145, 157; exogamy, 80–5, 142, 147; Kula partnership and, 185
coconuts, 26, 32, 35, 42, 52, 197
colonialism, Malinowski's attitude to, 16–17
conception, 102–6; *see also* illegitimacy; reincarnation
cooking, 38, 42–3
coral, 26, 31, 32
Coral Gardens and their Magic, 1, 6, 23, 75

249

Index

For Product Safety Concerns and Information please contact our EU
representative GPSR@taylorandfrancis.com
Taylor & Francis Verlag GmbH, Kaufingerstraße 24, 80331 München, Germany

* 9 7 8 1 1 3 8 0 6 4 0 0 3 *